BUSHWHACKER BELLES

The Sisters, Wives, and Girlfriends of the Missouri Guerrillas

LARRY WOOD

PELICAN PUBLISHING
NEW ORLEANS

First printing, 2016
Second printing, 2024

ISBN: 9781455621569

E-book ISBN: 9781455621576

Eliza Gabbert photo courtesy of Bushwhacker Museum.

Printed in the United States of America
Published by Pelican Publishing
New Orleans, LA
www.arcadiapublishing.com/pelican

BUSHWHACKER BELLES

Contents

	Preface	7
	Acknowledgments	11
	Introduction	13
Chapter 1	The Political Climate in Missouri	17
Chapter 2	She Adder and Rebel Damsel	25
Chapter 3	More in Common than a Name	33
Chapter 4	The Heart and Soul of Bushwhacking	41
Chapter 5	Mary Vaughn and Her Relations in the Brush	57
Chapter 6	Anna Fickle: Bribery and Murder	71
Chapter 7	Mary Ann Harlow: Bloody Bill Anderson Informant	79
Chapter 8	Bill Anderson Supporter or Bill Anderson Victim?	85
Chapter 9	Bitter Rebels but Fine-Looking Girls	95
Chapter 10	Wife of a Bill Anderson Guerrilla	107
Chapter 11	Confederate Mail Handlers	115
Chapter 12	Fannie Houx and the Excitement Surrounding Her Case	121
Chapter 13	Susanna Justice: Guerrilla Spy	133
Chapter 14	Professors of the Christian Religion	139
Chapter 15	The Handsome and Fascinating Mollie Goggin	149
Chapter 16	The Very Bad Bond Women	157
Chapter 17	The Post Oak "Prostitutes"	163
Chapter 18	Notorious and Active Rebels	181

Chapter 19 Four-Time Jailbird "Lizzie" DeWitt 191
Chapter 20 Dancing with a Rebel Flag 197
Chapter 21 To Be Hung by the Neck Until Dead 207
Chapter 22 Rebel Arms Supplier 215
Chapter 23 The Rebel Vixens of Chariton County 221
Chapter 24 Convicted by Her Own Admission 229
Chapter 25 The Ordeal of Tabitha Rider 233
Chapter 26 Who Were These Women? 241
Notes 257
Bibliography 281
Index 287

Preface

War has historically been considered the purview of men, but women have played significant roles in many of America's conflicts. This, of course, has been particularly true of recent wars, as females increasingly perform combat functions previously reserved for males. However, even during the Civil War over a century and a half ago, women played crucial parts. Occasionally they disguised themselves as men, donned uniforms, and fought alongside men. More often, they supported the war effort by performing auxiliary functions. Some served in official capacities as nurses, cooks, and washer-women, while others acted covertly as spies and messengers.

For the first one hundred years or more after the Civil War, little attention was paid to the role that women played in the conflict. Scholarship over the past half-century has largely filled the void. Mary Elizabeth Massey's 1966 work, *Bonnet Brigades* (later republished as *Women in the Civil War*), was one of the first serious studies of women in the Civil War. Massey found that most women participated in the war unintentionally, and hers was a study of how the war affected women, not how women affected the war.

Subsequent work, on the other hand, tends to focus on the role the Civil War played in empowering women, examining the endeavors women undertook during the war as avenues of liberation. For example, Victoria E. Bynum's 1992 book, *Unruly Women: The Politics of Social and Sexual Control in the Old South*, explored how the disorderly behavior of poor, powerless women in North Carolina during the Civil War gave them a voice in the public arena and threatened to disrupt the male-dominated social order. Laura F. Edwards' *Scarlett Doesn't Live Here Anymore*, published in 2000, showed that the struggles of poor, Southern women during the Civil War era had political implications, even though the women were not consciously striving for power or independence. In 2002, DeAnne Blanton and Lauren M. Cook, in *They Fought Like Demons: Women Soldiers in the American Civil War*, provided a wide-ranging and fascinating look at women who donned uniforms or otherwise disguised themselves as men and fought as soldiers. Published in 2010, Stephanie McCurry's *Confederate Reckoning: Power and Politics in the Civil War South* built on the work of Bynum and others to show that, although women were considered outside politics and war, the Civil War forced both Confederate and Union authorities to deal with them.

Perhaps no other state saw a greater proportion of its women involved in the Civil War, especially in covert roles, than the slave-holding border state of Missouri. Although Missouri stayed in the Union, the sentiments of its citizens were sharply divided. The state was soon drawn into a bitter guerrilla conflict marked by sabotage, raids, and personal vendettas. The war in their own back yard drew the state's civilians, including women, into the conflict. Neighbor was often pitted against neighbor. Southern-sympathizing women with guerrilla family members or close friends often fed and sheltered the partisan fighters in their homes.

Other Southern women in Missouri took an even more active role in helping the Rebel cause by spying and carrying information to bushwhackers or to Confederate soldiers. Because of the virulent and personal nature of the guerrilla warfare, more women in Missouri clashed with Union authorities during the Civil War than in almost any other state. Many were arrested, some accused of what the Union considered serious offenses and tried by military commission.

Countless books and articles have been written about the guerrilla warfare in Missouri, chronicling the lives and military "careers" of many of the individual guerrillas. In fact, some of their stories, such as that of William Quantrill, have been told repeatedly. Yet historians and writers have paid little notice to the role played by family members of the guerrillas, particularly their female loved ones. A few generally unreliable accounts of some of the supposed exploits of the female abettors of Missouri guerrillas were published during the late nineteenth century. These paint the women as either romantic heroines or depraved she-devils, depending on which side the author identified with. During the early twentieth century, a few old women who had been associated with the guerrillas as girls wrote reminiscent accounts that perpetuated the idea, first promulgated during the war, that women had little role in the conflict except as victims of a cruel Union Army.

Michael Fellman's 1989 work, *Inside War: The Guerrilla Conflict in Missouri During the American Civil War*, was one of the first scholarly works to look beyond the military narrative and examine the social and psychological impact of the guerrilla warfare in Missouri. It contained a chapter dealing specifically with women. While allowing that women sometimes willingly participated in Missouri's guerrilla conflict, Fellman overall accepted the portrayal of the females as victims of barbarous warfare in the state. Most subsequent scholars explore the part played by women in the guerrilla conflict in Missouri only incidentally within the larger context of examining the role and influence of women in the Civil War in general.

Only a few authors besides Fellman have looked at Missouri women during the war. Joseph Beilein, Jr., in his 2006 master's thesis, "'*The Presence of These Families Is the Cause of the Presence There of the Guerrillas': The Influence of Little Dixie Households on the Civil War in Missouri*," examined a few female-headed households along the Missouri River that served as places of refuge and support for guerrillas. Countering the idea that Missouri women during the Civil War were primarily victims, Beilein expanded on Bynum's concept of unruly or "disorderly" women to argue instead that the women acted with agency and freewill to affect the outcome of the war. However, Beilein's study was limited to a handful of subjects. In 2006, *Confederate Heroines* by Thomas Lowry profiled 120 Southern women, including a number of Missouri women, tried by Union military proceedings during the Civil War. However, Lowry presented some of the stories as illustrative sketches rather than thorough accounts; several of the remarkable cases he chronicled involved women who were not arrested for aiding guerrillas but rather for offenses such as smuggling mail into St. Louis prisons. In addition, many interesting cases of women arrested for aiding guerrillas never came to trial and were therefore not included in Lowry's study.

LeeAnn Whites argued cogently in her 2011 journal article, "Forty Shirts and a Wagonload of Wheat," that the guerrilla warfare in Missouri was a systemic rebellion against the occupying Union Army in which women played vital roles in aiding the male fighters. Her study was limited to the Kansas-Missouri border in the Jackson County area. Author Thomas Curran gave a presentation in 2011 at the Missouri State Archives on a research project entitled "Confederate Women and Military Justice in the St. Louis Area." Although Curran's study included a few women who helped guerrillas, his project, as the title of the presentation suggests, focused mainly on activities in and around St. Louis. Stephanie's Rohr's 2014 master's degree project entitled *Bushwhacker Belles: Exploring Gender, Guerrilla Warfare, and the Union Provost Marshal Records* expanded on the thesis advanced by White that women played a vital role in aiding the Missouri guerrillas. Rohr's non-thesis, like White's article, focused on a few women in the Kansas City area and was not a comprehensive or thorough study. Instead, the important value of Rohr's project is that it promises to facilitate scholars and historians' future study of the women abettors of the Missouri guerrillas through construction of a Web site that will provide links to primary documents, particularly provost marshals' records, pertaining to the women.

The stories of the individual Missouri women who clashed with Union authorities during the Civil War specifically for harboring, feeding, or otherwise aiding guerrillas have scarcely been told. Here I profile more than thirty such women. Many of their stories are being told for the first time. My main reason for writing the book is simply that I find the individual stories fascinating, but at the same time I believe these case studies will lead to critical observations about the guerrillas' female associates as a group that might add something to our understanding of them. The introduction will suggest the direction of the inquiry, and Chapter 1 will provide a framework for understanding the rise of guerrilla warfare in Missouri and the importance of the guerrillas' female associates. The final chapter will offer some conclusions. In between, the reader will meet the intriguing women who are the primary subjects of the book.

Acknowledgments

I researched this book more via the Internet and without traveling to libraries and other research centers than for any of my other recent nonfiction books. Therefore, I perhaps do not have as many people to thank who helped me with the research than I might otherwise have.

Still, there are a number of people I would like to acknowledge. I borrowed a few books on interlibrary loan through the Joplin Public Library. I wish to thank the library reference staff, particularly Patty Crane and Jason Sullivan, for fulfilling my requests. I want to thank Ann Christian for providing information and documents pertaining to the Fox family of Chariton County and John Deeben of the National Archives for providing transcripts of the trials by military commission of several of female subjects of this book. A number of people and institutions provided images for the book, notably George Longacre, Will Tollerton of the Bushwhacker Museum, Jaime Bourassa of the Missouri Historical Museum, and Alan Chilton of the Hulston Library at Wilson's Creek National Park. In addition, I downloaded a number of images from the Library of Congress Web site.

I should also acknowledge some of the Web sites and databases that made possible my research. Especially important were the subscription service www.Fold3.com; the Web site of the Missouri State Archives, which has increasingly made much of its material available online to the general public; and www.familysearch.org (Web site of the Church of Jesus Christ of Latter-day Saints), which provides access to census records and many other genealogical records free of charge.

I wish to thank my wife, Gigi, for her continued support and encouragement and for helping me with a couple of maps.

Lastly, I extend my appreciation to my editors, Mark Mathes and

Jessie Campbell, for their thorough review of the manuscript and excellent suggestions for improvement. I know the finished product is better because of their input.

Introduction

On September 3, 1863, Major L. K. Thacher, commanding the Union post at Westport, just south of Kansas City, wrote to Major Preston B. Plumb, provost marshal of the District of the Border, explaining that he had arrested a Mrs. Watson and her two daughters. The three women had been reported to him as "common prostitutes" who were in harmony with bushwhackers. As further justification for the arrest, Thacher added that Mrs. Watson had a son who had been with the "herd of fiends who massacred the citizens of Lawrence."

The Mrs. Watson whom Thacher took into custody was, in all probability, forty-one-year-old Martha Watson. Her daughters, Ellen and Sallie, were seventeen and thirteen at the time of Thacher's letter. Her two eldest sons were twenty-one and nineteen.[1]

Although such Union accusations of immorality among the female associates of the Missouri guerrillas were not rampant during the war, they were not altogether uncommon. The portrayal of the women as sexually promiscuous gained footing after the war. In 1891, for example, a correspondent to a St. Louis newspaper asserted that the Rebel women of Missouri, or the "bushwhacker belles" as he called them, engaged in all sorts of adventures to help the Southern cause during the Civil War. "Some of them risked not only their lives but their honor—aye, and lost it, too, tossing it gladly into the scale, believing that the end would justify the means. Sometimes the deed of shame was done to save a life, sometimes to destroy one, and sometimes to get a piece of news or a hundred gun caps and a bag of buckshot." The idea that many of the women who supported Missouri's guerrillas were "disorderly" in their sexual conduct has persisted to some degree in modern scholarship.[2]

Akin to the notion of female associates of the guerrillas as sexually dissolute was the idea that they were mean, uneducated women who were willing to go to any extreme to help their knights of the bush. During early December of 1864, for instance, Captain W. B. Kemper, assistant provost marshal at Liberty, said he had heard Zerelda Samuels, mother of Frank and Jesse James, proclaim that she was proud of the deeds of her sons, including their participation in the recent Centralia Massacre and that she "prayed to God to protect them in their work." Kemper concluded that Mrs. Samuels was "one of the worst women in this state."[3]

The perception of the Southern women of Missouri as violent, hostile, and adventurous in their support of guerrillas continued after the war. In 1869, a former Union soldier, writing under the name Leon Boyd (likely an alias), authored a series of articles for the *Carthage (Mo.) Weekly Banner* about the Civil War in southwest Missouri and its surroundings. In discussing the role of women during the war, he allowed that both Union and Confederate women had endured trials and hardships during the war, but then he went on to add, "Of all the rebels in the land, the most malignant, bitter, unrepenting and outspoken were women; not only here, but all through the South, as any soldier can tell you." Citing the example of Miss Louisa Challis and Mrs. Catharine Wade of Jasper County, Boyd said, "These women ranged over the whole Southwest and boasted that they often rode sixty miles in a day, acting as scouts and spies almost through the whole war."[4]

After the war, ex-Rebels embraced the idea that Southern-sympathizing women of Missouri undertook dangerous missions on behalf of the guerrillas, but they naturally framed the women's actions as heroic feats. Sometimes they claimed the women's deeds of derring-do surpassed those of the bushwhackers themselves.

According to legend, for instance, a detachment of Federals was sent from Newtonia to capture guerrilla leader Bud Shirley, brother of Myra Maybelle Shirley (aka Belle Starr) at his Carthage home, but Belle learned of the plan while in Newtonia. She supposedly galloped thirty-five miles cross-country on horseback and reached Carthage in time to warn her brother of the Federals' approach, overcoming the soldiers' considerable head-start. A number of years after the war, ex-Quantrill guerrilla William H. Gregg stated, "The part played by the women of the South exceeds in self-sacrificing glory that of the men."[5]

Were the female aiders and abettors of the Missouri guerrillas as wanton as Union observers sometimes accused them of being? Were they as heroic and adventurous as their own side sometimes portrayed them? These are just a couple of the questions that will be examined in light of the case studies that follow.

A number of other issues will also be explored. Were the women who helped the Missouri guerrillas coerced victims, or did they act of their own free will? If they acted freely, what motivated them? From what area of the United States did they or their families come to Missouri, and where in Missouri did they live? How did they behave when they were arrested or when they otherwise clashed with Union authorities, and how did Union soldiers treat them? What did the women have in common, and in what ways did they differ? In short, who were the women who helped guerrillas in Missouri during the Civil War?

Based on the stories that follow of women who were arrested for providing just such help, the last chapter will provide some tentative answers to these and other questions about the so-called bushwhacker belles.

Missouri County map showing the counties of "Little Dixie" in gray.

Chapter 1

The Political Climate in Missouri

Before we meet the bushwhacker belles, it will help to understand the political climate that led to their emergence.

Slavery was of course part of the landscape. But the women who helped guerrillas didn't necessarily come from slaveholding families. Only about one-eighth of Missouri families held slaves at the outset of the Civil War. The proportion was somewhat greater along the Missouri River counties where guerrilla activity was the most prominent during the war and where most of the women arrested for supporting guerrillas lived. Even in these so-called "Little Dixie" counties, non-slaveholders formed the large majority of the white population. Only in Lafayette County, the largest slaveholding county in the state, did the proportion of slaveholding households approach even half of the county's total households. Still, whether they owned slaves or not, most Missourians with Southern roots paid lip service to the institution of slavery.[1]

But was this slave economy that mainly benefited wealthy landowners worth going to war over? The yeoman farmers who comprised most of the state's rural population needed another reason for fighting. Southern leaders in Missouri provided that motivation by appealing to an emotion that was stronger and more immediate than support of an abstract principle or an institution that did not directly benefit the average citizen. Missourians must fight, so the argument went, to protect their homeland, their homes, and their families from rape and rapine at the hands of the Federal government. The invading Union Army threatened not just the institution of slavery but also that most sacred of institutions—the family—and posed an especial menace to women, the very embodiment of family.

The specter of the rape of white women by black men had long been used in Missouri and other slaveholding states to incite white men. Many heralded the prospect of freed male slaves and invading Federal soldiers as a sexual threat. This helped galvanize opposition among Southern-sympathizing men to the so-called Northern war of aggression that "Black Republicans," as abolitionists were often called, had instigated against the South. A Northern newspaperman traveling with Iowa troops in Missouri early in the war observed, "The Missourians believe very generally that we came here to steal their niggers, hang the men and ravish the women."[2]

Physical assault on Missouri women by either slaves or Union soldiers was actually quite rare during the Civil War. That said, Union soldiers invaded homes when no man was present. Troops spoke obscenely in front of women. They threatened families. These acts of what Fellman has called "symbolic rape" were cause for outrage. The sexual imagery they evoked helped solidify opposition to the Federal invasion of Missouri. So, too, did the pillaging, burning, and "rape of the land" early in the war by jayhawkers like Charles "Doc" Jennison and Jim Lane.[3]

In his inaugural address in January of 1861, several months before war erupted in Missouri, Governor Claiborne F. Jackson labeled the Northern states aggressors and advocated the thorough organization of a state militia to protect the lives and property of Missourians from a possible Federal invasion. He called on Missouri to "consult her own interest" and "to stand by her sister slaveholding states." His use of the feminine pronoun in reference to Missouri was not accidental. Figuratively, the state was understood to be female, a motherland that men should protect, just as they should protect women themselves.[4]

The state's individual citizens, however, were understood to be male. Only men could vote or otherwise participate in politics. The social role of women outside the home was limited. Men represented their households in political and most social functions, while women's lives revolved almost exclusively around the home. Worshiped as goddesses of the hearth but denied any real power, women stood outside politics and war—the "weaker sex" who needed protection. Their role during war was merely to support their husbands, sons, brothers, and fathers; keep the home and family going; and then welcome back their heroes.[5]

One of the more visible roles women were allowed to play in the war effort was the making of flags and uniforms. Women became closely associated with these patriotic symbols. The flags and uniforms they presented to their men at the beginning of the war served not just to identify units and ranks but also to remind the men why they were fighting. Even Quantrill's guerrillas supposedly had their black flag, lovingly made and presented to them by Anna Fickle, whose story is chronicled later in the book. Although the tale of the black flag might be apocryphal, it shows the mythic value attached to patriotic symbols. The guerrillas were fighting not just for themselves but for Anna Fickle and the women and motherland she represented.[6]

In fact, guerrilla warfare arose in Missouri precisely because many of the men who signed up to fight in Governor Jackson's Missouri State Guard at the outset of the war found that their desire to protect their homes, their families, and their homeland outweighed any devotion they might have had to the overall Southern cause. The Missouri State Guard had been created specifically to protect Missouri, and many militiamen balked at following their commanding general, Sterling Price, into the Confederate Army in late 1861 and early 1862. When their initial term of enlistment expired, many simply went home to try to resume their former occupations.

Some of the officers, still nominal members of the disintegrating Missouri State Guard, went back into their home territories on recruiting expeditions, seeking once again to fill out their units. Many of these recruiting officers eventually joined the Confederate Army once they finished organizing their units. The Confederate Army itself later sent officers from Missouri back into their home state on recruiting missions. Leading mere bands as they sought to fill out their companies, the recruiting officers waged a war of plunder and sabotage against the occupying Federal Army. Many were in no rush to get back to the regular theater of war in the South. The proximity of their homes to their field of operations often drew their families and friends into the partisan warfare.[7]

Although the guerrilla leaders usually held commissions as Confederate recruiters, Federal authorities refused to recognize them

Confederate General Sterling Price.(Courtesy of the Library of Congress.)

and their men as regular Confederate soldiers. They were, therefore, not protected by the rules of war. Instead, they—and the civilians who helped them—were considered outlaws.

As Fellman has pointed out, protecting womanhood was at the very heart of the unspoken guerrilla code, but Union men also placed women on an exalted shrine outside the realm of politics. They did not expect to have to deal with women during the war. In fact, Union authorities in Missouri did not have to deal with women very often during the early stages of the war. On the infrequent occasions in 1861 and 1862 when women were discovered helping guerrillas or otherwise acting as collateral participants in the war, they were usually not taken seriously. Either they were not arrested, or, if they were arrested, they were usually dismissed without charges.[8]

Of course, one of the reasons that Missouri women were seldom arrested early in the war for aiding guerrillas is that guerrilla warfare was not prevalent at first. It did not become widespread until the summer of 1862 and did not peak until two years later. Acts of sabotage like bridge burning that were committed in 1861 were considered serious crimes, and the perpetrators of such acts were treated as outlaws. Guerrillas were generally viewed more as a troublesome nuisance, though, than a real threat to the Union war effort in Missouri.

Another reason women were arrested infrequently early in the war was that Union authorities were slow to recognize the vital role civilians played in sustaining the partisan fighters. When they began recognizing the important part civilians played, they resisted the idea of targeting women and families as a way of undermining the guerrilla presence in Missouri. Protecting women was even written into the Union Army's laws of war.

Neither side wanted to be seen as making war on women.[9]

A noticeable shift in Union policy toward the treatment of female associates of the guerrillas occurred around the spring of 1863. On May 3, Benjamin F. Parker, colonel of Confederate partisan rangers, wrote to General James G. Blunt, commanding the District of Kansas. He railed against Blunt's policy of arresting and banishing Southern ladies of the district merely "for vindicating the sacredness of their sex against the slanders and insults of the base and unmitigated scoundrels, calling themselves United States soldiers."[10]

Blunt dismissed Parker's complaint as the ranting of a barbarian. He replied that he had instructed his officers commanding troops in the border counties of Missouri to destroy or expel from the district every Rebel sympathizer who gave aid to guerrillas. "These instructions," the general stressed, "will not exempt females from the rule. Experience has taught that the bite of the she adder is as poisonous and productive of mischief as the bite of any other venomous reptile."[11]

Shortly afterward, Blunt's District of Kansas was split into the

District of the Border and the District of the Frontier. Brigadier General Thomas Ewing, Jr., was put in command of the District of the Border. It encompassed much of northern Kansas and part of western Missouri, with headquarters at Kansas City. Adopting an even more zealous campaign than Blunt to eradicate guerrillas, Ewing began rounding up female loved ones of the guerrillas to banish them from the district. Many of them, including the sisters of Bloody Bill Anderson, were imprisoned in Kansas City. When the structure collapsed on August 13, killing five young women, the guerrillas were understandably outraged. Ewing did nothing to soften their fury when he issued Order No. 10 on August 18, officially proclaiming the policy he had already instituted. It read:

> Officers will arrest, and send to the district provost-marshal for punishment, all men (and all women not heads of households) who willfully aid and encourage guerrillas. . . They will discriminate as carefully as possible between those who were compelled, by threats or fears, to aid the rebels and those who aid them from disloyal motives. The wives and children of known guerrillas, and also women who are heads of families and are willfully engaged in aiding guerrillas, will be notified by such officers to remove out of this district and out of the State of Missouri forthwith.[12]

After guerrillas struck back by sacking Lawrence, Ewing issued Order No. 11, an even more severe policy. It required all citizens living in Jackson, Cass, and Bates counties and the northern part of Vernon County, except those within one mile of a Federal post, to either establish their loyalty and move to a military station—or leave.[13]

The policies that Blunt and Ewing adopted in the spring and summer of 1863 reflected the growing intolerance of Union authorities toward the female associates of guerrillas. Arrests of women accelerated. Only about forty women came into the custody of Union officials in St. Louis from the beginning of the war until the end of 1862, and not all of them were imprisoned. By comparison, at least one hundred seventy women, most from the state of Missouri, were jailed in St. Louis area prisons in 1864 alone. Many of them were arrested for helping bushwhackers. Indeed, the large majority of the women profiled in this book were arrested during 1864, the peak year of guerrilla activity in Missouri.[14]

The Union's arrest and prosecution of women represented an explicit recognition that they could not be ignored and would have to be dealt with. No longer could they be dismissed as outside the realm of politics and war. To be prosecuted was to be taken seriously. Even being required to take an oath was significant, because it meant that a woman was being recognized as a citizen. White women had always been allowed to take oaths, but being required to do so was an unusual acknowledgement of their political personhood.[15]

Few scholars today would disagree with the idea that the Civil War helped empower women, at least temporarily. The female abettors of the Missouri guerrillas were no exception. The activities they engaged in forced men—both the Union soldiers who opposed them and the partisan fighters who relied on their help—to take them seriously.

We will take them seriously, too. Let's meet the bushwhacker belles and hear their stories—their backgrounds, testimony about their supposed crimes, their own words, their punishments, and the rest of their stories.

Chapter 2
She Adder and Rebel Damsel

In 1863, halfway through the Civil War, Union troops in Missouri were growing frustrated with their inability to drive Confederate partisans out of the state. The Federals had begun to target the guerrillas' civilian support system. And even women, who'd largely been left alone until now, were no longer off limits.

Clay County was a Confederate stronghold. Food, clothing, and comfort were in short supply. Lurena "Lou" McCoy was nineteen, with two kids at home and her husband fighting for the South. After he slipped home for a visit, Lou decided to help the cause. She made a gray uniform for a guerrilla.

Federal soldiers interrogated her for the whereabouts of her husband, Confederate soldier Moses McCoy—and about the uniform she was making. Her husband's hurried visit and the humble cloth landed Lou in a mess of trouble. She was one of the bushwhacker belles.

In a 1912 article for *Confederate Veteran Magazine*, Lou, now sixty-eight years old, recalled her arrest in Clay County during the war. Besides making a suit of clothes for the Southern recruit, she had refused to tell Federal soldiers where her husband was. Her memory of events, forty-nine years after they happened, was sharp, but there was a bit more to the story, at least from the Union side, than what she told the magazine.[1]

Sometime near the first of March in 1863, Confederate recruiting officer Joe Hart appeared in the Clay County area with an irregular band that included Moses McCoy. Lou identified her husband as a captain in Colonel Jo Shelby's Confederate cavalry brigade, and she explained that the men were not only on a recruiting mission but had also returned home to see their families. Lou was left alone since early in the war to take care of two kids, and still only nineteen years old in 1863. She was no doubt glad to see her husband and his friends, but the visit ended up getting the young woman in serious difficulty.[2]

On or about March 15, Lou's sister Lydia was visiting the McCoy home a couple miles east of Missouri City when, according to Lydia, Lou went into town and brought back a tailor named James Moffett because she wanted to make a suit of clothes—a gray uniform—for Joe Hart. When Lou returned with Moffett, Hart and another guerrilla named Louis Vandiver were at the McCoy home. Moffett took Hart's measurements and left.

After the material for the suit was cut, Lou went to the Missouri City home of Elizabeth Wallis around the first of April and asked her to finish the coat.

It was wartime, and money was scarce. They bartered. In exchange for Mrs. Wallis's work, Lou offered to give her meat or other food items. Mrs. Wallis agreed, and she completed the coat except for buttonholes and buttons. Meanwhile, Lou went to Nowlin's store in Missouri City and bought trim for the coat; she presumably cut the buttonholes herself and sewed on the buttons and other trim after Mrs. Wallis returned the coat to her.[3]

A local Union militia captain, Darius Sessions, somehow learned of Lou's involvement in making a suit of clothes for a Southern soldier. On May 15, he arrested Lou at her home and confiscated the coat. The coat, however, was little more than a pretext. The main charge against Lou was that she had helped Hart's band of guerrillas.

Sessions offered to parole her on the spot if she would reveal her husband's whereabouts, according to Lou's story many years later. She refused. Sessions and his detachment started with her toward the US arsenal at Liberty Landing as their prisoner. As the Federals escorted her through the streets of Missouri City, Louis Vandiver's sister witnessed the spectacle. She sent word of Lou's arrest to her brother and other members of Hart's band.[4]

At Liberty Landing, arsenal commander Captain Joseph Schmitz of the Twenty-fifth Missouri Volunteer Infantry began gathering evidence against Lou. What about the confiscated coat? Elizabeth Wallis said Lou had told her that she was having the coat made for her brother. Lydia Alder on the other hand, suggested the only coat she knew about was the one her sister Lou had made for Joe Hart. Lydia said she saw the suit of clothes at her sister's house after it had been completed. She did not know who had cut it out or where, but she said she saw Hart leave the McCoy premises with it. When she was shown the coat that had been confiscated, she said it was not the same one that she had seen her sister give to Hart.

So, it's quite possible that Lou McCoy had a hand in making two different coats around the same time. Then again, it's just as likely that Lou claimed the coat was for her brother when it was really for Hart. Years later, in her recollection of the events surrounding her arrest, Lou made no mention of two different coats. If there was only one coat, however, Lydia must have been lying as well. If so, her motivation for doing so is not clear since she had already implicated her sister with the first part of her testimony.[5]

At any rate, Schmitz drew up a formal statement of charges against Lou. The first charge was that she had given aid and comfort to the enemy. The specification was that she had fed and harbored Joe Hart's band during the month of March.

The second charge was disloyal conduct. The first specification was that she had spoken in favor of the rebellion and of persons engaged in the rebellion. She was reported to have said on or about March 15, "I have fed Hart and will feed him again and…if I had no children, I would turn out in the brush myself and help Hart." The second specification was that, when she was arrested, she had in her possession "certain wearing apparel fashioned after the manner of the colors of the Rebels now in arms against the U.S. of America."

Among the witnesses who signed the statement of charges against Lou was James Moffett, the tailor who had fitted Hart for his suit.[6]

On May 17, after completing his investigation and drawing up the charges against Lou, Schmitz put the prisoner on a steamboat headed for St. Joseph, headquarters of the District of North Missouri. Meanwhile, according to Lou's later story, Moses McCoy was south of the Missouri River heading back to the Confederate Army. Then word of his wife's arrest reached him. Outraged by the news, he called at the camp of noted Jackson County guerrilla leader William Quantrill and asked for some men to accompany him back into Clay County. Quantrill furnished the warriors.

McCoy and about fifteen other guerrillas re-crossed the river on the morning of May 19. They were bent on revenge. Although most of the men accompanying McCoy had been recruited by Hart, Hart himself had temporarily left the group to make a trip to the St. Joseph area. Ferdinand Scott led the partisans who came into Clay County on the 19th. Others members of the gang, besides McCoy, included Frank James, Fletch Taylor, and Louis Vandiver.

The guerrillas went to the McCoy neighborhood east of Missouri City and called for breakfast at the home of a local man. They announced that they were members of Quantrill's band, and their boisterous conduct led the man to believe they were drunk. After they left, the man hurried to Missouri City to report their presence in the area to the Union soldiers stationed there. According to Lou, the man was a friend of the guerrillas who told his visitors he must report them in order not to get in trouble himself. They told him to go ahead because that was what they wanted.[7]

Upon hearing the man's report of guerrillas in the area, Captain Sessions of the local militia and Lieutenant Louis Grafenstein of Schmitz's Twenty-fifth Missouri Infantry started immediately out of town. They took three soldiers to investigate.

The bushwhackers lay in wait at the side of the road about a mile and a half east of town. When the soldiers approached, the band sprang up out of the brush. They opened fire, knocking Sessions and a soldier named Benjamin Rapp down with the first blasts. Grafenstein was hit soon afterwards.

The guerrillas closed in on the three injured men as the other two soldiers escaped. Rapp was robbed and left for dead, and Sessions was shot two or three more times through the head. Grafenstein, while trying to surrender, was shot twice through the head as a woman stood by begging for his life. Captain Schmitz's official report described the savagery.

The guerrillas trailed the remaining two soldiers into Missouri City by a circuitous route. They found Rapp was still alive, having been picked up along the road, brought into town in a wagon, and treated in a hotel. Upon hearing the news, one of the guerrillas went to the wounded man's bedside, pulled out his pistol, and fired three more rounds into the helpless soldier. Left for dead a second time, Rapp miraculously survived again.[8]

The guerrillas pillaged the town. Then they moved off to the north, Schmitz reported, and rendezvoused with Joe Hart. Hart told them he had come straight from St. Joseph, where he had managed a brief visit with Lou McCoy, then on parole in the city.

According to Lou's later story, however, her husband and some of the guerrillas re-crossed the Missouri River after the Missouri City raid and went back to Quantrill's camp. They reported that Sessions was dead and Lou McCoy was still a prisoner. The guerrilla leader captured a Union provost marshal and held him as a ransom for her freedom.[9]

Upon first reaching St. Joseph, Lou McCoy was taken before district commander Colonel Chester Harding, Jr. He read the charges against her, and she admitted she had fed and harbored Rebel soldiers.

Calling her a "she adder" and a "rebel damsel," the *St. Joseph Morning Herald* said she told Harding that "her friends were in the brush to protect themselves from insult, rapine, and murder" and that she would continue to help them as long as she could. "That is the kind of grit we like to see in God's last best gift to man," said the *Herald*, "but we prefer to see her exerting herself for honest men rather than thieves and murderers. Miss McCoy should 'star it' in the South awhile." Despite Lou's sassy attitude, Harding told her she could be released upon taking an ironclad oath to the Union, but she refused unless the most objectionable parts of the oath were marked out. Harding declined her demand and retained her in custody.[10]

Lou was held at first at the residence of a Federal captain named Dunn, but the limits of her confinement were soon extended upon her word of honor to include the city of St. Joseph. After she had been in St. Joe a few days, Harding called her back into his office and again offered her a parole in exchange for her oath. She again refused. Finally, after she had been in St. Joseph almost a week, the colonel offered her what she called "a mild, light oath," and she took it. Immediately after taking the oath, she was informed that she needn't have done so, because Quantrill had already negotiated her freedom in exchange for his releasing the Union provost marshal he had captured.[11]

Much of Lou's story rings true. Parts of it seem romanticized, such as her absolute refusal to take a strict oath. The extent of Quantrill's involvement in the Missouri City episode and its aftermath is also perhaps overstated. What we know for sure is that the terms of her oath

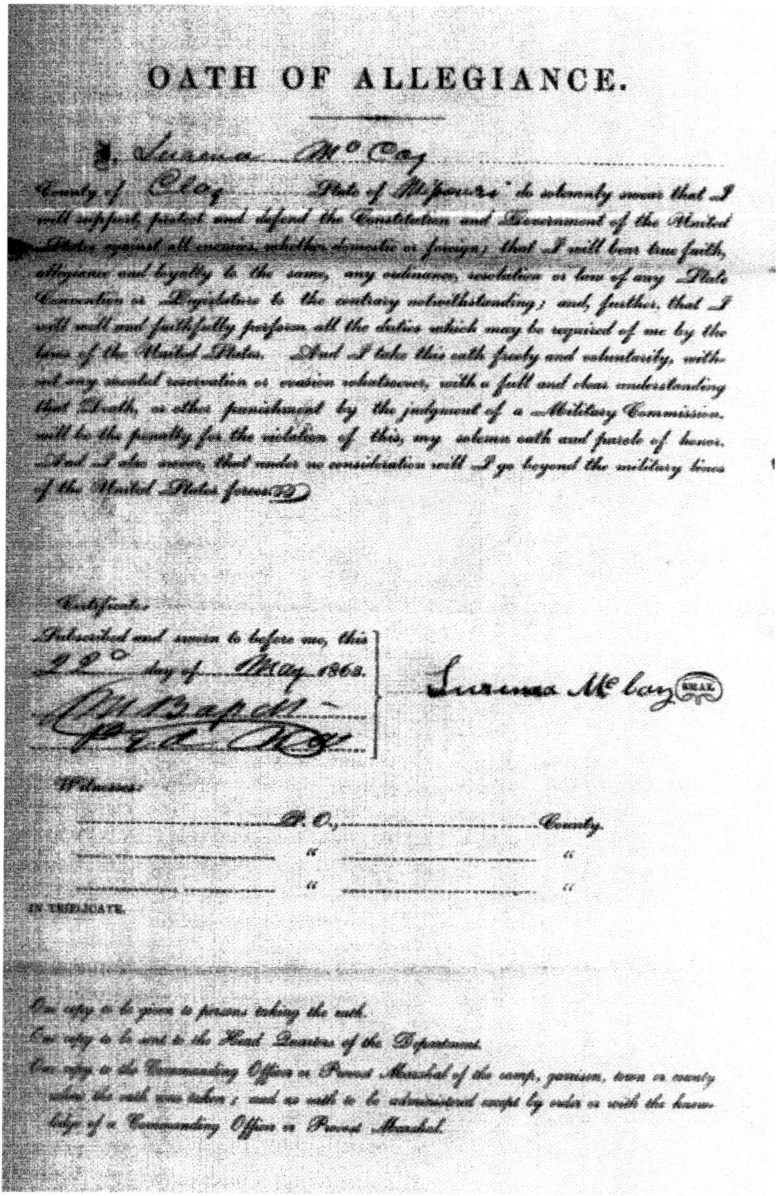

OATH OF ALLEGIANCE.

I, Lurena McCoy

County of Clay State of Missouri do solemnly swear that I will support, protect and defend the Constitution and Government of the United States against all enemies, whether domestic or foreign; that I will bear true faith, allegiance and loyalty to the same, any ordinance, resolution or laws of any State Convention or Legislature to the contrary notwithstanding; and, further, that I will well and faithfully perform all the duties which may be required of me by the laws of the United States. And I take this oath freely and voluntarily, without any mental reservation or evasion whatsoever, with a full and clear understanding that Death, or other punishment by the judgment of a Military Commission, will be the penalty for the violation of this, my solemn oath and parole of honor. And I also swear, that under no consideration will I go beyond the military lines of the United States forces.

Certificate

Subscribed and sworn to before me, this 22d day of May 1862.

Lurena McCoy (SEAL)

Witnesses:

P. O., County.

IN TRIPLICATE.

One copy to be given to persons taking the oath.
One copy to be sent to the Head Quarters of the Department.
One copy to the Commanding Officer or Provost Marshal of the camp, garrison, town or county where the oath was taken; and no oath to be administered except by order or with the knowledge of a Commanding Officer or Provost Marshal.

The oath Lurena McCoy took, which she later claimed was a "light" oath. (From Union provost marshals' records.)

and parole were about as ironclad as such documents normally were during the Civil War. She signed both on May 22, 1863. The oath stated that she solemnly swore to support the US, to bear true allegiance to the same, and to perform all duties required of her. It further stated that she understood she could receive any sentence up to and including death for violating the oath. The parole specified that she would not in any manner promote the rebellion, provide aid or support to the enemies of the United States, or have any communication of any kind with those engaged in hostilities against the US government.[12]

Reflecting many years later on her arrest and the circumstances surrounding it, Lou allowed that Captain Sessions no doubt felt he was only doing his duty in arresting her, but his action was a cruel wrong and a mistake that cost him his life. Speaking of Moses McCoy, Lou declared, "Like a true defender of home, he restored his wife to her children and her fireside and then went back to his post in Shelby's command to fight for his country. . . .Mr. McCoy would have been less than a man and unworthy of a wife if he had permitted such an injustice to go unpunished."[13]

After her parole, Lou McCoy came back to Clay County and apparently lived in relative peace for the next year and a half. However, she certainly did not switch her loyalties to the Union. She did not altogether give up her activities on behalf of guerrillas or Southern soldiers either. In the fall 1864, she was once again arrested on suspicion of disloyal activity. Although the details of her arrest are sketchy, it had something to do with her activity during General Sterling Price's raid into Missouri in September and October. Recollecting the incident years later, Lou said only that she was accused of coming in advance of Price on his raid. She added that her husband had, in fact, come in advance of Price but that she had not. Presumably what Lou was actually arrested for was feeding and otherwise helping her husband and other Confederate soldiers from Price's army.[14]

Union authorities also arrested a number of other civilians from the Clay County area about the same time they arrested Lou, with the prospect of shipping them all south. Captain W. B. Kemper, assistant provost marshal at Liberty, began gathering evidence against them. Writing to the Department of the Missouri headquarters in St. Louis on December 2, 1864, Kemper informed Colonel Joseph Darr., Jr., acting provost marshal general, that he had sworn testimony against Mrs. Moses McCoy and family and he felt sure it would satisfy the colonel in her cases. Kemper said he also had a letter written by Lou to Mr. Reed of Clay County. "Reed is strictly a loyal man," Kemper added, "and has not been able to live at home during the past summer and fall." Although the contents of Lou's letter to Reed are unknown, the missive apparently implicated her in disloyal activities or expressed disloyal sentiments.[15]

On January 29, 1865, Lurena McCoy signed a sworn statement on behalf of herself and a number of other civilians who were to be shipped south. They had to certify that they had been read banishment orders to areas beyond the US forces (Special Orders No. 9, issued by the Department of the Missouri headquarters on January 9). According to Lou's later recollection, she left Liberty near the middle of February in company with twelve other families from Clay and Jackson counties, escorted by a detachment of Union soldiers. The group was taken to Pine Bluff, Arkansas, where a new escort received them for their continued journey south.[16]

At the mid-point of the war, Lou had been arrested and released upon taking an oath of loyalty after just a few days of confinement. Now, she was being shipped south on charges seemingly no more serious than those she'd faced in 1863. By late 1864 and early 1865, Union officials had lost patience with the Missouri guerrillas—and with the women who helped them.

The Rest of the Story

Lou McCoy did not return to Clay County after the war. She made her home in Texas, as did many other Missouri expatriates of Southern sentiment.

Moses McCoy died just a few years after the war ended, and Lou was remarried to William P. Lucas.

Lou had three children by McCoy and four additional children by William Lucas. She married a third time to Calvin B. Gentry when she was relatively old, and she died in Tarrant County, Texas, the Fort Worth area, in 1916.[17]

CHAPTER 3
More in Common than a Name

Saline County, named for the salty springs along the Missouri River, was bushwhacker territory. It was part of an area known as "Little Dixie" because of the concentration of small plantations producing cash crops like hemp and tobacco. Most of the white settlers had come from Kentucky and Tennessee. About one-third of the county's residents were slaves.

In the summer of 1863, Federal cavalry searched the county for guerrilla chief Bill Jackson. They particularly wanted him because he was the son of former Missouri governor Claiborne F. Jackson, who had tried to take the state out of the Union.

This is the story of how Lieutenant William D. Blair chased Jackson in Saline County in late August. Instead, he found three Jackson women who were unrelated to Bill Jackson but who nonetheless tried to hide his whereabouts.

They paid the price as bushwhacker belles.

On or about August 26, Lieutenant Blair of the Fourth Missouri State Militia Cavalry led a scout past the Mary Jackson residence in the neighborhood of Saline City shortly before noon. A black woman standing in the doorway beckoned him, and he stopped to see what she wanted. The woman told the Federal officer that Bill Jackson was in the woods nearby with four men and that Mary Jackson and her family had fed the bushwhackers earlier the same day.

Suddenly a young woman appeared. She ordered the servant away while Blair was still talking to her. The young woman, twenty-six-year old Betty Jackson, was one of Mary Jackson's daughters, and Blair testified she later told him no one who would report on her friends was going to stay around her.[1]

Blair and his scouting party promptly rode to the indicated

spot in the woods and found signs that a band of men had recently been there. Convinced that the servant had been telling the truth, Blair set off in pursuit of the guerrillas.[2]

The Federals were unable to overtake the bushwhackers and gave up the chase. They returned to the Jackson home about five o'clock the same afternoon. Confronting Mary Jackson, Blair demanded to know whether she had fed Bill Jackson's gang earlier in the day. She admitted she had. She had declined to feed the men at her house; instead, she had sent them to the woods with the assurance that she would send food to them there "if they must have it."[3]

Betty Jackson's sister Sue confessed that she and another sister, Nannie, had delivered the victuals to Bill Jackson in the woods. Bill Jackson and his men were her friends, she was not ashamed of taking food to them, and she would fight for them, too, if she had any kind of arms.[4]

Betty Jackson confirmed that she was the one who had run off the black woman who had told the Federals Bill Jackson's location earlier in the day. Bill Jackson and his guerrillas were her friends. She didn't care who knew it. She planned to feed them at every opportunity.[5]

Blair arrested Mary, Betty, and Sue Jackson on August 27 and took them to Marshall, where they were held for several days before being transferred to district headquarters at Jefferson City, pending legal proceedings against them.

On September 14, all three women were paroled under the condition that they report when called. The terms of Betty's and Sue's paroles confined them to the limits of Jefferson City, while their mother was allowed the freedom of Cole County. The next day, orders were issued that the Jackson women should be tried by military commission at Marshall in their home county of Saline.[6]

Mary Jackson's trial began on the morning of October 6. Lieutenant Blair was the main prosecution witness. John Lincoln, a private in the Federal scouting party, sustained his commanding officer's testimony concerning the soldiers' chase after Bill Jackson's guerrillas. After the soldiers returned to Mrs.

Lieutenant (later Captain) William D. Blair arrested the Jackson women. William D. Blair, #11477, in the collection of Wilson's Creek Battlefield. (Courtesy of National Park Service.)

Jackson's house, Lincoln heard her say to Lieutenant Blair that she had fed Bill Jackson but she would never have gone to the door if she had known it was Bill Jackson at her dooryard fence.[7]

Conducting her own cross examination, Mary Jackson tried to get Lieutenant Blair to admit she had told him that she at first ordered Bill Jackson away and that she only fed him after he threatened her. Blair responded that he recalled only that she had said she did not want to feed the guerrillas at her home but would feed them in the woods.[8]

Mrs. Jackson called James Bailey, a worker on her farm, as a defense witness. Bailey testified that Mary Jackson had refused to feed Bill Jackson's guerrillas and their horses when they first came to her house and had told them to leave. Bill Jackson said he would "be damned if he was not going to have it, if he had to take it by force."[9]

Mary also submitted a written statement in her defense. She acknowledged feeding Bill Jackson's men but claimed she did so under compulsion. She then added in language of the time: "As to harboring them, she as an individual denyes ever having dun any such thing." Mary further claimed that she had always been opposed "to that sistem of warfare" and had never done anything for the guerrillas "but what they forced her to do."[10]

Despite her protestations of innocence, Mary Jackson was convicted of feeding and harboring guerrillas after a trial that lasted only a couple of hours.

The trial of her daughter Betty, charged with uttering disloyal sentiments, began immediately afterwards. Lieutenant Blair was again the chief witness for the prosecution. He said that Betty Jackson denied having seen Bill Jackson's men on the day in question but she admitted they were her friends and that she was the person who had driven the black woman away. Betty offered no defense except for her written statement.

As for the general charge of uttering treasonous sentiments, Betty pleaded helpless womanhood. The statement read, "Her being a lady, and unaccustomed to being held responsible for anything she might say, she did not really know what was loyal or disloyal." Betty denied the allegation that she had called Bill

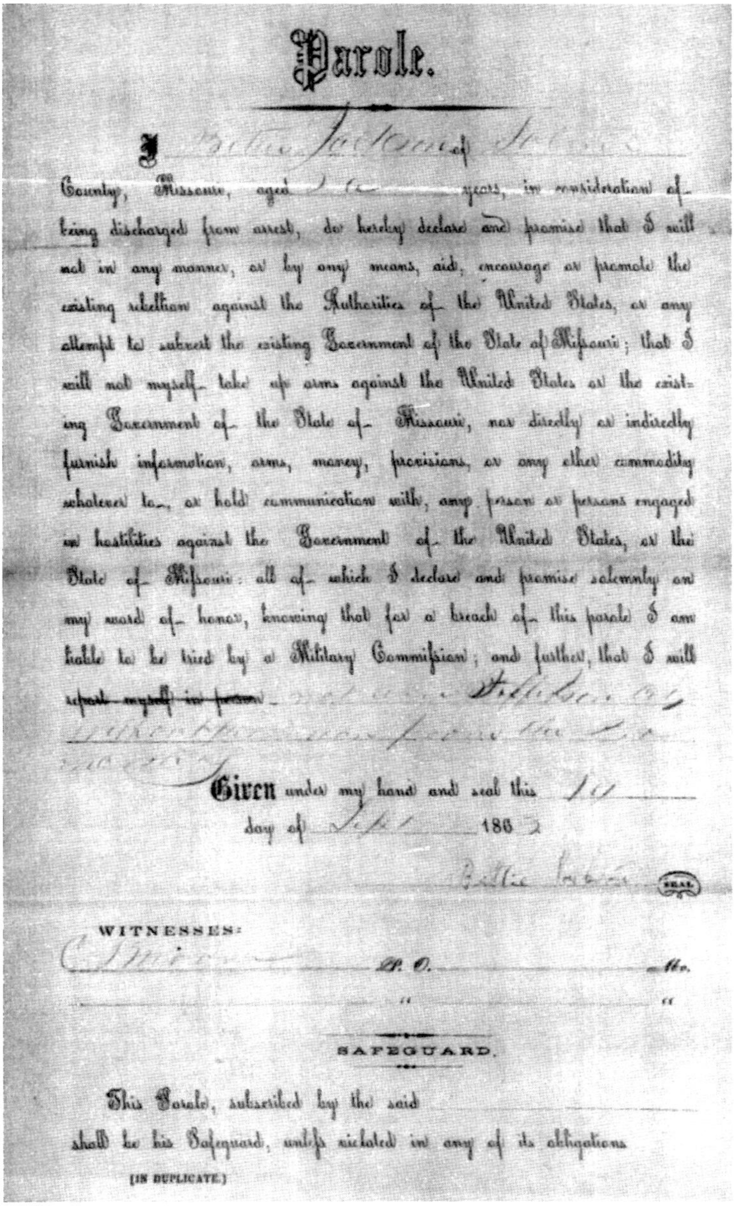

Parole.

I Bettie Jackson of [illegible] County, Missouri, aged [illegible] years, in consideration of being discharged from arrest, do hereby declare and promise that I will not in any manner, or by any means, aid, encourage or promote the existing rebellion against the Authorities of the United States, or any attempt to subvert the existing Government of the State of Missouri; that I will not myself take up arms against the United States or the existing Government of the State of Missouri, nor directly or indirectly furnish information, arms, money, provisions, or any other commodity whatever to, or hold communication with, any person or persons engaged in hostilities against the Government of the United States, or the State of Missouri: all of which I declare and promise solemnly on my word of honor, knowing that for a breach of this parole I am liable to be tried by a Military Commission; and further, that I will ~~report myself in person~~ [illegible]

Given under my hand and seal this 10 day of Sept 186[illegible]

Bettie Jackson [SEAL]

WITNESSES:

[illegible] P. O. Mo.

" "

SAFEGUARD.

This Parole, subscribed by the said shall be his Safeguard, unless violated in any of its obligations

(IN DUPLICATE.)

Betty Jackson's parole, restricting her freedom to the limits of Jefferson City. (From Union provost marshals' records.)

Jackson her friend or had said she would feed him. When she ran the black woman off, she had said only that no one should stay around her who would bring her into trouble.

Like her mother, Betty closed her statement with a plea for leniency and a willingness to take the oath of allegiance, but she, too, was convicted of the charge against her.[11]

Sue was charged with feeding and harboring bushwhackers as well as uttering disloyal language. She was tried after her older sister. Lieutenant Blair was once again the prosecution's star witness. Sue did not deny making statements to him and his men that might have been construed as disloyal.

During Blair's cross-examination, however, she claimed she spoke as she did only because his men used insulting language toward her. Blair's rebuttal? He was the only one to whom she talked.

In her written statement, Sue acknowledged carrying victuals to Jackson on the day in question, but only because, "owing to the imperitive command of Jackson, it had to be dun, and she hapened to be the one appointed to do it." She never harbored bushwhackers. She never said she would fight for Jackson. She said only that she could fight, meaning she could fight those who insulted her. She had no recollection of saying Jackson and his gang were her friends.

She claimed to be only fourteen years old (when she was at least eighteen or nineteen). She, like her mother and her sister, closed her statement with a plea for leniency. Faring no better than they did, she was convicted on both charges against her when a verdict in her case was rendered on October 7.[12]

All three women were sentenced to be banished from the state. Brigadier General Egbert B. Brown, commanding the District of Central Missouri, approved the findings and sentences in late October. Brown ordered the women sent to St. Louis to await the ruling of Major General John M. Schofield in their cases, although no record of their transfer has been located. In late November, General Schofield, commanding the Department of the Missouri, approved the findings and sentences.

General John M. Schofield commuted the sentences of the Jackson women. (Courtesy of the Library of Congress.)

However, he commuted the sentence of Mrs. Jackson and canceled the punishment of her two daughters. Mrs. Jackson was required to give bond in the sum of $1,000 as a security for her "future good conduct" and to take an oath of allegiance to the Union, while her daughters were required only to take oaths. Schofield ordered that the women be released from custody upon fulfilling the required obligations.[13]

Mary Jackson had claimed she only helped Bill Jackson because he made her. Betty pleaded for leniency because she was a woman. Sue said she was a mere girl who only used disloyal language because the soldiers insulted her. All were common arguments employed by the bushwhacker belles. All failed in the case of the Jackson women. Their only salvation was that the year was 1863. Commanding generals still hesitated to impose banishment or lengthy imprisonment on women. That would soon change.

The Rest of the Story

Mary Jackson and her husband, Thomas, were still living in Saline County by 1880. Mary died shortly afterward, and Thomas died a few years later. Both are buried in Saline County's Sappington Grove Cemetery.

What happened to the couple's daughters Betty and Sue after the Civil War has not been traced.[14]

CHAPTER 4

The Heart and Soul of Bushwhacking

Of all the female allies of the Missouri guerrillas, perhaps none are more legendary than the Mayfield sisters of Vernon County. Situated on the Kansas border south of Kansas City, Vernon County suffered considerable damage during the Civil War. The courthouse and the whole town of Nevada were burned in 1863, and the county was almost completely depopulated by General Thomas Ewing, Jr.'s infamous Order No. 11. In Vernon County, as elsewhere in the state, women and children suffered along with the men. The story of the Mayfield sisters typifies as well as any the bravery and adventure with which the women faced their hardships.

In 1887, twenty-plus years after the war, the author of the *History of Vernon County*, wrote about the Mayfield women. After allowing that their "highly thrilling" experiences "ought to be related in full, without exaggeration or embellishment," he went on to pen an exaggerated and embellished account of their wartime exploits. We can perhaps forgive the author's occasional embroidery, because compared to many other county histories of the era, the *History of Vernon County* is quite reliable. A few years later a correspondent to the *St. Louis Globe-Democrat*, repeating several of the same episodes chronicled in the county history, penned a less accurate and equally romantic version of the Mayfield women's exploits that fueled and distorted the legend. Stories about the Mayfield girls have endured into the modern era, adding to the inviolability, if not the truth, of the legend. But what is really known for sure about the Mayfields?[1]

John Mayfield and Ella Justine Burrus migrated from Tennessee to Missouri about 1836 and settled in Newton County. In 1850, their family included Hiram, Brice, Amanda (who usually went by her middle name, Ella, while her mother went by Justine), Lenora, John (whose middle name was Crawford and who was usually called

Crack), and Clarinda. For some reason, seven-year-old Sarah "Sallie" Mayfield, was not living with her parents but instead was staying in the John Hoyt household not far away.[2]

In 1856, the family moved to Vernon County, settling in the Montevallo area, and John Mayfield died there in 1858. Twenty-one-year-old Lenora, nineteen-year-old John, and thirteen-year-old Jane (listed as Clarinda in the previous census) were still living at home in 1860. Twenty-five-year-old Brice Mayfield was married, and he and his wife, Margaret, were also living in Justine's home. Twenty-three-year-old Ella was married to Joseph F. Phillips, and the couple was living nearby. Lenora's soon-to-be husband, John Gabbert, was also living in the Montevallo area with his family, including his father, William, and his twenty-four-year-old sister, Eliza. Seventeen-year-old Sallie Mayfield was already married, and she and her husband, David P. Giboney, were living across the Barton County line with a two-year-old son, William. The eldest Mayfield son, Hiram, had either returned to or stayed in Newton County and was working as a farmhand there.[3]

When the Civil War ignited, Brice Mayfield and his younger brother Crack joined the Missouri State Guard and served in Captain James M. Gatewood's company of Colonel Dewitt C. Hunter's Seventh Cavalry Regiment, composed mostly of Vernon County men. They saw action at Wilson's Creek in August of 1861 and at the skirmish on Dry Wood Creek in early September. During the latter action, Union forces captured Crack Mayfield, then released him on parole shortly afterward.[4]

In the winter of 1861-62, Brice Mayfield, returning from his service in the State Guard, came back into Vernon County "with some kind of recruiting authority," according to the county history. It is probable that Mayfield had, in fact, been commissioned to recruit in his home territory, as many Missouri soldiers were at this stage of the war, especially if they had served as officers during the early days of the State Guard. (Mayfield's rank in the state force is unknown.) Whether Mayfield drew his recruiting authority from the Confederate Army or the Missouri State Guard is uncertain. His older brother, Hiram, served in the Confederate Army after his term of enlistment with the State Guard expired, but there is no record that Brice ever did so.[5]

Regardless of the military authority for his mission, Brice Mayfield apparently spent more time bushwhacking than recruiting, as was the case with many Missouri soldiers sent back into their home area to recruit. According to the county history, he and his brother Crack turned to "irregular warfare against the Federals in this part of the State" as soon as they reappeared in the county after their stint with the State Guard:

> Their deeds and adventures, if fully related, would fill a considerable volume. They were splendid horsemen, not troubled with conscientious scruples regarding the manner in which they acquired their steeds, shrewd in forming their plans and cool and thorough in their execution, and bold and daring fighters.[6]

The Mayfield brothers became noted throughout the western border counties of Missouri from the Osage River south to the Arkansas line and "gained for themselves the admiration of a large share of the Confederate element of Southwest Missouri." The author allowed that some of their exploits were exaggerated, but then he proceeded to relate a few of their more dubious deeds.

During the early spring of 1862, while a company of the Sixth Kansas Cavalry was stationed at Montevallo, seven Federals reportedly rode out to a creek a half mile west of town. While they watered their horses, Brice Mayfield, Crack Mayfield, and John Gabbert surprised them and took them prisoner. The bushwhackers held the Union soldiers for several days at Dunnegin's Grove a few miles southwest of Montevallo while they tried to negotiate a prisoner exchange. The Mayfields' sister Ella and Gabbert's sister Eliza were dispatched to the Federal commander at Montevallo. They offered to swap the Union soldiers for Henry Taylor, a guerrilla leader then being held prisoner at Fort Scott, but the commander rejected the proposed exchange. The Federal soldiers, according to the county history, were soon afterward taken to Dry Wood Creek in western Vernon County, "turned loose and advised to go to 'bleeding Kansas' and stay there."[7]

The sisters and other female relatives of the Mayfield boys fed, clothed, and sheltered their knights of the bush, as family members of the Missouri guerrillas almost always did. But the Mayfield women went a step further. They acted as go-betweens as they did in their attempt to negotiate Henry Taylor's release or otherwise actively aided their husbands and brothers. The women's plucky reputation rivaled or exceeded that of their male relatives. As the county history said, "The Mayfield sisters were scouts, spies, guides, and couriers as the occasion demanded."[8]

On February 7, 1862, Kansas troops killed Sallie Mayfield's husband, David Giboney and left his body to rot for three days before he was finally buried in a shallow grave near a small stream.

Almost a month passed.

Sallie was nineteen, mother of two—and a sudden widow. Standing four feet ten inches, with light hair and hazel eyes, she might have looked unassuming, but she was no shrinking violet. About March 5, she dug up her husband's body by herself. She hauled his remains to a Montevallo cemetery and reburied the body on March 10, after an additional five days of exposure. Bushwhacker belles suffered cruelties of war just like their men.[9]

In early August of 1862, a number of Southern partisans of Vernon County were killed or captured during Confederate colonel John T. Coffee's recruiting campaign in the area. The captives were taken to Springfield and imprisoned. Later in the month, Ella Mayfield and Eliza Gabbert made a trek to Springfield on their own to intercede on behalf of the prisoners. One of the detainees, a young man named John McNeil, who had been captured twice previously and released each time upon taking an oath of allegiance, was particularly anxious about his fate should his identity be found out. Ella Mayfield saved him by pretending to be his lover and pleading with Union provost marshal T. A. Switzler to release her beau. According to the county history, Switzler yielded to the supplications of a pretty woman, and "McNeil was released upon taking another oath, and went away with his alleged 'sweetheart,' a woman he had never seen before!"[10]

A Union wagon train traveling in late December of 1862 from Fort Scott, Kansas, to Bentonville, Arkansas, camped in Neosho, Missouri, at Christmastime. Two men of the escort named Sam Kaiserman and Jack Hudson visited the home of a man named Parnell on Shoal Creek north of Neosho, where a number of young women were gathered. A local lad named Coyer accompanied them. The three men spent Christmas night there.

Eliza Gabbert was associated with the Mayfield girls and participated in some of their exploits. (Courtesy of the Bushwhacker Museum.)

Parnell lived in the Mayfields' old Newton County neighborhood, and Brice and Crack happened to be in the vicinity. Upon learning of the presence of the two soldiers at Parnell's house, the brothers determined to capture or kill them.

Early on the morning of the 26th, the Mayfields, dressed in Federal blue, rode up to the Parnell home and hallooed the house. Presuming the visitors to be fellow soldiers, Kaiserman and Hudson stepped out to greet them. Brice and Crack drew their revolvers and opened fire. They mortally wounded Hudson.

Unscathed, Kaiserman was able to drag his fallen comrade back inside, as the Mayfields dismounted and charged up to the house. Seventeen-year-old Coyer went to the door. He was shot and killed instantly. Kaiserman returned fire and killed both Mayfield brothers, Crack falling first and Brice falling across his younger brother's body. Both died almost instantly.

All four of the dead men were transported to Neosho. The Mayfields, recognized by some of the citizens there, were buried in a common grave. When Kaiserman got back to Fort Scott, he received a hero's greeting. An enterprising photographer took pictures of the "slayer of the Mayfield boys" and sold them as souvenirs.[11]

Lenora Mayfield's husband, John Gabbert, was killed April 25, 1863, by a Federal scouting party on the road between Montevallo and the Gabbert farm southwest of town. According to the county history, Gabbert was twenty-four years old at the time and his wife "much younger," but this is an error. In fact, Lenora was also twenty-four, the same age as her husband.[12]

Ella Mayfield, like her sisters Sallie and Lenora, spent time separated from her first husband during the early 1860s, although there is no evidence that Joseph Phillips was killed by Union soldiers as were Dave Giboney and John Gabbert. The *History of Vernon County* says only that Ella and her husband were "separated by the war."

Either the couple was divorced or else Phillips must have died. At least Ella behaved as if such were the case. Sometime in the spring or summer of 1863, she married David Majors, a bushwhacker from Cass County[13]

The last week or so of May 1863 turned bloody quickly.

On May 24, 1863, guerrillas under Vernon County partisan leader William Marchbanks killed two Union men from Cedar County in Nevada as the Federals were on their way home from Fort Scott. When word of the killings reached Cedar County, a squad of Union militia from that county and neighboring St. Clair County invaded Vernon County under Captain Anderson Morton. They burned the town of Nevada in revenge on the morning of May 26.

Early the same morning, a band of about twenty-five guerillas from the Montevallo area, unaware of Morton's presence in Vernon County, had ventured into Cedar County on a raid. Organized by forty-eight-year-old William Gabbert but led by Jackson County bushwhacker William Bridgeman, the guerrillas burned several dwellings belonging to Union men and came back to Vernon County loaded down with plunder. Meanwhile, Morton, returning to Cedar County after completing his fiery work in Nevada, struck the trail of the bushwhackers near Montevallo and followed them to the Gabbert home near the small community of Bellamy, where they surprised and routed the guerrillas, killing seven, including Bridgeman. The rest of the partisans, including William Gabbert and Dave Majors, managed to escape. Morton burned the Gabbert home and regained most of the loot the bushwhackers had carried off from Cedar County.[14]

Ella Mayfield was one of the first on the scene at the Gabbert place after the guerrillas had been shot to pieces and fled. According to the county history, she "with her own hands washed the ghastly faces and prepared the bloody corpses of the bushwhackers for sepulture; and she and her sisters assisted in their burial." Tending to the dead and dying was expected of most young women of the Civil War, but what Ella Mayfield did next is the stuff of legend.[15]

She was still helping with the interments when a messenger brought word that she was urgently needed in Fort Scott on a matter of life and death. Mounting a swift horse at three o'clock in the afternoon, Ella rode to the house of a Southern-sympathizing friend four miles north of Fort Scott; she covered the entire distance "without drawing bridle" and arrived at nightfall.

After Brice Mayfield's death the previous December, his widow, Margaret, had vowed that the guerrillas would avenge her husband's death if his killer ever fell into their hands. By way of identifying the man they wanted, the bushwhackers had managed to obtain one of the souvenir photos of Kaiserman. They got it from a doctor in Fort Scott named Davis. Ella learned upon reaching her friend's house that Union soldiers had called on Dr. Davis for return of the photo. They threatened to kill him if he did not produce it in twenty-four hours.[16]

Remounting her steed, Ella galloped through the night and arrived at her mother's home a little after daylight. Within an hour, she had procured the photograph and was once again blazing a trail toward Fort Scott astride her trusty horse.

She arrived just in time for Dr. Davis to produce the picture. She saved his life, so the story goes, "having ridden 125 miles in 24 hours, day and night, across the country, fording streams and threading intricate byways, with but two hours rest and repose."[17]

"Dave Majors was a rough rider and a fierce fighter," and Ella shared in many of her husband's adventures. Once she was in camp with him and his band of guerrillas on Cynthia Creek southwest of Montevallo.. A company of Cedar County militia suddenly charged upon them, scattering the bushwhackers in every direction. Instead of running, Ella grabbed her husband's saddle and revolvers and hid with them in a nearby thicket. "She concealed herself for two days and nights, without food and but little water, and with no companionship save that afforded by the skunks, opossums, and prairie wolves, which visited the abandoned camp to feed upon some fresh meat left by the bushwhackers in their flight," according to the county history.[18]

On May 20, 1864, Justine Mayfield's house was burned, and shortly afterward she planned to go south into Arkansas, escorted by Dave Majors and his band of bushwhackers. They helped her load a wagon with provisions and make other arrangements for the trip. Federals attacked the guerrilla party on the morning it was to set out, so they postponed the journey. A few days later, the partisans again made preparations to depart.

They were at an abandoned log cabin two miles northwest of Bellamy getting ready to leave when a second Federal attack scattered the bushwhackers camped in front of the cabin. One of the guerrillas, John Hinman, sprang to his saddle but had trouble getting his horse's reins unhitched from the small bush to which they were fastened. Dave's wife, Ella Mayfield, rushed from the cabin, heedless of the bullets that whizzed around her, to try to help Hinman. Suddenly, the horse broke loose, and Hinman whirled the animal around and galloped forward right into Ella, knocking her to the ground and trampling over her. Ella picked herself up, her face covered with blood, but she was little worse for the wear and even helped dig a grave and bury a bushwhacker named Joe Ray, who had been killed in the attack. Concluding his account of Ella's various adventures, the author of the county history declared, "There is not room here to give the thrilling experiences of Ella Mayfield in full, interesting as they may be to a certain class of the readers of this volume."[19]

Although Ella was the most active of the Mayfield sisters in her support of guerrillas during the Civil War, Sallie became the most noted after the war, largely because of a case of mistaken identity.

A version of the tales involving Ella Mayfield that misnamed the intrepid heroine as Sallie Mayfield was published in the *St. Louis Globe-Democrat* in 1891. It was subsequently reprinted in other newspapers across the country, elevating Sallie to a legendary status that surpassed her more adventuresome older sister.

Not only did the newspaper account attribute Ella's feats to Sallie, but the story also exaggerated many of the details of Ella's exploits, as originally chronicled in the county history. For instance, the 125 miles that Ella supposedly rode in 24 hours became 120 miles in 12 hours in the Sallie version of the story published in the newspapers, and the ride Ella had made with only "two hours rest and repose" Sallie managed to accomplish, in the newspaper adaptation, "without an hour's rest or a wink of sleep."[20]

Only one episode involving the Mayfield sisters' partisan activity can be documented. It was a run-in that Sallie Mayfield and her younger sister Clarinda Jane (often called "Jennie") had with Federal authorities in the summer of 1864. The facts surrounding the case paint a considerably tamer picture of Sallie than her legend holds, and the affair scarcely rivals the supposed exploits of Ella Mayfield. Despite this, it shows that the Mayfield women were, indeed, fast friends of the bushwhackers and resourceful in accomplishing their ends.[21]

Sallie remarried a man named Waitman or Weightman, sometime after Dave Giboney's death in February 1862 and prior to the summer of 1864. (Her second husband was possibly the Weightman that the *History of Vernon County* identifies as a member of Marchbanks's band of guerrillas.) In the summer of 1864, Sallie was living in Newton County, although her husband was away from home in the Confederate Army.[22]

In July 1864, Sallie returned to Vernon County to visit her mother and other members of the Mayfield family. On the 23rd, Sallie, her sister Jennie, her cousin Nancy Burris, and a fourth young woman named Nannie McConnell walked from the Mayfield home to pick apples at an orchard four miles away. They had gone about two miles when they were overtaken by six armed bushwhackers riding alongside the women. The men identified themselves as members of Marchbanks's command, although Jennie Mayfield later claimed they were "entire strangers" to her.

They asked whether the women had seen any Federal soldiers in the area, and the young ladies replied that they had not. As the women approached their destination, the bushwhackers spotted some Union soldiers in the orchard and promptly took to the brush, leaving the women to deal with the Federals on their own. The soldiers turned out to be a detachment of the Third Wisconsin Cavalry on a scout from Camp Curtis north of Nevada. They arrested the women on suspicion of aiding and abetting guerrillas.[23]

As the women were being taken back to the Federal camp near Balltown, Nannie McConnell escaped. The next day, July 24, Captain Robert Carpenter, the camp commander, sent the other three women under escort to Fort Scott. The escort also carried a letter from Carpenter to Colonel Charles W. Blair, commanding at

Fort Scott. He recommended that the women be banished from the district:

> These Ladies it is well known to all in this entire country have from the very first of Bushwhacking aided and abetted with all their energies & in every possible way the Bushwhackers & Thieves which infest this country. They have fed them, given them shells, carried them news, taken care of their Sick and wounded. In fine, they have given them a home & Supplied them with ammunition. They have been the very heart & Soul of Bushwhacking in this vicinity. They have been known to ride 25 & 30 miles to give warning to our enemies of any danger from the approach of Federal Troops. And just as long as Such women are allowed to live within our lines, just So long we may try in vain to exclude Bushwhacking, for they will Harbor about as long as we tolerate these women. We have fought the Rebs for the last two years & these women have always been their most effective aiders & abettors & if we are ever to rid this country of these midnight assassins & murderers, I must protest against these women being allowed to remain within our lines. If justice could be meted out to them, Hanging is too good for them. If these ladies take the notion, they will get away if not vigilantly guarded. They say they won't go South.[24]

After the prisoners reached Fort Scott, Colonel Blair wired Department of Kansas headquarters at Fort Leavenworth inquiring as to what should be done with them. He received a reply on July 26 with instructions to send them to Leavenworth. The next day, Blair forwarded the three women as directed, under the guard of Captain John Hayes. Blair also sent a letter to Major H. H. Heath, provost marshal at Leavenworth, seconding Captain Carpenter's recommendation that the women be banished from the district. Blair enclosed the captain's letter as evidence in the case, and he added, "There were three or four brothers & cousins of these Mayfield women who were noted desperadoes & bushwhackers, but they have all been killed off, leaving the women to represent the family in this regard."[25]

A fourth young woman, Ella Sims, was also sent to Leavenworth under Hayes's guard. Blair, however, recommended leniency in her case. Even though he felt confident she was a Southern sympathizer, he did not think she had actively aided bushwhackers; plus, she and her family were now living close to a Federal post where she could be closely watched.

Ella had been taken prisoner in Vernon County a week or two earlier, after a letter she wrote to her brother at Mexico, Missouri, was intercepted by Federal authorities. In the letter, she wrote of her "exquisite pleasure" in seeing guerrilla leader Henry Taylor and his men come into the county, and she told her brother of all the goings-on in their old neighborhood of Montevallo. Among the tidbits of information she imparted was news of the forthcoming wedding of "Miss Jane Mayfield to the honorable Mr. McWaters, bushwhacker, but you know that is a recommendation to anyone in this country."

Twenty-year-old William Edward McWaters, who lived in neighboring Cedar County around 1860, was a notorious guerrilla during the Civil War who became an even more infamous outlaw after the war. According to post war accounts, Jennie aided McWaters in many of his wartime exploits. The light-haired, blue-eyed Jennie stood four feet eight inches tall, two inches shorter than Sallie, but she was at least as daring and intrepid as her older sister, if the post war stories are to be believed. One outlandish claim even had her accompanying McWaters to Lawrence during Quantrill's notorious raid. (We do not know for sure whether the anticipated wedding between McWaters and seventeen-year-old Jennie Mayfield ever took place.)[26]

The female prisoners from Vernon County reached Leavenworth in late July and were held there for about three weeks. On August 20, Major Heath prepared to send Sallie Waitman, Jennie Mayfield, Nancy Burrus, and two other women to the District of Central Missouri headquarters at Kansas City for the disposition of their separate cases. In the transferal papers that Heath filled out, he advised Captain J. C. W. Hall, provost marshal at Kansas City, that Miss Burrus, Miss Mayfield, and Mrs. Giboney (i.e. Sallie Waitman) were "strongly tinctured with disloyalty, as their conversation, while under guard here, testifies." Later the same day, Nancy Burrus took sick, so the Federals held up the plans to send her to Kansas City and temporarily retained her at Leavenworth.

Miss Burrus was later paroled at Kansas City upon giving an

oath of allegiance. The exact fate of Ella Simms after reaching Leavenworth is unclear, although the Vernon County history said that she ultimately died either in prison or while on the way home.[27]

Jennie Mayfield and Sallie Waitman, however, were sent to Kansas City as scheduled, and they arrived there on or before August 22. On that date, Captain Hall wrote to Colonel J. P. Sanderson, provost marshal of the Department of the Missouri headquartered in St. Louis, asking what disposition to make of the women and enclosing the evidence against them, including Captain Carpenter's statement. Hall said he had no place to keep the women and no knowledge of their case beyond the enclosed evidence. However, he added, if Sanderson was in the habit of sending females south without trial for aiding and abetting bushwhackers, "I would regard them as proper subjects for such treatment."[28]

Hall received word back from Sanderson on or about August 27 that the Mayfield sisters should be sent to Gratiot Street Female Prison. Shortly thereafter they were transferred to St. Louis and arrived at the Gratiot facility on September 5. Union officials deposed both sisters on September 9.[29]

Sallie Waitman toned down her rhetoric once she reached St. Louis. As far as she knew, her husband was in the Confederate Army in General Green's brigade (presumably Martin Green's brigade). She didn't know whether he was still with Green or not. She had never helped bushwhackers, and she didn't even know any. Yes, guerrillas had come to her house two or three times but that they had only drunk water. She had never fed them, and they had never asked for anything to eat. The reason she didn't report them was that she lived too far from the nearest Federal post until the spring of 1864. Since then no bushwhackers had visited her house. She also blamed bushwhackers for having stolen two horses from her in the spring of 1862. She had two brothers in the Rebel army who had been killed earlier in the war. But she currently had no relatives in the Southern army except her husband and did not sympathize with the South, only with her husband. Sallie went so far as to say she desired to see the authority of the Federal government restored, and she was willing to take the oath of allegiance.[30]

Jennie Mayfield was hardly as contrite as her older sister.

Although she denied, like Sallie, that she or her family had ever fed or otherwise aided bushwhackers, she admitted to being a Southern sympathizer who "would be willing to help their cause if in my power." She added that she did not want to see the South put down and the authority of the US government established over the entire country.[31]

Sometime in September or early October, the Mayfield women transferred from Gratiot Street Prison to a temporary female prison on St. Charles Street. In the meantime, Union officials continued to examine the evidence in their case. One officer concluded the women were no doubt Southern sympathizers, but the evidence against them was insufficient to sustain a court martial. Another suggested release on oath and bond as "the best plan to pursue." On October 19, 1864, Union officers decided to banish the Mayfields to Illinois and require them to reside north and east of Springfield.[32]

Conditions at the St. Charles Street Prison were much worse than at the Gratiot Street Female Prison. This fact might have influenced what happened next. Before the plan to banish the Mayfield women could be carried out, the resourceful sisters took matters into their own hands. In the wee hours of the morning on October 21, using a screwdriver fashioned from a table knife, the women managed to remove the fastener from the door of their third-floor room. Then, carrying their shoes, they slipped quietly down the stairway to the front door at the bottom of the stairs. They waited until the guard pacing his beat outside the building had passed, and then they unbolted the door. As soon as they heard the guard round a corner and start walking along another side of the building, they pushed the heavy door open and quickly slipped out, closing the door behind them. They hurried into the street and skipped away.[33]

The young women wandered the streets of St. Louis until daylight. Unacquainted with the city and afraid to ask for directions, they encountered many close calls, according to the Vernon County history, until they discovered a railroad, which they followed west almost to St. Charles and finally reached the home of some friends in western St. Charles County. After remaining there awhile, they proceeded to the home of their mother, who had recently moved to Morgan County.[34]

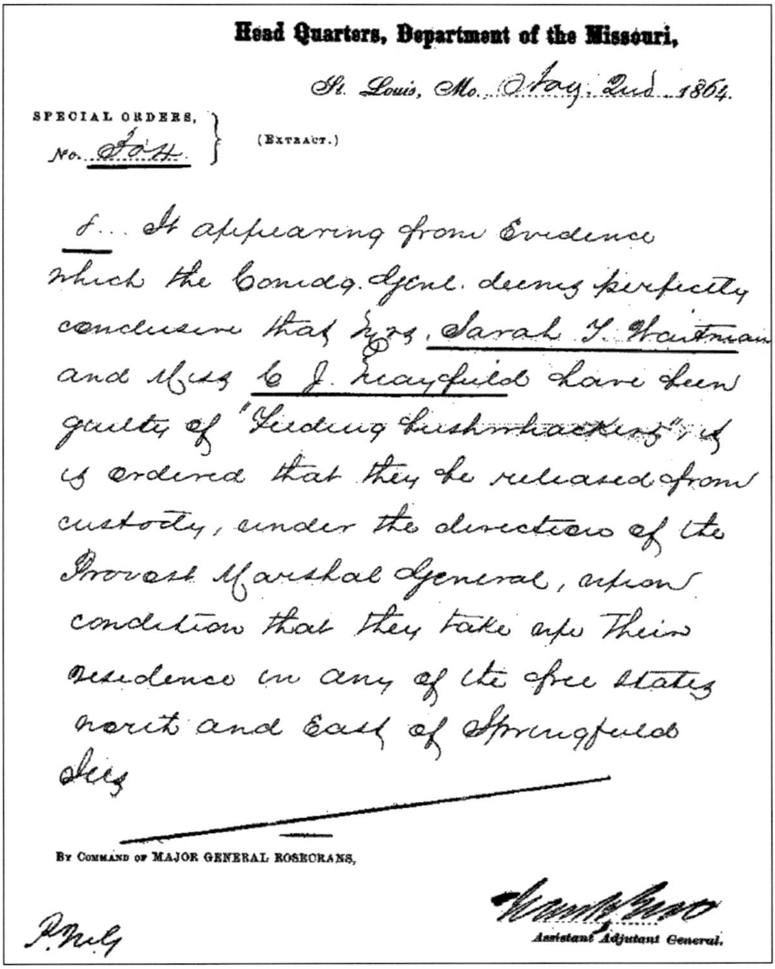

Head Quarters, Department of the Missouri,

St. Louis, Mo. May 2nd 1864.

SPECIAL ORDERS, No. 104. } (EXTRACT.)

8... It appearing from Evidence which the Comdg. Genl. deems perfectly conclusive that Mrs. Sarah T. Waitman and Miss C. J. Mayfield have been guilty of "Feeding bushwhackers", it is ordered that they be released from custody, under the direction of the Provost Marshal General, upon condition that they take up Their residence in any of the free States north and East of Springfield Ills

BY COMMAND OF MAJOR GENERAL ROSECRANS,

Assistant Adjutant General.

Sallie Mayfield Waitman and Clarinda Jane Mayfield escaped before their order of banishment could be carried out. (From Union provost marshals' records.)

The escape of the Mayfield women was not discovered until between six and seven in the morning, when the door to their room was found ajar. The fastener, screws, and makeshift knife were found in their room. Jailer William Dixon gave an alarm and then hurried to a nearby railroad depot to see whether the fugitives tried to board a train. He was too late. Later the same day, he was required to explain the escape and answer the alleged lapses in security that might have contributed to it.[35]

Not all the proper authorities were informed of the Mayfield girls' nocturnal escapade. After considering the charges against the Mayfield sisters, General William Rosecrans, commanding the Department of the Missouri, decided the evidence was "perfectly conclusive" that Sallie Waitman and Jennie Mayfield had been guilty of feeding bushwhackers. On November 2, his assistant adjutant general, Captain Frank Eno, issued an order on his behalf releasing the pair "upon the condition that they take up their residence in any of the free states north and east of Springfield, Ill." The order was returned to the general's office the same day with the notification that the two women had escaped from the St. Charles Street prison "some time since."[36]

Meanwhile, Ella Mayfield went south to Arkansas with her husband, Dave Majors, during or near the time of her sisters' incarceration. Majors was killed near Kingston in January 1865.

Although the Mayfield sisters' Civil War adventures might not have been quite as startling as some post-war accounts would lead us to believe, they were remarkable enough without adornment.

The Rest of the Story

After the war, Ella returned to Vernon County. By 1870, she lived with her third husband, George Hinch, in the Montevallo area, and the couple had no children living in the household. Ella later moved to Jackson County and died there in 1912.

Her mother, Justine, also came back to Vernon County, where she died in 1872.

Sallie's second husband, Waitman or Weightman, apparently died near the end of the war or shortly afterward, because Sallie married her third husband, a man named Morgan, about that time. By 1880, she lived in Clay County as the head of household with five children, including William Giboney from her first marriage.

At the time the *History of Vernon County* was published in 1887, Sallie was reportedly living in Kansas City, but her date of death is unknown.

Lenora, who had two kids by her first husband, was remarried to Henry Vickers shortly after the war ended and had three more kids. She died in Texas in 1917.

Jennie Mayfield's fate after the war is unknown.[37]

CHAPTER 5
Mary Vaughn and Her Relations in the Brush

Forty-seven-year-old Mary Vaughn was arrested at Westport by Federal authorities in early February 1865 on suspicion of giving aid and information to bushwhackers. Her affidavit several days later said she was a Union woman and always had been. Other witnesses, including at least one Union soldier, vouched for her loyalty. Considering the hardship and terrible loss she and her family had suffered at the hands of Federal authorities, the statements in the wake of her arrest seem almost incredible.

Either Mrs. Vaughan was one of the most forbearing women of America's Civil War, or she was very good at hiding her true feelings.[1]

Mary Fuqua and Josiah Vaughn married in Knox County, Illinois, in 1832. About 1837, they migrated to Missouri with their two sons and settled in southwest Jackson County in the area of the Little Blue River between Hickman Mills and Little Santa Fe. Eight more children were born to the marriage after they reached Missouri.[2]

When the Civil War exploded, the two oldest sons were already living in California. The fourth- and fifth-born sons, Dan Vaughn and James "Jim" Vaughn, took up the Southern cause. It's probable that one or both of them joined the Missouri State Guard during the early stages of the war, but this is not known for sure, since Missouri State Guard recordkeeping was spotty and many of the records that *were* made were later lost. Regardless, they and perhaps their next-older brother, Thomas Vaughn, soon fell in with notorious Confederate guerrilla leader William Quantrill.[3]

Sometime during 1862, Federal troops shot twenty-four-year-old Thomas Vaughn in the brush. It's not clear whether he was a member of Quantrill's gang or any other guerrilla band at the time. Mary Vaughn later claimed her third-born son had never been in the

Rebel army and was "murdered for his money upon the highway." Thomas Vaughn left a widow, Nancy Jane; two infant sons, Richard and Josiah; and an eight-year-old stepson, Charles Gray.[4]

Almost from the outset of the Civil War, the official Union position toward Confederate guerrillas in Missouri was that they were nothing but outlaws. In practice, guerrillas were not dealt with summarily early in the war. As the conflict wore on, however, Union officials became increasingly frustrated by their inability to eradicate the bushwhackers, and they adopted increasingly harsh policies toward the Southern partisans. This was especially true in Quantrill's stomping grounds of Jackson County. Union authorities in 1863 not only clamped down on the guerrillas themselves but also began routinely arresting their family members as a way of trying to break their support system and drive them from the state. The Vaughn family was one of those targeted.

On March 28, 1863, a band of bushwhackers that included Dan Vaughn, Dick Yeager, and Samuel Clifton waylaid the steamer *Sam Gaty* on the Missouri River at Sibley in northeast Jackson County. Under the command of the notorious George Todd, the guerrillas killed several black men and two soldiers. They also stole a large amount of supplies. After the raid, Vaughn, Yeager, Clifton, and a man named Anderson (probably Bill or Jim Anderson) retreated to Chapel Hill in Lafayette County, where they met up with Vaughn's fifteen-year-old sister and Clifton's new wife, Margaret.

On or about April 12, the four men, accompanied by Margaret, returned to Jackson County to the home of Mary Vaughn. There, Margaret's eighteen-year-old sister, Martha (who was married to Bernard Lindsey), prepared supper for the newcomers. On April 18, Margaret and Martha ventured into nearby Westport. A few days later they were arrested as spies by Major W. C. Ransom. Margaret was charged with treason for aiding, feeding, and passing information to guerrillas. She was also charged with being an accomplice to murder and robbery for harboring her husband, her brother, and their cohorts after the attack on the Sam Gaty and for receiving money taken from one the Union soldiers killed during the raid. Martha was charged with spying and feeding guerrillas, but she was not charged in connection to the Sam Gaty attack. The Vaughn sisters were imprisoned at Fort Leavenworth after their arrest.[5]

Not long after the Vaughn sisters were captured, Union officials confiscated a letter, dated April 30, that a young woman had sent to Margaret from Chapel Hill. It's not clear whether the sisters had already been moved to Leavenworth at this point, but the letter writer was aware that Margaret and Martha were in Union custody. After teasing Margaret about receiving free room and board from the government, the young woman wrote, "Tell your sister that she ought not to have fed such a bad man as Dan Vaughn." Then she added, "Well, Mag, I think you had as much right to be a bushwhacker's wife as a Fed's, don't you?"[6]

The Vaughn sisters languished at Leavenworth. Their brother Jim ventured across the state line into Kansas, ostensibly to visit a former sweetheart. On his return trip, he stopped at a barber shop in Wyandotte for a haircut on May 25. While in Wyandotte, he was recognized and betrayed by a former acquaintance, and a squad of Union soldiers filed into the shop and arrested him as he sat in the barber chair.

Twenty-year-old Vaughn was taken to Kansas City and given a hasty, drumhead court martial the same day. Convicted as a spy for being a Confederate guerrilla inside Union lines, he was sentenced to death by General James G. Blunt. The next day, May 26, Vaughn was removed from the guard house near the corner of Main Street and Missouri Avenue. He was driven by wagon, guarded by soldiers on all sides, to a hill not far away near the present-day intersection of Wyandotte Street and Twelfth Street, where a gallows awaited his hanging. Vaughn's face wore a sad expression as the wagon pulled up, but he steeled himself as he dismounted. He ascended the scaffold, took a few trinkets and some money from his pockets, and handed them to a Union officer. He requested that they be forwarded to his sisters at Leavenworth.[7]

Young Vaughn met his fate with resignation and even defiance. "I'll die a true Southern man," he threatened the small crowd gathered to witness his execution. He added that some of them could expect to suffer for his death.

A black hood was draped over the condemned man's face, and he was led to the raised trap door. "You're not going to push me off, are you?" he asked as he stepped onto it. After standing on the trap for a moment and mumbling something about his last look, he told the executioner to "let her slide." The door was sprung, launching him into eternity. Vaughn was pronounced dead after fifteen minutes and his body cut down after seventeen. The corpse was placed in a plain wooden coffin and buried about a hundred yards from the gallows.[8]

Jim Vaughn had warned that his death would be avenged. The very next day, Confederate partisan colonel and Quantrill associate Benjamin F. Parker executed at least four Federal officers in retaliation for the hanging.

By the late spring of 1863, the guerrilla conflict in Missouri was turning increasingly into a war of retribution.[9]

On June 26, 1863, exactly a month after Vaughn's execution, his sisters were moved from Fort Leavenworth to Kansas City and placed under guard at the Union Hotel. Additional female relatives of Quantrill's guerrillas were rounded up. The hotel filled, and some prisoners were placed in a building at 1409 Grand. On August 13, this building collapsed. Four young women died, including a sister of Bill Anderson. A fifth was mortally wounded.

The Vaughn girls were evidently not in this building, or, if they were, they escaped serious injury. Shortly thereafter, they were released, or they might even have been released prior to the collapse.[10]

The collapse of the female prison, of course, outraged the guerrillas. Many claimed it had been deliberately orchestrated by Federal officials. The tragedy served as a driver for Quantrill's raid on Lawrence, Kansas, eight days later. Dan Vaughn likely took part in the infamous sacking on August 21, but this is not definitely known.

What is known for sure is that two of the Vaughn sisters were arrested again a little over a year later. On August 31, 1864, soldiers from the Department of Kansas arrested seven people in Jackson County: Martha Lindsey, her two kids (Susan and Emma Lindsey), her sister Susan, her sister-in-law Nancy, and Nancy's sons Richard and Josiah. They were taken back to Leavenworth. Their charges were aiding and giving information to bushwhackers.

On September 23, they were sent to Kansas City for a disposition of their case. Mary Maxwell, who lived in the Vaughn neighborhood, and two of her daughters were arrested and sent to Leavenworth about the same time the Vaughn girls were arrested. The Maxwells were returned to Kansas City at the same time as the Vaughns.[11]

On October 3, Captain J. C. W. Hall, assistant provost marshal at Kansas City, wrote to Colonel J. P. Sanderson, provost marshal general of the Department of the Missouri headquartered at St. Louis. Hall recommended that the women and their kids be "removed to some other locality, where their presence will not be a constant irritation to loyal people." He said the evidence against the women was "not of a very satisfactory or positive character."[12]

"Nevertheless," he went on, "no doubt exists in my mind of their complicity with the bushwhackers of this county. Many of their immediate relations are now in the brush and others have been killed while actively engaged as bushwhackers and marauders, and their reputation for disloyalty is notorious."[13]

On October 13, the Vaughn women were sent back to Leavenworth "for safekeeping." Their case was still pending in early November when Dan Vaughn captured several Federal soldiers. He negotiated with Union authorities for an exchange of prisoners. On November 4, Captain Hall issued Special Order No. 76. This order specified that Susan Vaughn and Nancy J. Vaughn, whom Hall misidentified as a sister of Vaughn, would be held as hostages pending the release of John Bay and B. M. Cox, two soldiers of the Second Colorado Cavalry being held by Vaughn. Should Vaughn kill the prisoners, the two women would be kept in custody until Vaughn's capture or death; but if the soldiers were released, the women would likewise be released to their Jackson County home.[14]

Hall dispatched a copy of the order by messenger to Vaughn and sent a copy to Major H. H. Heath, provost marshal general of the Department of Kansas. He requested that the Vaughn women be closely guarded.

His implication was clear: bushwhacker belles could not be trusted.

Vaughn received his copy the next morning, November 5. He wrote back the same day, agreeing to release the soldiers in exchange for Nancy Vaughn and his two sisters, Susan Vaughn and Martha Lindsey.

Vaughn said a man named Muir would act as a go-between in the exchange and that the women should be released into Muir's custody. Vaughn told Hall that if he failed to deliver the women to Muir, two other Union soldiers whom Vaughn was still holding would "forfeit their lives."[15]

Later the same day, November 5, Vaughn scribbled a pass for the two Federal soldiers. He directed all Confederates and bushwhackers in the region to allow the soldiers to pass beyond the Rebel lines so that they could be exchanged for his sisters and his mother. He threatened, "If Muir does not bring back the women, I will kill him."[16]

Since Vaughn mentioned his mother in the pass but not in his letter to Hall, it is unclear whether he truly believed his mother was being held prisoner with his sisters, but if he did believe this, he was mistaken. Union prison records of Vaughn's sisters and sister-in-law in the fall of 1864 make no mention of his mother. Mary Vaughn's own statements taken a few months later suggest she was not a prisoner during the time in question. However, she lived, at least part time, in a house on or near the post at Hickman Mills under Union protection. It is possible her son might have construed this as imprisonment.[17]

During the time Hall was negotiating with Dan Vaughn, the captain was also still in communication about the case with the office of the provost marshal general at department headquarters in St. Louis. Sometime in early November, Hall added a notation to the October 31st roll of prisoners held at Kansas City. It said the provost marshal general recommended the release of the Vaughn women because of "want of evidence" and "to save the lives of two soldiers captured by D. Vaughn, bushwhacker and brother of the Vaughns herein mentioned, also brother of Mrs. Lindsey."[18]

On November 7, Captain Hall wrote Heath at Leavenworth, "Daniel Vaughan, Bushwhacker, has complied with Special Orders No. 76, a copy of which I sent you. I therefore request that the female prisoners sent you on the 13th for safekeeping be released and permitted to return to their respective homes."[19]

Colonel Sanderson had recently died and been replaced by Joseph Darr, Jr., as provost marshal general of the Department of the Missouri. On November 12, Darr returned the evidence in the Hall-Dan Vaughn prisoner exchange negotiations with a recommendation that the case be referred to the district commander at Kansas City for "such action as he may see proper to take." This was apparently a reference only to the case of Dan Vaughn, as his sisters had already been released at this point.[20]

They would not enjoy their freedom for long.

After Susan, Martha, and Nancy were released, Mary Vaughn apparently left the place where she had been staying at the Hickman Mills post. She and Susan returned to her old home a half mile away.

Sometime in November or early December 1864, Dan Vaughn came to the house with two other bushwhackers. Susan talked with her brother, but neither he nor the men with him got down from their horses, according to her later statement. Mary Vaughn spoke to her son as well, but his visit was less than welcome. In fact, Mary even reported her son's visit to Union authorities sometime after he left.[21]

It is also likely, however, that Mrs. Vaughn's choice to inform on her own son after he was safely away from her house was at least partly a ploy to deflect suspicion away from herself. The Vaughn home was a regular resort for bushwhackers, said some of her Union neighbors. In early January 1865, Union authorities began gathering evidence against Rebel sympathizers living in the Hickman Mills area. Henry Tull swore out an affidavit stating that "Mrs. Rucker, Mrs. Vaughn & Mrs. Flannery and their families are intimate with and on friendly terms with the Bushwhackers and entertain them day and night whenever they call upon them."[22]

It is possible Tull was referring to Nancy Vaughn, but his neighbor James H. Harris left no doubt which Mrs. Vaughn he meant when he reported to Union officials on January 24 that "Mrs. Vaughn (mother of Dan)" was one of many Rebel sympathizers living in the Hickman Mills vicinity.[23]

On or about January 28, 1865, some bushwhackers came to Nancy Vaughn's house while Nancy was at the home of a neighbor, fifty-year-old Lydia Taylor, about three-quarters of a mile away. The guerrillas cooked and ate at Nancy's house.

Suddenly, the visit turned deadly. They were discovered and attacked by five Federal soldiers. The bushwhackers killed two soldiers in the skirmish and escaped.

Nancy paid the price for her hospitality. The surviving Federal soldiers burned both Nancy's and Lydia Taylor's houses. With no place of her own, Nancy Vaughn sought shelter for herself and her children with Mary Vaughn, who had gone back to her house at the Hickman Mills post.[24]

Henry Tull reported that Dan Vaughn regularly visited many of the homes in the Hickman Mills neighborhood. It is not certain that the bushwhackers who ate at Nancy Vaughn's place were a part of Vaughn's band, but his guerrillas were definitely still raising hell in the general vicinity. On the evening of January 31, they raided the small town of Aubry just across the state line in Johnson County, Kansas. Little more than a wide place in the road, Aubry was also raided by Quantrill in 1862. The *Olathe Mirror* reported the latest incident:

> Dan Vaughn and his band of cutthroats are having things pretty much their own way; they go and come at will and are not interfered with in the least. On Tuesday night of last week they entered the town of Aubrey, in this county, burnt several dwellings, killed an unarmed man from Fort Scott, who was stopping there overnight, and rode leisurely off chuckling with delight at their fiendish work.[25]

After Nancy Vaughn moved in with her mother-in-law in late January, the two women and their children, at the direction of the Hickman Mills post commander, were moved almost immediately to Westport. The entire household was arrested there on February 3, 1865, and taken to Kansas City. Lydia Taylor and her children were arrested a few days later.[26]

On February 11, thirty-two-year-old Nancy Vaughn gave a deposition at Kansas City. Yes, she was the widow of Thomas Vaughn. She was "tolerably well acquainted" with the people who lived in the vicinity of Hickman Mills. She named several men she considered loyal. She singled out several others, such as Isaac Flannery and Dan Vaughn, whom she knew to be bushwhackers. She also mentioned two women, Lizzie Rule and the widow Flannery, as "bad rebel(s)." Nancy was a Union woman: "I have never done anything against Federal troops or the Federal government," she declared. "All my troubles have arisen by me having relations that are friends to the Rebels and Bushwhackers and who at the same time pretend to be friends to Federal troops."[27]

The same day, February 11, Lydia Taylor also gave a statement.

It contradicted Nancy Vaughn's claim of loyalty. Lydia knew the widows Mary and Nancy Vaughn, and she also named several other women in her neighborhood, including Lizzie Rule and the widow Flannery. She denounced all of them as "the worst kind of Rebels." Mary Vaughn was "the best woman in the lot, and I believe she would say or do very little for the Rebels and Bushwhackers if she could help herself and was out of this country." As for the others, she said very little on their behalf. All her problems resulted from the "wicked people with whom I have been compelled to live and associate."[28]

Three days later, on February 14, Mary Vaughn admitted about her son, Dan Vaughn, "He is I suppose now in the Brush." She also confirmed that her sons-in-law, Bernard Lindsey and Samuel Clifton, were either in the brush or in the Confederate Army. Lindsey had stopped at her house in the fall of 1864 during General Sterling Price's raid through Missouri, while his wife—Mary's daughter—was imprisoned at Leavenworth. Clifton also came through the area during Price's raid and called at Mary's house. Unlike Lindsey, he did not continue south with Price but took to the brush instead. As far she knew, "He may still be with the bushwhackers."[29]

Mary knew most of the people who lived in her neighborhood. Like Lydia Taylor, she labeled some as loyal and some as disloyal. She denounced Polly Maxwell, Mary's daughters' fellow prison inmate the previous fall, as "a Rebel and a bad woman. She feeds and aids Bushwhackers & has always done it." Mary said her son Dan had given Polly Maxwell sixteen dollars to buy him a pistol. Mary concluded that her husband, Eli Maxwell, served in the Southern army but that she had been passing herself off as a widow and had taken up with a former Union soldier named Howard.[30]

Daniel A. Stephens, a Federal soldier familiar with the Hickman Mills neighborhood, was also deposed on February 14. He knew two local women, a Mrs. Harper and a Mrs. Kelly, to "harbor and feed Bushwackers willingly and render to them all the assistance and comfort in their power." Stephens added, "Old Mrs. Mary Vaughn, Dan Vaughn's mother, is in my belief a much better woman than either of them. She is really a better woman than old Mrs. Lydia Taylor is. I have no confidence in the loyalty of old Mrs. Taylor or in that of Mrs. Harper or Mrs. Kelly. I have some little confidence in Mrs. Vaughn's loyalty, if she was removed from her old locality."[31]

Stephens said Virginia Taylor, Lydia's daughter, was a "notorious Rebel, and one of the worst young women I ever knew." He also had a low opinion of Mrs. Nancy Vaughn. "I have every reason to believe and do believe that she will aid and assist the Bushwackers and has done so repeatedly whenever it was possible to do so without detection. She is a firm, fast friend to them & they all well know it, they have often been found at & seen from her house by the Federal Troops."[32]

On March 16, 1865, Mary Vaughn, Nancy Vaughn, and their

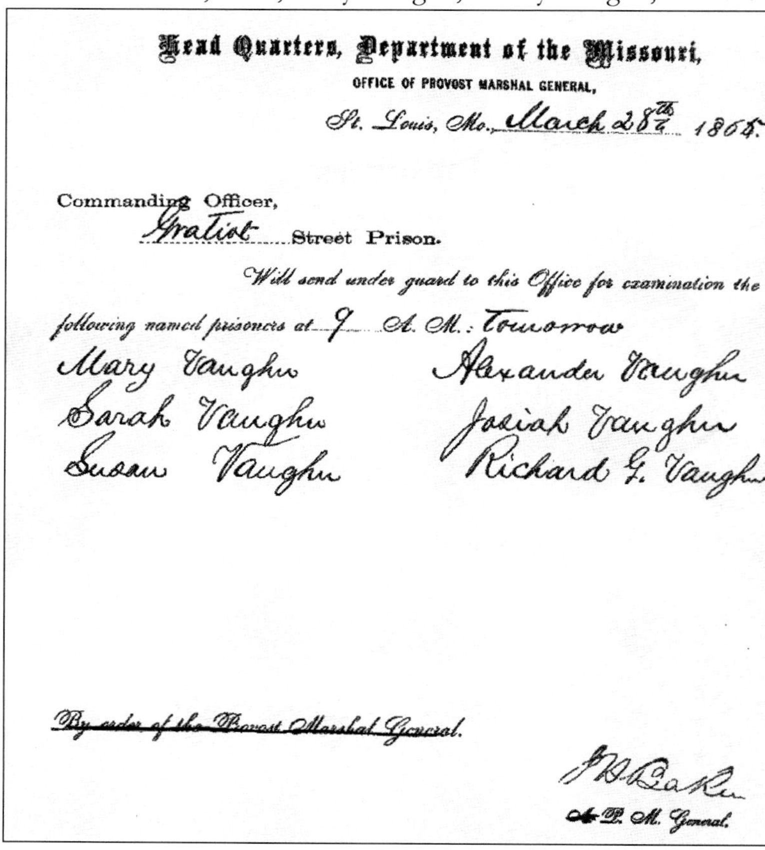

Head Quarters, Department of the Missouri,
OFFICE OF PROVOST MARSHAL GENERAL,
St. Louis, Mo., March 28th 1865.

Commanding Officer,
Gratiot Street Prison.

Will send under guard to this Office for examination the following named prisoners at 9 A. M.: Tomorrow

Mary Vaughn Alexander Vaughn
Sarah Vaughn Josiah Vaughn
Susan Vaughn Richard G. Vaughn

~~By order of the Provost Marshal General.~~

J. D. Baker
A. P. M. General.

Order transferring Mary Vaughn and her family from Gratiot Street Prison to the provost marshal's office in St. Louis. (From Union provost marshals' records.)

children were transferred to the Gratiot Street Female Prison in St. Louis.

Nancy died the next day.

On March 29, Mary said she had often seen bushwhackers in her neighborhood and they sometimes had eaten at Nancy's house. She had not impugned her daughter-in-law in her first statement, but now she did, perhaps because Nancy was dead. [33]

Mary admitted that Rebels had frequented her own house in 1861 and she sometimes fed them but only because she felt she had to. She left home to get away from them. From April 1862 until August 1864, Mary lived in both Kansas and Illinois. She had only returned to Jackson County from Illinois in 1864 to settle a debt. She remained only because she was unable to collect the money due her. During Price's raid in the fall of 1864, some Southern soldiers had taken her only horse and all the flour, cornmeal, and meat she had on the place. She had never willingly furnished anything to any of them except her own sons and sons-in-law, whom she had indeed fed. "I have tried hard to act as a loyal woman," she declared, "and I submit myself willingly to be dealt with as my actions merit."[34]

Do we believe Mary's careful balance between contrite and disloyal? Was she saying these negative things about Southerners just to get on the good side of the Union soldiers who were interrogating her? No doubt she said to a certain extent what she thought the soldiers wanted to hear, but at the same time her statements have a ring of sincerity. Perhaps Daniel Stephens, the Federal solider, was right when he said that Mary would have been a loyal woman if not for her ties to family and neighborhood.

In addition to taking care of her own children, Mary had assumed the care of her grandsons Richard and Josiah since their mother's death. She had no charge of Charlie Gray, Nancy's son from a previous marriage; she suggested sending him to an uncle and aunt, William and Miranda Whitehouse, who lived in Jackson County.[35]

Fifteen-year-old Susan Vaughn gave a brief statement in St. Louis on the same day her mother did. She said when her brother Dan rode up to the door at her mother's house the previous fall in the company of two other bushwhackers, it was the first time she had seen him in two years. This, of course, confirms Mary's claim that she was not living in Missouri from 1862 to 1864. Susan said none of the Vaughns' neighbors willingly harbored or fed bushwhackers. She recalled one time, while visiting her sister-in-law, when two bushwhackers came near Nancy's house but fled when they saw three Union soldiers nearby.[36]

An undated note written by an unidentified Union official was attached to the statements the Vaughns made in Kansas City. It had been forwarded with them to St. Louis. The unknown writer recommended the women be banished from the state but doubted the wisdom of sending them south. Instead, he suggested they be sent somewhere east of the Illinois River and north of the Ohio for the remainder of the war. The war ended before Union authorities finally took action in the Vaughn women's case. But neither the end of hostilities nor the unknown Union official's recommendation softened their punishment. Mary and Susan Vaughn were sent south on April 30, 1865.[37]

In mid-May of 1865, Union authorities made arrangements for Charlie Gray to be sent from the Gratiot Street Prison to his aunt and uncle at Raytown. His transfer papers say his mother died at the female prison on March 17, but do not mention the other Vaughns, who had already been banished.[38]

As the Civil War wound down in Missouri, Union authorities offered amnesty to bushwhackers who would lay down their arms and take an oath that they would no longer bear arms against the US. Many guerrillas in west central Missouri began surrendering at Lexington. On May 26, Dan Vaughn was among a group of Southern men who surrendered to Union authorities there. He is listed on the surrender roll as a private in Stand Watie's regiment, which casts doubt on whether this was indeed Josiah and Mary Vaughn's bushwhacker son. However, his surrender at Lexington and his residence of Jackson County prior to the war, as given on the roll, strongly suggest this was the same Dan Vaughn.[39]

The Rest of the Story

After the Civil War, most of the Vaughns returned to or remained in the Jackson County area. Around 1870, Josiah Vaughn was living in the Lee's Summit area. His and Mary's two youngest children, Alexander and Sarah, both of whom had been imprisoned with their mother during the Civil War, were living with him.

Martha Vaughn Lindsey, who had lived with her husband in her parents' household in 1860, lived next door to Josiah in 1870. She and Bernard now had five children.

Also living in the Lee's Summit area not far away was Martha's sister Susan, who had married William Gilham in 1867. The couple had one infant son.

Across the line in Cass County but still not far away were Margaret Vaughn Clifton, her husband Samuel, and their two daughters.

During the war Mary Vaughan had suffered unimaginable loss. One son was killed by Federal soldiers in 1862, and she left Missouri to get away from the bitter conflict within its borders. While she was away, two of her daughters were thrown in prison, and another son was hanged as a bushwhacker. Upon her return, two daughters and her daughter-in-law were imprisoned. Near the end of the war, Mary herself was arrested, taken to a St. Louis prison, then shipped south.

What happened to Mary after the war is not known for sure, but she apparently died prior to the 1870 census. Perhaps the hardships she had endured during the Civil War finally wore her down.[40]

And as for the bushwhacker Dan Vaughn, he lived for many years in Texas after the war. He died a respected citizen in Fort Worth in 1913.[41]

Chapter 6
Anna Fickle: Bribery and Murder

Twenty-three-year-old Anna Fickle, her Confederate boyfriend, and an elderly woman in the Lexington area hatched a plot to free a captive bushwhacker. Standing four feet seven inches with light hair and gray eyes, the petite Anna would charm a Union guard and throw in a $30 gold bribe. They'd kill the guard and free the shackled prisoner.

Then something went wrong.

This is her story.

William T. "Bloody Bill" Anderson ranted about Anna Fickle in the summer of 1864. She is one of the few belles of the brush identified by name in the *Official Records*. Her citation and particularly her association with Bloody Bill Anderson account for the fact that she is better known than most of the other women who aided the Missouri guerrillas during the Civil War.

Indeed, she was already legendary by the time the volume of the *Official Records* in which she is mentioned was published in 1893, thanks in large part to romantic accounts of William Quantrill and his associates by authors like John N. Edwards and J. W. Buel. So the name Anna Fickle, unlike that of a number of the other subjects of this book, is no doubt already familiar to many readers.

But what do we really know about her aside from legend?[1]

A native of Missouri, Anna (also called Ann or Annie) grew up in Lafayette County. Situated along the Missouri River in "Little Dixie," Lafayette was the largest slave-holding county in the state, and Confederate sympathies dominated.

Anna was living in Lafayette County with her parents, Henry H. and Frances Fickle, and six siblings around 1850. The family still resided there ten years later. When the Civil War ignited, Anna's younger brother Joseph enlisted in the Missouri State Guard. In early 1862, he joined Quantrill's irregular company.

According to Buel, later the same year, after Federal authorities had declared guerrillas to be outlaws, Anna fashioned and gave to Quantrill the legendary black flag under which his guerrilla band supposedly fought throughout the remainder of the war. She presented it with a glowing speech. It is difficult to judge how much, if any, of Buel's account of the flag episode to believe. His main source for the story was the unreliable former Quantrill guerrilla George Shepherd. Shepherd tended to overstate his own role in the adventures he related. He wove into the summer of 1862 flag episode details from an incident involving Fickle that actually occurred a year and a half later.[2]

Visiting and eating at the homes of sympathizers could be dangerous—deadly—for bushwhackers. And the Union troops who pursued them.

Seventeen-year-old Otho Hinton was captured and two other bushwhackers killed on December 20, 1863, at the home of a Mrs. Neill twelve miles south of Lexington. Hinton was taken to Lexington, where he was held prisoner.

Several residents, including Anna's father, were also arrested for feeding and harboring guerrillas. Hinton himself testified that guerrillas frequently ate at the Fickle residence. Mr. Fickle was released on parole shortly after his arrest. Hinton, however, was closely guarded at Lexington, awaiting trial for being a bushwhacker.[3]

Hinton belonged to the squad of Quantrill lieutenant Andy Blunt, who was romantically involved with Anna. On or about February 20, 1864, an elderly lady named Ann Reid, Anna, and Blunt hatched a scheme to free the prisoner. Anna's role was to enlist the cooperation of a young Federal soldier named William Sabins she knew. She bribed him $30 in gold. Sabins arranged for Hinton to eat dinner on the evening of February 22 at the home of Mrs. Reid. Mrs. Reid lived near the Masonic College in Lexington, where Hinton was being held.

The prisoner and his guard arrived as scheduled. At 7:00 p.m., Mrs. Reid stepped into another room. This was a prearranged signal to Hinton. Hinton announced that he was ready to return to the guardhouse. Fettered with a ball and chain, he walked toward the front door, where Blunt and two sidekicks named James Waller and

Masonic College in Lexington where Otho Hinton was held and where Anna Fickle was likely held after her arrest for helping Hinton to escape. (Courtesy of the Battle of Lexington State Historic Site.)

John Burns lay in wait. Their plan was to kill the guard and free Hinton from his shackles.

Unknown to the other conspirators, however, Sabins double-crossed the schemers. A squad of soldiers stationed outside the house spotted Blunt and his partners and demanded to know their business. One of the soldiers recognized Burns as a former Union militiaman turned bushwhacker. The Federals opened fire on the desperate trio, killing Burns. At the first sound of the commotion outside, the guard inside the house shot and killed Hinton before he even reached the door. Meanwhile, Blunt and Waller escaped, killing a Federal soldier named Asher in the process. They, too, were killed the following month.[4]

Immediately after the scheme to free Hinton unraveled, Anna Fickle and the seventy-eight-year-old Ann Reid were arrested for their part in the plot. They went to prison at Lexington. Anna was reportedly thrown into a dungeon. While she awaited the disposition of her case, her brother Joseph and three other bushwhackers were killed in April southwest of Lexington not far from the Fickles' Greenton-area home.[5]

On May 16, Anna and Mrs. Reid were sent to district headquarters at Warrensburg. Mrs. Reid must have been released shortly afterwards in consideration of her advanced age, as no record of any further proceedings against her has been found in Union provost marshals' records. Anna was held for trial at Warrensburg. She was accused of violating the rules of war, giving aid and comfort to the enemies of the government, aiding and abetting a prisoner to escape, and murder. The murder charge stemmed from Blunt's killing of the Federal soldier named Asher.[6]

Anna's trial by military commission began on June 1. William Sabins, the prosecution's star witness, testified that Anna Fickle had acted as an intermediary between him and Blunt's gang. He said she had smuggled him a file to cut Hinton's chains.

On cross-examination, Anna accused Sabins of being the one who had first come up with the scheme to free Hinton. He flatly denied the allegation. She did get Sabins to admit, however, that the original plan had been for him to use the $30 bribe to solicit Hinton's guard's cooperation. The witness also stated that Anna had balked when the conspirators broached the idea of killing the guard.[7]

Perhaps the latter admission swayed the officers hearing the case. After retiring to deliberate on June 2, they came back with a verdict of not guilty on the most serious charge, murder. However, they convicted Anna on the other three charges and sentenced her to confinement in a military prison for the duration of the war. After reviewing the proceedings of the military commission, General Egbert B. Brown, commanding the District of Central Missouri, returned the papers on June 7 to the judge advocate of the commission with instructions to reconsider the findings and sentence in the case. Brown said that the evidence clearly showed complicity in Asher's murder on the part of Anna. If the officers of the court could not agree on a conviction of first degree murder, he authorized them to consider a charge of second degree murder. On June 21, the commission came back with a verdict of guilty of murder in the second degree and sentenced Anna to ten years in the state penitentiary at Jefferson City.[8]

In late June, Anna took sick. On June 27, she was temporarily paroled and moved, "in consequence of her serious illness," from the guardhouse to the residence of Wiley Farmer. Dr. James S.

Edwards, assistant surgeon of the Seventh Cavalry Missouri State Militia, attended her.[9]

On June 28, Brown approved the military commission's new findings in Anna's case. He ordered both the prisoner and the case records be sent to departmental headquarters in St. Louis, pending the final promulgation of her sentence. Brown said there was no suitable facility for her continued confinement in Warrensburg.

Department commander General William Rosecrans confirmed the findings in the case on June 30 and forwarded the findings to President Lincoln for his final approval. In early July, Anna, apparently having recuperated enough to travel, was escorted to St. Louis. Travel was likely by wagon to Sedalia and then possibly by train. She arrived on July 4 at the Myrtle Street Prison, a former slave pen in downtown St. Louis that the Union had confiscated at the beginning of the war for use as a military prison.[10]

On July 7, Bloody Bill Anderson wrote or dictated several blustering letters from the brush in the Lafayette County area. He sent them to Lexington newspapers for publication. In one of the letters, addressed to General Brown, Anderson raged against Anna's imprisonment, apparently unaware that she had already been removed to St. Louis:

> General: I have not the honor of being acquainted with you, but from what I have heard of you I would take you to be a man of too much honor as to stoop so low as to incarcerate women for the deeds of men, but I see that you have done so in some cases. I do not like the idea of warring with women and children, but if you do not release all the women you have arrested in La Fayette County, I will hold the Union ladies in the county as hostages for them. I will tie them by the neck in the brush and starve them until they are released, if you do not release them. The ladies of Warrensburg must have Miss Fickle released. I hold them responsible for her speedy and safe return. General, do not think that I am jesting with you. I will have to resort to abusing your ladies if you do not quit imprisoning ours.

Undaunted by Anderson's threats, Brown forwarded the letters to General Rosecrans "as a curiosity and specimen of a guerrilla chief's correspondence."[11]

Meanwhile, Anna Fickle found herself in limbo, awaiting the final disposition of her case. On July 16, Colonel J. P. Sanderson, provost marshal general of the department, returned the record of the proceedings in her trial to General Rosecrans. He recommended sending her to Jefferson City for confinement, in keeping with the

Absalom Grimes, who made an "across the street" acquaintance with Anna Fickle while they were both being held at the Gratiot Street Prison. (Courtesy of the Missouri History Museum.)

commission's verdict. However, Rosecrans's judge advocate, Lucien Eaton, informed Sanderson on July 18 that Anna could not legally be sent to the state penitentiary "until the pleasure of the president in the case can be known."[12]

Shortly after her arrival in St. Louis, Anna was moved from Myrtle Street Prison to the female prison across the street from Gratiot Street Prison. Confederate mail runner Absalom Grimes, who was confined in the hospital of the Gratiot Street Prison that summer, recalled years after the war that during Anna's stay at the female prison he made "an 'across-the-street' acquaintance" with her, because the windows of the hospital were directly opposite the female facility.[13]

On August 8, Rosecrans received word that President Lincoln had

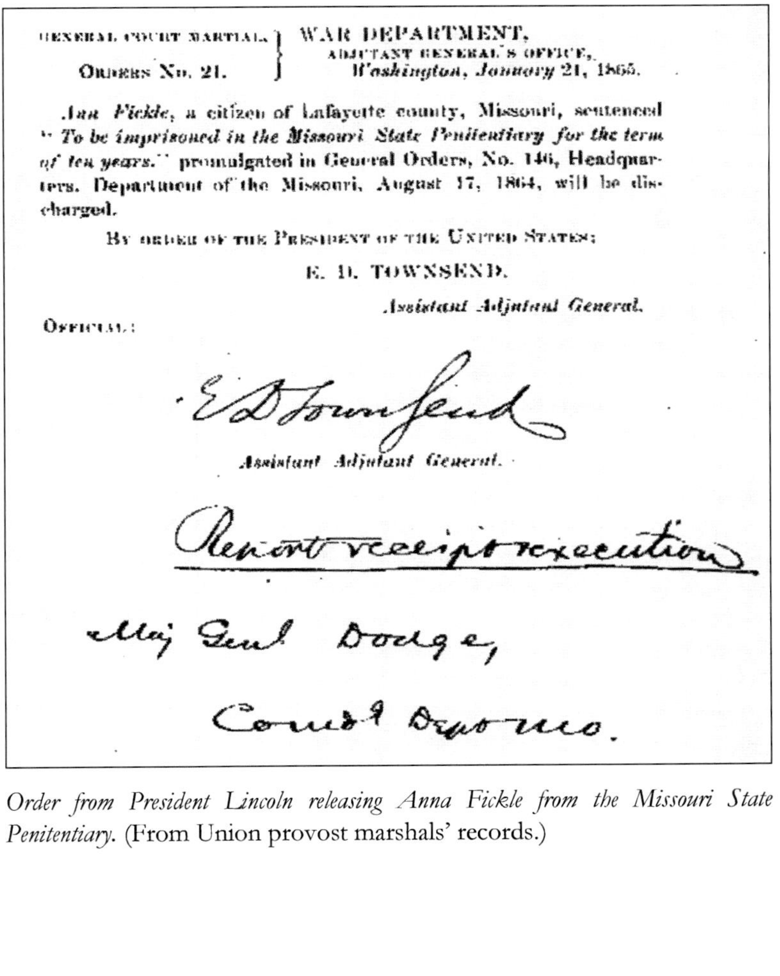

GENERAL COURT MARTIAL ORDERS No. 21.

WAR DEPARTMENT,
ADJUTANT GENERAL'S OFFICE,
Washington, January 21, 1865.

Ann Fickle, a citizen of Lafayette county, Missouri, sentenced "*To be imprisoned in the Missouri State Penitentiary for the term of ten years.*" promulgated in General Orders, No. 146, Headquarters, Department of the Missouri, August 17, 1864, will be discharged.

BY ORDER OF THE PRESIDENT OF THE UNITED STATES:

E. D. TOWNSEND.

Assistant Adjutant General.

OFFICIAL:

E D Townsend

Assistant Adjutant General.

Report receipt & execution

Maj Genl Dodge,

Comd'g Dept Mo.

Order from President Lincoln releasing Anna Fickle from the Missouri State Penitentiary. (From Union provost marshals' records.)

approved the findings in Anna's case. On August 17, Department of the Missouri headquarters issued General Orders No. 146, which promulgated her sentence of ten years in the state penitentiary. On September 20, she was sent to Jefferson City for confinement. Grimes recalled that, after he arrived at the state prison in November, he attempted to renew his long-distance friendship with Anna by writing her a note that a prison trusty promised to deliver.

On January 21, 1865, the US War Department, by Lincoln's direction, issued an order discharging Anna. Lincoln often mitigated sentences during the war. Upon her release in early February, she was sent south for the duration of the war, according to the *History of Lafayette County*.[14]

The Rest of the Story

Anna returned to her home territory after the war and married former Confederate soldier George W. Parker on November 28, 1867, in Lafayette County. She remained there the rest of her life.

In 1870, she and George had one child, and ten years later they had four children. By 1910, Anna, now a widow, was still living in Lafayette with two of her grown children in the household.

Anna died in June 1920. She is buried beside her husband in the Odessa Cemetery in Odessa, Missouri, a town that was not established until several years after the Civil War. About a half mile to the north, thousands of motorists every day speed past on Interstate 70 unaware of the unique and interesting role that Anna played in the Civil War in Missouri.[15]

CHAPTER 7

Mary Ann Harlow: Bloody Bill Anderson Informant

Anna Fickle was not the only Lafayette County woman who was involved in trying to effect the freedom of a bushwhacker held prisoner at Lexington in 1864. Not long after, another bushwhacker belle made a daring attempt to save a Confederate guerrilla.

She may have looked unassuming, at just four feet, eight inches tall with light hair and hazel eyes. But Mary Ann Harlow was no delicate damsel. She took matters into her own hands.

Spring 1864. Miss Fickle's plot to liberate Hinton had just ended in fiasco. Confederate bushwhacker Marion D. Erwin was arrested and convicted as a bushwhacker and spy. He landed in the guardhouse at Lexington. He was sentenced to be shot on June 24th.

On June 23rd, famed Bloody Bill Anderson and his band were camped near Wellington. Mary Ann heard about the upcoming execution and decided to do something about it. She sent a man to Bloody Bill's camp. Her messenger told the guerrillas of Erwin's impending fate and urged them to save the condemned man, suggesting perhaps they could kidnap some Union citizens and hold them as hostages for the release of Erwin.[1]

Although he didn't know Erwin, Anderson promptly took up the challenge. He and his gang arrested Wellington postmaster Davis K. Duck and two other local Union men. Bloody Bill sent word to Lexington threatening to kill the three men unless Erwin's death sentence was lifted. Convinced that the desperate Bill Anderson was not bluffing, Union authorities halted the execution before it could be carried out on the 24th. The following day General Egbert B. Brown officially suspended the sentence. However, he ordered that six prominent Southern-sympathizing citizens of the Wellington area be arrested and held as hostages to ensure the three Union men were not harmed.[2]

Meanwhile, Erwin was retained in custody, and Anderson tackled the issue of his continued confinement in his letter to General Brown dated July 7:

> As to the prisoner Ervin you have in Lexington, I have never seen nor heard of him until I learned that such a man was sentenced to be shot. I suppose that he is a Southern man or such a sentence would not have been passed. I hold the citizens of Lexington responsible for his life. The troops in Lexington are no protection to the town, only in the square. If he is killed, I will kill twenty times his number in Lexington. I am perfectly able to do so at any time.
>
> Yours respectfully,
> W. Anderson
> Commanding Kansas First Guerrillas.[3]

Anderson had already released Duck and the other two captives by the time he penned his now-infamous letters. He soon left the Lexington area, crossed the Missouri River, and went on a killing spree that lasted all summer. Erwin was released near the same time Anderson left the area.

Word reached Federal authorities of Mary Ann Harlow's possible role in the kidnapping of the three Union men. Lieutenant J. M. Gavin, assistant provost marshal stationed at Lexington, built his case against her. On July 5, he took depositions from Isaac W. Whitsett and his wife, Mary Jane, neighbors of the thirty-eight-year-old Mrs. Harlow. According to the Whitsetts, Mrs. Harlow sent a messenger to the bushwhacker camp on the evening before Erwin's scheduled execution to suggest that the guerrillas arrest Union men and hold them as hostages to save him. Isaac Whitsett added that she said she would deny the deed if she were accused of it. He said she asked him to deny it also. The Whitsetts said that they knew of no other disloyal acts by Mrs. Harlow.[4]

On July 18, Jonas Hines swore he knew Mary Ann Harlow to be a Rebel who was in the habit of giving aid and comfort to bushwhackers. He knew nothing about her sending word to them to rescue Erwin. Hines added that Mary Ann was the wife of Creath Harlow, who had been in the Southern army.

Bloody Bill Anderson. Mary Ann Harlow was accused of soliciting his help in a scheme to rescue condemned prison Marion D. Erwin. (Author's collection.)

On July 23, Robert Troutman said only that he knew Mary Ann had given aid to bushwhackers. On August 1, Davis Duck, the Wellington postmaster, testified that Mary Ann was "an out and out Rebel." But he did not know for sure whether she had instigated his arrest by Anderson. On August 13, John Piper stated that he considered Mary Ann a disloyal woman, but he knew nothing of any specific disloyal acts she might have committed. Willis H. Worley made a very similar statement on August 18, as did J. P. Williams on the 19th.[5]

In mid-August, Lieutenant Gavin received orders to forward Mary Ann and all the evidence that had been gathered so far to district headquarters. On August 17, she was sent to Warrensburg, an all-day trip by wagon.

General Alfred Pleasonton, General Brown's successor in command of the district, ordered on August 22 that Mary Ann and her case be forwarded to St. Louis to be disposed of as General William Rosecrans, the commanding general of the department, saw fit. The order was carried out the next day.

When she arrived in St. Louis, Mary Ann was housed initially at Myrtle Street Prison but was soon moved to the Gratiot Street Female Prison.[6]

Mary Ann was taken to the provost marshal's office for examination not long after her arrival at Gratiot. A transcription of the interview does not survive, but the examiner's partial summary shows a few details. Here is what she said.

She had never given aid to the rebellion. She did not belong to any secret Southern society. Further, she did not urge the bushwhackers to arrest Union men to be used as hostages for the release of Erwin. She would like to see the Union restored "under the old laws, if we can get them," but otherwise she favored the Southern Confederacy.

Mary Ann's examiner turned his findings over to Gustavus Cohn, chief of the examining bureau, who forwarded the case to department headquarters. He thought the evidence fully justified a trial despite her denial.[7]

Accordingly, on October 5, General Rosecrans ordered Mary Ann held for trial by military commission. She was officially charged with "consorting with and aiding bushwhackers," the specification being that she did "willfully and maliciously advise and counsel said bushwhackers" to arrest loyal Union men and hold them as hostages for the release of Erwin. The proceedings against her began on or before October 12.

Two days later, however, Lieutenant Albert G. Clarke, judge

advocate of the military commission, referred Mary Ann's case back to judge advocate general Major Lucien Eaton with a request for further instructions, because Isaac and Mary Jane Whitsett, the primary witnesses against the accused, had moved to Indiana and could not be located. On October 15, Eaton informed Captain Frank Eno, Roesecrans's assistant adjutant general, that the witnesses in Mrs. Harlow's case were inaccessible. Eaton recommended that, since Mary Ann was "clearly an unsafe person," she should be sent to reside east of the Mississippi River and north of Keokuk, Iowa.

The court martial against Mary Ann was accordingly suspended, and she was included in an order of banishment, dated October 17, removing her and a number of other women accused of disloyalty to the free states north and east of Springfield, Illinois.[8]

Nine days after Mary Ann's banishment, Bloody Bill Anderson was killed in Ray County while leading a wild charge against a detachment of Missouri State Militia. Marion D. Erwin, released after Anderson intervened on his behalf at Mary Ann's urging, was recaptured in Howard County in early 1865. Taken to Macon City, he was executed as a bushwhacker.

The Rest of the Story

Like many of the bushwhacker belles banned from Missouri during the Civil War, Mary Ann Harlow came back to her old neighborhood to take up the thread of her life that had been unlaced by the violent conflict within her state. In 1870, she and her husband, Creath, were living in the Wellington area of Lafayette County with two children in the household.

Ten years later, Mary Ann was a widow still in the Wellington area, now living with the Jessie Moore family.

In 1900, she was seventy five years old, living with Lewis and Sallie Eichler in nearby Bates County. She was listed in the census as an aunt of either Lewis or Sallie.[9]

CHAPTER 8
Bill Anderson Supporter or Bill Anderson Victim?

Nancy Longacre fed and housed plenty of people at her home in western Missouri—Federal soldiers, bushwhackers, stagecoach drivers, and railroad workers.

It was 1864, three years into the Civil War with no end in sight. Nancy, forty-three, had two sons serving in the Confederate Army. She stood four and a half feet, same as her daughter Martha.

Violence seemed to circle Nancy's homestead like a buzzard. Mail and stagecoach robberies. Boarders robbed by bushwhackers at her home. One railroad worker was robbed of everything but his underwear and socks there.

The countryside around Nancy's Johnson County home was a Southern stronghold at the edge of Little Dixie, but some of her neighbors supported the Union. They watched suspiciously as bushwhackers and Confederates visited her.

She knew Bloody Billy Anderson. When his gang slaughtered a dozen Union troops, Nancy was suspected of tipping off the bushwhackers.

Nancy swore she was a victim of Anderson herself and loyal to the Union.

Federal officers did not believe her.

Perhaps the truth lived somewhere in the middle.

Nancy M. Tucker married Benjamin I. Longacre in 1847 in Jackson County. Around 1850, the couple was living in Jackson Township of Johnson County (northwest corner) with their two infant children and Benjamin's three sons by a previous marriage.

A decade later, Benjamin had recently died, and his oldest son, John, had already left home. The household was otherwise intact, and the family was still living in Jackson Township. Among the children in the home was ten-year-old Martha Longacre, a blue-eyed girl with light hair just like her mother's.[1]

After the Civil War broke out, Nancy's stepson William joined the Missouri State Guard and served three months. In August of 1862, he was enlisted into the Confederate Army in Jackson County by Colonel Gideon Thompson. Many of those enlisted by Thompson had previously ridden with Quantrill. It's not known for sure whether Longacre was one of them.

In May 1863, the twenty-one-year-old Longacre was captured in Marion County, Arkansas, and sent to Gratiot Street Prison in St. Louis for taking up arms against the US. When interrogated, he said he had one brother who was also in the Southern Army. This was probably a reference to Elbert Longacre, who was a year younger than William.[2]

William Longacre's fate after his imprisonment in the spring of 1863 is uncertain, but a year later, his stepmother, Nancy, got involved in a matter that resulted in her arrest and transport to St. Louis as well.

Bloody Bill Anderson, fresh from wintering in Texas, arrived in central Missouri in the spring of 1864. He joined guerrilla leader Dick Yeager and began operating in Cooper and Johnson counties just south of the Missouri River.

On the evening of June 11, the bushwhackers were camped in the vicinity of northwest Johnson County.

Corporal Joseph Parman and fourteen soldiers of the First Missouri State Militia Cavalry, on a scout from Holden, camped the same night about two or three miles west of Kingsville near the Longacre home.

On the morning of the 12th, Parman and his squad moved off to the northeast, but they were soon overtaken and attacked by Anderson and Yeager's guerrillas. The bushwhackers had just robbed a mail stagecoach a half mile west of the Longacre home earlier the same morning.

Disguised as Federal soldiers, the bushwhackers killed twelve of the Union troops. Only Parman and two others managed to escape to the woods. Parman reported the attack as soon as he reached Holden. The guerrillas numbered eighty to one hundred men, and the attacking party about forty. Parman felt sure the guerrillas had been tipped off as to his whereabouts, because they had his small squad virtually surrounded before the attacking party showed itself in the rear.[3]

Who could have tipped them off?

Suspicion immediately fell on Nancy Longacre, since Parman had just left her home shortly before the attack. The day after the attack, Captain John Wyckoff, the corporal's company commander, ordered Mrs. Longacre and her family to leave their home. He did not arrest them or immediately report the family.

Union authorities linked the attack to Mrs. Longacre a month and a half later. Her Union-friendly neighbors said she had a reputation of staying in touch with bushwhackers. Captain James Eads reported seeing guerrillas at the Longacre home. Bushwhackers had robbed the stage—and even railroad workers who boarded at the Longacre home.

The order came: Find her and arrest her immediately.

Here is how it happened.

In response to an inquiry from the Lexington headquarters of First Missouri State Militia Cavalry commander Colonel James McFerran, Captain James Eads penned a letter explaining the action in the Longacre case. Eads had been Wyckoff's second-in-command at the time of the Parman incident. Although he regretted that Wyckoff had not yet made a full report of the matter, he agreed with the eviction of Mrs. Longacre from her home.

Eads said the Longacre family had a reputation among all their Union neighbors of being in touch with bushwhackers. He claimed he himself had seen signs that guerrillas stopped at the Longacre home—and that the family had admitted as much. He told the colonel the stage had been robbed several times near the Longacre house. Railroad workers boarding at the house had also been robbed.

On the night before the attack on Parman, he continued, Bill Anderson and Dick Yeager were at the Longacre residence. They robbed all the strangers there. The next morning they robbed all the passengers on the mail coach. Eads said Anderson had learned the whereabouts of Parman from someone at Mrs. Longacre's home.[4]

On July 26, McFerran forwarded Eads's letter to district headquarters at Warrensburg. Two days later, assistant adjutant general James H. Steger, on behalf of district commander General

Alfred Pleasonton, replied to McFerran. He directed him to find Mrs. Longacre. He was to notify district headquarters or arrest the family immediately if they were near McFerran's command (i.e. Lafayette County). If he arrested them, he was to send them to Warrensburg.

Steger added that anyone known to have given information to bushwhackers should not be merely ordered to leave the neighborhood. He wanted them arrested and sent to Warrensburg.[5]

On August 1, Captain Eads informed Colonel McFerran that Nancy Longacre was near Kingsville or Holden about twenty miles west of Warrensburg. McFerran told district headquarters the

Colonel James McFerran, whose investigation led to the arrest of Nancy and Martha Longacre. (Courtesy of the Missouri History Museum.)

woman was outside his command.

Captain Steger then ordered Captain Melville U. Foster, commanding the garrison at Holden, to arrest Nancy Longacre and her family. Foster took them into custody on August 9, sending Nancy, her fifteen-year-old son, Thomas, and her fourteen-year-old daughter, Martha, to district headquarters at Warrensburg.[6]

Steger ordered provost marshal Captain Richard L. Ferguson to find enough evidence to expel the family. Ferguson relayed the orders to Captain Foster on August 11.

Several days after ordering Ferguson to gather evidence against the Longacres, General Pleasonton hadn't heard anything, and he wanted to know the status of the case. Captain Ferguson replied on August 15th that he had still not heard back from Captain Foster.[7]

Whether Foster finally came through with the necessary evidence or Pleasonton simply grew impatient is not certain. But a day or two later, Nancy and her daughter, Martha, were sent to St. Louis on charges of harboring and giving information to bushwhackers. Both were interviewed there on August 29 by assistant examiner George J. W. Nexsen.[8]

Nancy told Nexsen she had two stepsons and one nephew in the Southern army. Still, she was not a Southern sympathizer—and would like to see the Union restored.

Had bushwhackers or partisan rangers ever visited her house? She said that a party of men stopped one time as they were passing. She did not know any of them. Later, workers boarding at her house told her they were bushwhackers.

Had bushwhackers ever robbed anybody at her house? She said that some men robbed her boarders. She later learned the robbers were part of Anderson's band. They did not take anything from her but they did steal money from her son. They also started to take his clothes but allowed him to keep them when she appealed to them that he was an orphan boy.

Had she ever aided bushwhackers? She admitted to giving breakfast to about twenty members of Tippett's band one time during late summer 1863. She said she did not report the bushwhackers but that her boarders did—or at least they told her they would.

She said she did not know any bushwhackers personally.

Did she share information with bushwhackers about Corporal

Parman's squad? She said she did not. She admitted she did not know for sure whether Martha gave such information. Her daughter had denied doing so.

Nancy said Federal soldiers had come to her house on several occasions. She thought she had even fed some of the soldiers who were later killed by Anderson. She concluded the interview by saying she had always opposed bushwhacking and was willing to take an oath of allegiance.[9]

Martha, like her mother, said she opposed bushwhackers and added that she didn't think it was right "to carry on their avocation." In fact, Martha's testimony mirrored Nancy's so closely that one might reasonably conclude that the mother and daughter had thoroughly rehearsed their stories ahead of time—or else they were both telling the truth.[10]

Nancy and her daughter were initially housed at Myrtle Street Prison. They were transferred to Gratiot Street Prison by September 7, when they were listed on the prison's morning report.[11]

Nancy's and Martha's statements denied any part in helping bushwhackers. So, authorities in St. Louis continued gathering other evidence in the Longacre case.

On September 21, St. Louis resident Alonzo W. Miller testified that he first met Nancy Longacre the previous February when his horses tired and he stopped at her house to let them rest. Miller was a railroad contractor whose duties included driving the mail coach between Warrensburg and Independence. Nancy allowed him to stay. She told him about previous robberies at her home. She wanted him to send the mail on to the next station for fear that he might be robbed at her house. She told him the mail coach had previously been robbed in her neighborhood. Union soldiers had threatened to burn her house if it happened again.

Miller further stated that on June 12, the day Parman's men were killed, the bushwhackers—the Anderson gang—had held up the stage a short distance west of Mrs. Longacre's home. They hijacked the mail and everything he owned. They left him in just his underwear and a pair of socks. He went back to Nancy Longacre's house, and she gave him clothes. She, too, had been robbed the same day by the same gang.

Photo thought to be Martha "Mattie" Longacre as a young girl. (Courtesy of George Longacre.)

Every time he was at Mrs. Longacre's house, Miller added, he had heard her denounce bushwhackers. In addition, he named three Union men from her neighborhood whom he had heard speak favorably of her. They said she was not guilty of the charges against her. Miller also pointed out that the mail had been robbed in Mrs. Longacre's neighborhood even after she had been evicted.

Mrs. Longacre's livestock had been assessed and taken to Warrensburg to pay for damages that he felt she did not rightly owe, Miller concluded.[12]

How would the Federal leadership deal with mother and daughter? "The old lady" would be held for trial, ordered Joseph Darr. The child would be released.

But Martha would not see freedom immediately.

Despite Miller's statement on Nancy's behalf, solicitor J. Warren Bell referred her case to acting provost marshal general Joseph Darr, Jr. on September 29. Bell recommended holding "the old lady" for trial and releasing Martha at once, since there was "no testimony whatsoever against the child." But Darr decided to await the result of the mother's trial before releasing the girl.[13]

In early October, Darr forwarded Nancy's case to department headquarters for trial, and her court martial began on or about October 7. In early November, the defendant was acquitted, and commanding general William Rosecrans ordered her release on the 5th. After the order was carried out on the 7th, Nancy requested to be readmitted for an additional day (presumably so that arrangements for her travel or housing could be made). The request was granted. Colonel Darr ordered both Nancy and her daughter released on the 8th.[14]

Like Mary Ann Harlow, Nancy Longacre was arrested for helping Bloody Bill Anderson. Unlike Mary Ann, Nancy was acquitted of the charge. Even Union authorities recognized that not all the bushwhacker belles were equally guilty.

The Rest of the Story

Nancy and Martha returned to Johnson County. Mother and daughter would live the rest of their lives there. Formed in 1834, the county is in western Missouri and today part of the Kansas City region.

Around 1870, Nancy and Martha were living near Kingsville with Martha's brother, Thomas, and her stepbrother, Albert.

In 1880, Nancy was living at Kingsville with her uncle John Tucker. She died there ten years later and is buried at nearby Bluff Springs Cemetery

Martha married Edward Baker in 1878. She, too, lived the rest of her life in the Kingsville area. She died in 1932 just shy of her 82nd birthday. She rests beside her husband in Bluff Springs Cemetery, not far from her mother's gravesite. Kingsville was a small town since before the Civil War. It still is, with a population under 300.[15]

CHAPTER 9
Bitter Rebels but Fine-Looking Girls

Of all the women mentioned in Union documents in association with Bill Anderson, the ones who obviously had the closest connection to him were his younger sisters, Mary Ellen "Mollie," Josephine "Josie," and Martha Jane "Mattie." Given the notoriety of Bill Anderson and his younger brother Jim for their heinous deeds, it would not be surprising if their sisters had also earned despicable reputations in Union circles. But such was not the case.

One newspaper report late in the war, for example, stated that while Mollie and Mattie Anderson were "decidedly rebellious in their sentiments," they were "very genteel and modest young ladies."[1]

The Anderson sisters were born in Randolph County, Missouri, during the mid- to late-1840s. The family moved to Kansas in 1857, settling near Agnes City along the Santa Fe Trail a few miles east of Council Grove.

Mischance hovered over the family like a pall. A couple of years after the Andersons arrived in Kansas, Bill's next-younger brother, Ellis, was either killed by Indians or disappeared. He was never heard from again.

Tragedy struck the family a second time in the summer of 1860, when the mother, Martha Anderson, was killed by lightning.[2]

The father, William C. Anderson, had become friends with local judge A. I. Baker. Baker, like Anderson, lost his wife about 1860 or 1861. Not long after Mrs. Baker's death, the thirty-six-year-old judge became romantically involved with sixteen-year-old Mollie Anderson.

Mollie's father and Baker had a falling-out.

Baker accused Bert Griffin, a relative of the Andersons, of horse theft in the spring 1862. He broke off his relationship with Mollie Anderson about the same time.

Anderson was furious over the accusation of horse stealing and the jilting of his daughter. Horse stealing was a grave charge—a hanging offense—in 1862. Having your daughter's reputation sullied was serious business in any era. Anderson showed up drunk at Baker's house on May 12 threatening to kill the judge.

Baker shot and killed Anderson instead.[3]

In response to their father's death, Bill and Jim Anderson, who were accused of abetting Griffin in the horse theft, took their sisters and fled to the Missouri border. They left the girls at the home of an acquaintance in the Kansas City area on the Kansas side of the line.

The brothers took to the brush, operating as guerrillas in the border region. In early July the brothers and three sidekicks made a desperate and determined ride back to Agnes City.

The group arrived at the Baker place after dark on the night of the 3rd. One of the men who was unknown to the judge called him from his house. The rest of the gang opened fire on Baker, driving him into a cellar beneath a roadside store.

They piled barrels and heavy boxes on top of the cellar door. Then they set fire to the store and galloped away into the night. Baker may have died from the smoke and fire. One report suggested he might have shot himself instead to avoid an agonizing death.[4]

After the murder, the Anderson gang rode swiftly back to Missouri. They stopped several times to exchange horses at way stations along the Santa Fe Trail. They terrorized residents at each stop.

At 142-Mile Creek (present-day Allen), Jim Anderson threatened to kill Charles H. Withington but his older brother Bill restrained him. Withington had previously been a friend of the Anderson family, but he had sided with Baker after the William C. Anderson shooting. He had also implicated Bill Anderson as an accomplice of Bert Griffin in the horse stealing scheme.[5]

Back in Missouri, the Anderson brothers resumed their marauding and soon fell in with guerrilla chief William Quantrill.

Their sisters moved from house to house in the border region around Kansas City.

In late July of 1863, Bill Anderson took his sisters to the Mundy residence near New Santa Fe on the Missouri side of the line and left them there. Both parents of the Mundy family were dead. Several

women lived at the home at the time:
—twenty-seven-year-old Mattie Mundy,
—twenty-year-old Sue Mundy,
—their married sister, Lucinda Mundy Gray, whose husband was away from home, likely in the brush as a guerrilla,
—and Mollie Grandstaff, whose stay was temporary.[6]

Early in the war, Union authorities considered the Missouri guerrillas a mere nuisance that could be swiftly eradicated, but by the summer of 1863 the partisans had proved to be a stubborn problem. Quantrill, the most prominent guerrilla leader in the state, was a particular thorn in the Union's side. General Thomas Ewing, Jr., who commanded the District of the Border encompassing the Kansas City area, began a concentrated effort to drive Quantrill and his men out of the territory. One of the first steps was to clamp down on civilians in the area who helped the guerrillas. The Union determined that, if they could not drive out the guerrillas by force, they would weaken them by undermining their support system.

For the first time during the war, females who fed, harbored, or otherwise sustained the guerrillas were specifically targeted.

Mollie Grandstaff had recently come under suspicion of harboring guerrillas and receiving stolen property from them. A squad of Federal soldiers, learning her whereabouts, went to the Mundy residence to arrest her on or about July 25.

Shirts may have gotten all the women in trouble.

The soldiers found a large supply of shirts and other goods at the Mundy house. They thought guerrillas had stolen the cache during a recent raid on Shawnee, Kansas.

The Federals arrested all the women there.

According to one post-war account, Bill Anderson showed up to oppose the soldiers and fired above their heads as they rode off with the young women. He was afraid to fire low for fear of hitting his sisters.

Another account says Bill was arrested with the women. Mrs. Sue Womacks (nee Sue Mundy) recalled years after the war that Anderson was present at the house when the Federals arrived. The Union troops arrested Bill along with the young women, but he soon escaped.[7]

The Federals took all seven young women to Kansas City and imprisoned them in a brick building at 1409 Grand Avenue. Union authorities planned to remove the women from the district in accordance with General Ewing's recent clamp-down on civilians.

The women were held on the second floor of the building. The first floor was the headquarters of the Federal soldiers detailed to guard the prisoners, and it also housed a grocery. The vacant third floor had previously been used as the studio of artist Caleb Bingham, who owned the building. The structure had been called into service just a day or two before the Anderson sisters were arrested because the nearby Union Hotel, the primary residence for women prisoners, had become overcrowded with Southern girls.

On August 13, the Grand Avenue building collapsed, burying many of the female prisoners in a heap of bricks. A huge cloud of dust arose, and terrible screams and moans came from the rubble. A girl, thought to be Josephine Anderson, kept pleading for someone to take the bricks off her head, but she soon fell silent. As the dust began to clear, five lifeless bodies were dragged from the ruins,

Charity McCorkle Kerr was among the young women who died in the collapse of the female prison in Kansas City, which also claimed the life of Josephine Anderson. (From *Quantrill and the Border Wars.*)

including fifteen-year-old Josephine.

Her sister Mattie was found with a ball and chain around one ankle and two broken legs. The guards had shackled her earlier in the day for annoying them, and she wailed that she could have jumped to safety if she hadn't been chained.

Older sister Mollie escaped with minor injuries.

Mollie Grandstaff was also injured.

An angry mob gathered at the scene almost immediately, cursing and threatening the Union soldiers. Many Southern sympathizers even claimed the Union had deliberately orchestrated the collapse. Union officials only fueled the bitter feelings when they suggested the women might have contributed to the collapse themselves by tunneling around the foundation of the building in an effort to escape.

The truth appears to lie somewhere in the middle. The best evidence suggests that the soldiers did weaken the structure by removing one or more pillars but not for the calculated purpose of collapsing the building. They simply wanted to give themselves more space or to gain easier access to another part of the building.

Regardless of the reason for the collapse, the incident inflamed Southern sympathizers and aroused the guerrillas to a fever of revenge.

The death of Josie Anderson drove the already-desperate Bill Anderson to madness. According to legend, he started carrying a silk cord in which he tied a knot each time he killed a Union man. Some said he would go into battle foaming at the mouth and whispering Josephine's name.

Anderson and his fellow guerrillas used the prison collapse as a justification for the notorious Lawrence Massacre eight days later. On the morning of August 21, about 400 guerrillas under Quantrill rode into the abolitionist stronghold of Lawrence, Kansas, and glutted their vengeance. By the time the jubilee of slaughter was over four hours later, about 180 men and boys, most of them civilians, lay dead. Bill Anderson alone claimed to have killed fourteen men.[8]

Over a month later, a Union military commission tried some of the women.

On September 17, Mollie Grandstaff stood trial. She was found guilty of aiding bushwhackers and receiving and concealing stolen property. Bloody Bill's sister Mollie was tried and convicted on similar charges around the same time.

Their sentence? Banishment from Union lines. Union authorities sent them to St. Louis on November 24 for shipment to the South.

Upon reviewing their cases, however, Lieutenant-Colonel William H. Coyle, temporarily acting as provost marshal general of the department, recommended that the sentences be mitigated. He advised that the two young women be paroled on oath and bond and returned to Kansas City.

Shortly afterward, someone of higher authority (name illegible) endorsed Coyle's recommendation, adding in reference to the young women, "I will not have them sent south."[9]

Mollie Anderson signed the oath to the Union on December 10. She was released on $1,000 bond and sent back to the District of the Border. In Kansas City, she was required to sign another oath before authorities granted her freedom. On December 24, she gave

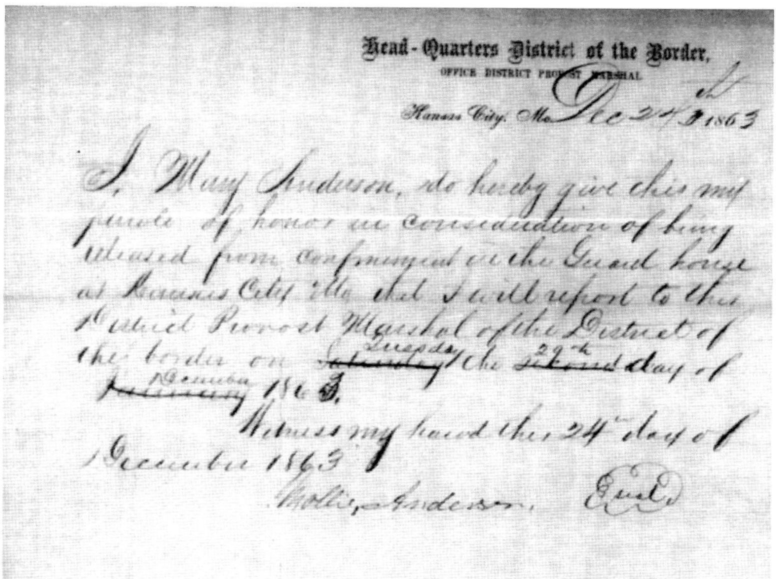

Head-Quarters District of the Border,
OFFICE DISTRICT PROVOST MARSHAL
Kansas City, Mo. Dec 24 1863

I, Mary Anderson, do hereby give this my parole of honor in consideration of being released from confinement in the Guard house at Kansas City Mo that I will report to the District Provost Marshal of the District of the border on ~~Saturday~~ Tuesday the ~~second~~ 29th day of ~~January~~ December 1863.

Witness my hand this 24th day of December 1863

Mollie Anderson.

Mollie Anderson's parole, dated December 24, 1863. (From Union provost marshals' records.)

her "parole of honor." She agreed that, in consideration of being released from the guardhouse, she would report to the district provost marshal on the 29th. She was then turned loose.[10]

Meanwhile, near the time Federal authorities transported Mollie Anderson to St. Louis, they released her sister Mattie Jane on parole. Mattie went back to her old stomping grounds in Kansas to live with C. H. Withington. Although Withington had clashed with the male members of the Anderson family, he apparently wanted to show the girl that he had no hard feelings toward her.

Things did not work out as he had planned. Perhaps he and Mattie clashed, or maybe she was just homesick for Missouri. On Christmas Day 1863, Withington wrote to Charles S. Hills, provost marshal of the District of the Border, that Jane Anderson could not remain "in this country." He said he would try to put her on the Santa Fe mail stage the next day "if they will take her." If not, he requested that Hills send someone to come and get her at the first opportunity. He added that Miss Anderson wanted to go to Lexington, Missouri.[11]

The movements of the Anderson sisters are sketchy in the months immediately following Mollie's release from Federal custody and Mattie's return to Missouri. The girls seemingly reunited near Lexington, where Mattie had asked to be sent. The Missouri State Guard had scored an important victory over Federal forces at the Siege of Lexington in the fall of 1861, but the town had been under secure Union control ever since.

Not so with the rest of the county. Although Lafayette County was home to a sizeable Union-supporting German population, most of the countryside was strongly pro-Confederate. Bill Anderson had made the place his headquarters when he'd first taken to the brush after his flight from Kansas in 1862. And now, two years later, according to one post-war report, his sisters spent four or five weeks there in the spring or early summer of 1864 nursing a wounded guerrilla, Warren Welch, back to health.[12]

During 1864, the girls seemed to follow Bill Anderson and his bushwhacker gang. Later in the summer, Anderson shifted his operations to Howard County. Located on the north side of the Missouri River halfway between St. Louis and Kansas City, Howard County was the very heart of Little Dixie.

Bill's sisters soon followed him. Sustained by a network of Southern-sympathizing citizens, they moved from one home to another with brief stays.

In the late summer or early fall, Mollie and Mattie stayed for a while with George W. Shaw near Rocheport.

Sometime around the first of October, Bill Anderson arranged for Porter Jackman, uncle of Confederate colonel Sidney D. Jackman, to move the girls to Jackman's nearby home. They boarded there with Jackman's wife, Mary "Polly" Jackman, for about three weeks. Bill Anderson, his brother Jim, and some of Anderson's other men stayed briefly at Jackman's as well. The Anderson brothers left sometime before their sisters, supposedly to go south.

When Mollie and Mattie left near the end of October, they announced that they were going south, too, to meet their brothers in Texas at their sister-in-law's house.[13]

On September 27, Bill Anderson and his men took twenty-three unarmed Federal soldiers off a train at Centralia in northern Boone County and executed them in what became known as the Centralia Massacre. As the long killing season of 1864 wore on throughout the summer and into the fall, Union authorities in Missouri focused more and more on one goal: finding and stopping the bloodthirsty Bill Anderson. They finally succeeded almost a month after the Centralia tragedy. On October 26, Federal troops in Ray County mowed him down as he led a mad charge into their lines.

The news of Bill Anderson's death changed the Anderson girls' plans to go south. About the first of November, they turned up incognito at the home of Mrs. Susan M. Bass. Mrs. Watson, wife of bushwhacker John S. Watson, arrived about the same time. The three asked permission to board there.

Mrs. Bass was acquainted with Mrs. Watson, but she did not know the other two young ladies. They introduced themselves as the Oldham sisters. They were, in fact, as Mrs. Bass later learned, Mollie and Mattie Anderson. They no doubt considered it too risky to reveal their true identities as the sisters of the late Bill Anderson. In Union circles, his execution of the Federal soldiers at Centralia and his other heinous deeds had earned him the reputation of an inhuman fiend.

The three women boarded with Mrs. Bell. It was a rocky couple of weeks. Bushwhackers came and went. Their host finally discovered the Anderson girls' true identities. When Mrs. Bass asked them to leave, they dared her to run them off.

Finally, Union leaders arrested the Anderson sisters.

They were hauled off to prison, yet they left behind problems for Mrs. Bell. This is her story.

Mrs. Bass later claimed the three young women were forced upon her, but she let them stay at her house, insisting that they each pay rent and board of three dollars per week.[14]

During the three-plus weeks that the young women stayed with Mrs. Bell, bushwhackers often visited her residence. They sometimes took supper, forcing Mrs. Bell's slaves to serve them. Sometimes they stayed overnight.

Mrs. Bell said she did not learn the Anderson sisters' true identity until they had been with her about three weeks. When she asked them to leave, they became defiant.

She did not report the bushwhacker activity at her house directly, she said, for fear of retaliation. About the time of her confrontation with the Anderson sisters, she did manage to report it indirectly (i.e. presumably through a third party). On this information, Lieutenant Joseph M. Street of the Ninth Missouri State Militia Cavalry arrested the Anderson sisters in late November at Mrs. Bass's home. He took them initially either to Fayette or Mexico, Missouri, but authorities soon sent them to Macon, headquarters of the District of North Missouri.[15]

Shortly after the Anderson girls' arrest, Mrs. Watson wrote a letter to Mrs. Bass seeking the return of all the personal property that the three young women had left at the Bass home. When Mrs. Watson got little satisfaction from her first letter, she wrote a second, more threatening, missive. It instructed Mrs. Bass to send all of her (i.e. Mrs. Watson's) things and all of the Anderson sisters' personal items. These included dresses, silk thread, bonnets, hats, gloves, letters, and a picture of Mattie. If Mrs. Bass did not comply, there would "be bad times shore."

John S. Watson also wrote to Mrs. Bass in the days immediately after the Anderson girls' arrest. In a letter dated November 28 he instructed Mrs. Bass to send thirty dollars in gold and fourteen dollars in silver that he or one of his comrades had left at the Bass house. He said he would send a bushwhacker named Carter to collect the gold and silver and that Carter would settle up with Mrs. Bass in greenbacks for the girls' room and board. Mrs. Bass later testified that Carter did, indeed, show up for the coinage and that, after she gave it to him, he "pitched $25 in greenbacks in my lap" as he rode away.[16]

A couple of weeks after their arrest, Union officials at Macon sent the Anderson sisters to St. Louis. They arrived under guard on the evening of December 10 and were placed in the Gratiot Street Female Prison.

The sisters made the St. Louis papers. Their descriptions in the competitive newspapers were similar. These newspapers were indeed very competitive—Republican was conservative, almost sympathetic toward South. Democrat was radical Republican. Yet the newspapers described the Anderson sisters as proper young ladies.

The *St. Louis Daily Missouri Republican* observed that the Anderson girls "are spoken of as persons of more refinement than could well have been expected in the relations of such a cutthroat and ruffian." The *Daily Missouri Democrat* considered them proper and reserved young ladies, despite their strong Southern sympathies.[17]

The *Democrat* further remarked that the Anderson girls were "quite young and handsome." Years after the war, a man who had known the Anderson sisters in Kansas echoed the same opinion, recalling that, even though they were bitter rebels, they were "fine looking girls."[18]

On January 19, 1865, Federal authorities shipped Mollie and Mattie Anderson south beyond the Union lines by way of Gaines Landing, Arkansas.

During the past five years, Mollie and Mattie had endured unimaginable grief. An older brother disappeared, never to be heard from again. Their mother was struck and killed by lightning. Their father shot and killed by a double-crossing Kansas judge. Sister Josephine crushed to death by the collapse of the Yankee prison. Another brother killed by Federal troops. If the two sisters hadn't already been "bitter rebels," they surely would be now. Yet they went on to lead surprising normal lives after the war.

The Rest of the Story

The Anderson sisters and brother Jim were destined to live together or nearby for most of the rest of their lives. They married, raised families, moved near one another, and seemed close until their deaths.

Mollie and Mattie Anderson did not return to Missouri after the war.

Instead, they took up residence, along with their brother Jim, in Grayson County, Texas, where Quantrill's guerrillas had spent the winter of 1863-1864 and where some of them had returned the following winter.

Mollie married Alexander V. Doak in Grayson County on June 18, 1865.

Mattie married E.G. Douglass on February 20, 1867, in the same county.

Jim married Mary Lucy Erwin on October 21, 1868, also in Grayson County.

All three couples were living in Refugio County on the Gulf Coast in 1870.

Jim's and Mattie's families lived in the same household. Mollie and her family lived nearby. The census taker listed Jim Anderson's occupation as a teamster.

By 1880, Jim was dead. Mollie's and Mattie's families were back in Grayson County.

In 1900, Mollie was living in Ardmore, Indian Territory, with her husband, who was a government contractor, and her son Claude (the only child still living at home), who was a medical student. Around 1900, Mattie and her family were living near Houston, Texas, in Fort Bend County, where her husband was head of a convict camp.

When Mollie became very ill in the fall of 1903, Mattie visited her sister at Ardmore and was by her bedside when she died. Mollie was buried in Rose Hill Cemetery at Ardmore.

Mattie died a few years later in Coryell County, Texas.[19]

CHAPTER 10

Wife of a Bill Anderson Guerrilla

Nineteen-year-old Imogene "Emma" Brumfield was arrested in Howard County on the day she learned her husband had been killed.

Less than a month after their wedding.

Imogene was taken into custody near the same time and place that Bill Anderson's sisters, Mollie and Mattie, were also arrested. The three were taken as prisoners to St. Louis together.

From there, however, their ways parted drastically. The Anderson girls were shipped south. Imogene Brumfield became one of the few Missouri women during the Civil War, if not the only one, who was banished to Canada.

Imogene moved from Canada to Lexington, Missouri, with her father, John B. Jordan, and the rest of the Jordan family in the summer of 1860. During the first three years of the Civil War, Jordan was generally considered loyal to the Union, and his daughter had a reputation in Lexington as "modest and well-disposed in her deportment and character."[1]

By late summer 1864, Imogene's loyalties shifted.

In September 1864, Imogene left home. Her story was that she planned to visit friends in Glasgow in western Howard County. Instead, she went to the southeast part of the same county to rendezvous with Benjamin F. Brumfield, a Bill Anderson bushwhacker. The area was an enclave of Southern sentiment, and earlier in the summer, Anderson had adopted it as his center of operations. He called Rocheport, just across the line in Boone County, his "capital."

Imogene had fallen in love with Benjamin, presumably during the early summer when the Anderson gang was operating in Lafayette County. During her sojourn in Howard County, Imogene boarded at first in the home of Mary Jackman, the widowed mother of

Confederate colonel Sidney Drake Jackman. Later Imogene moved to the home of Porter Jackman, Sidney Jackman's uncle.

Bill Anderson's sisters also stayed with Porter and his wife, Mary, part of the time that Imogene was there. Members of Anderson's band, including Brumfield, showed up from time to time as well.

On October 25, Imogene Jordan married the twenty-one-year-old Brumfield at the Porter Jackman residence. A justice of the peace named Piper performed the ceremony.[2]

Sometime after her wedding, Imogene moved to the nearby home of a Mrs. Breshears. On November 20, bushwhacker John Watson, the same man whose wife had introduced the Anderson girls to Mrs. Bass, and two other guerrillas showed up at the Brashears house. They told Imogene that Brumfield had been killed by Federal soldiers. Even as Imogene spoke with the bearers of the tragic news, Union soldiers were in the immediate vicinity. The three men made their getaway.

A party of soldiers arrived shortly afterward, and according to their later testimony, Imogene was irate. She denounced them as robbers and murderers. The soldiers arrested her on suspicion of giving information and encouragement to bushwhackers.[3]

Imogene was held in Glasgow about two weeks. On December 8th, Captain John D. Meredith escorted her to Macon, headquarters of the District of North Missouri. There she gave a statement to district provost marshal R. A. DeBolt. Imogene didn't mince words. She proclaimed herself a Southern sympathizer and admitted she knew Benjamin Brumfield was a bushwhacker when she married him.[4]

Federal detective James A. Pickett, who had previously interrogated Mrs. Brumfield, also gave a statement to DeBolt on December 9. Pickett said it wouldn't bother Imogene to be sent south because that was where she wanted to go. The detective also said Imogene had rejoiced over Bill Anderson's massacre of the Union soldiers at Centralia on September 27.[5]

Imogene was sent under guard on December 10 from Macon to St. Louis, 170 miles away. It was likely cold. The passenger car probably would have had some crude sort of heat—a wood or coal stove near the front of the car, perhaps. The same train carried Mollie and Mattie Anderson. In an article about the Anderson girls' incarceration at Gratiot Street Female Prison, a St. Louis newspaper remarked, "Mrs. Imogen [*sic*] E. Brumfield, widow of one of Bill Anderson's gang, was brought down at the same time and furnished with similar accommodations. Imogen was married but a short time before her husband was killed, but she does not appear to be inconsolable for his loss, as she remarked that there were 'plenty more men left.'"[6]

Word of Benjamin Brumfield's death and Imogene's arrest reached Imogene's married sister, Amelia Jordan Scoville, in Chicago in early December. On December 13th Amelia picked up her pen on

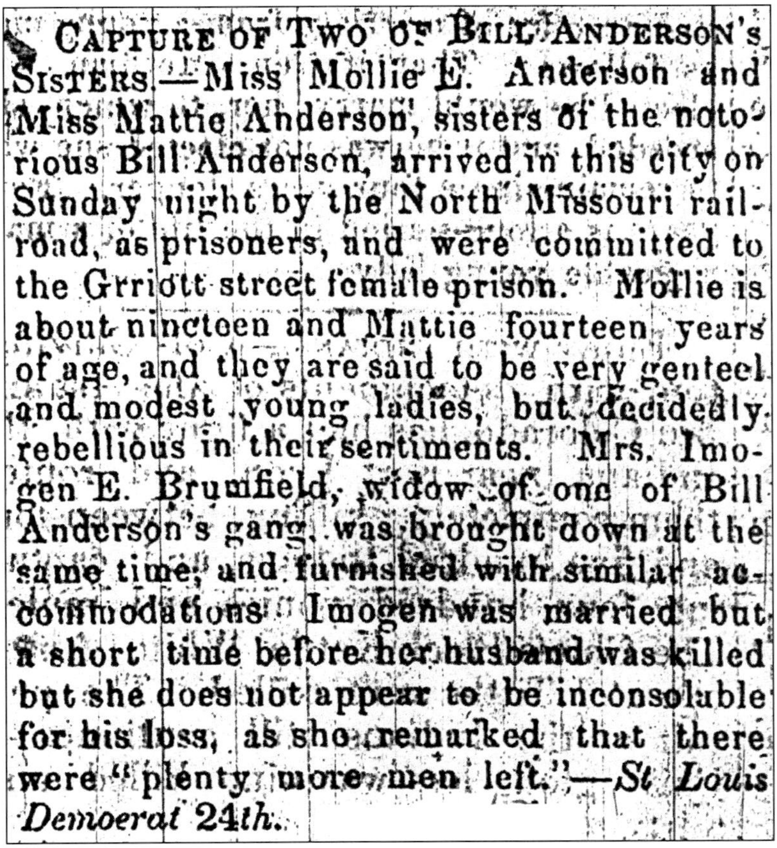

CAPTURE OF TWO OF BILL ANDERSON'S SISTERS.—Miss Mollie E. Anderson and Miss Mattie Anderson, sisters of the notorious Bill Anderson, arrived in this city on Sunday night by the North Missouri railroad, as prisoners, and were committed to the Grriott street female prison. Mollie is about nineteen and Mattie fourteen years of age, and they are said to be very genteel and modest young ladies, but decidedly rebellious in their sentiments. Mrs. Imogen E. Brumfield, widow of one of Bill Anderson's gang, was brought down at the same time, and furnished with similar accommodations. Imogen was married but a short time before her husband was killed but she does not appear to be inconsolable for his loss, as she remarked that there were "plenty more men left."—*St Louis Democrat 24th.*

Newspaper story detailing the capture and imprisonment of Imogene Brumfield and the Anderson sisters. (From the Mound City (Kans.) *Border Sentinel.*)

Imogene's behalf to ask for help from an influential acquaintance. It was the second time she did so. Two years earlier, the girls' father was briefly imprisoned at Lexington. Amelia had written to a man named Wilkins for her father, and now wrote to Wilkins again for her sister. Mrs. Scoville beseeched Wilkins to use his influence to bring about Imogene's release.[7]

What, if any, action Mr. Wilkins took is unknown.

Imogene got a chance to tell her own story on December 29th in an interview with assistant examiner George J. W. Nexsen. She admitted that Bill Anderson's men called at the Porter Jackman residence occasionally while she was staying there, but they seldom ate there. She denied telling John Watson and his two comrades that Federal soldiers were in the vicinity when they brought word of her husband's death. She claimed she did not use disrespectful language to the soldiers when they showed up.

Asked whether she was a Southern sympathizer, she at first said she had no sympathies for either side because she had nothing to gain or lose. But then she changed her answer:

Yes, she did sympathize with the South.

No, she did not wish to see it put down.

No, she had never carried Rebel mail or traded any sort of contraband.

No, she had never helped or encouraged bushwhackers other than her husband.[8]

Imogene tried to mitigate the circumstances of her arrest with the latter claims. But she did little to help her cause when she wrote a letter to her family on January 6, 1865, from her prison cell. She told her mother she was "still a prisoner and a very contented one. Nothing to say. Nothing to do. So nothing to write. Only that I have the exquisite pleasure of acting the part of a Biddie once a week." (This probably meant she was required to cook, clean, or perform other domestic duties.) Imogene told her mother that Mollie and Mattie Anderson were both sick with the measles and that she enjoyed waiting on them during their illness. "If there was nothing to prevent my happiness but being a prisoner," she concluded, "I would not mind remaining in prison for a year."

The letter went on. To her younger sisters, Ida and Clara, she wrote, "Tell me all about your school, but please do not mention any of your Union beaus, for it will only anger me to think you have such friends." She did not want to hear from or about anyone who expressed a sentiment against her deceased husband because her heart and soul were with his cause. If he were to have the same trial to undergo again, she would "desire him to die the same death."[9]

The letter was intercepted. It became evidence against her.

On January 9 she wrote another letter, this time to her sister Amelia. The tone was even more defiant than her previous one. Perhaps she felt freer to express her true feelings to her sister than to her parents. Or perhaps a few extra days of rumination on the pain Union authorities had brought her had whetted her bitterness to an edge. Imogene asked Amelia not to grieve for her because she wasn't grieving for herself. She lamented that it had been so long since she had heard from her "dear old home, dear old Canada," and she added:

> If I ever get out of this infernal region, I intend going there. God grant that I may never see the accursed shores of this states again, if it was not for that the only thing I ever loved is lying in its soil, sleeping his last long sleep. Would to God that I were a man. Please do not pronounce me crazed or wild. It is true I have almost lost all reason, but I have a little rebble sense left. Nothing more. Do not wonder what has caused it. If you had your husband killed, murdered, yourself taken prisoner by his murderers and not allowed to see him, not even to know where he is buried nor who performed the sacred offices which is due to the dead, you would be a demon, which I fess I am. If not one now, just on the verge.

Changing the subject, Imogene asked about Amelia's baby daughter, Leila. "Perhaps she will have the pleasure of seeing her aunt Emma this year," Imogene pined.[10]

While Imogene lolled in prison and nursed her rancor, friends and family on the outside worked on her behalf.

Seven Union men from Lexington signed their names to a letter dated January 6 asking authorities to show leniency in her case, for the sake of Imogene's parents. This is what their missive contained. They were acquainted with Imogene. They had "never heard anything detrimental to her as a lady or otherwise" prior to her leaving her father's home in September. She left without the knowledge or consent of her parents. Her conduct had brought "deep distress and sorrow" upon them. Mr. Jordan planned to return to Canada with his family. If it was consistent with the nature of the charge against Imogene, could he be allowed to take his daughter with him? If she were allowed to return to Canada under banishment the young woman might yet be saved from ruin.[11]

On January 13, after reading the transcript of Nexsen's interview with Imogene Brumfield, chief examiner Albert G. Clarke forwarded the transcript to the provost marshal general. He recommended the young woman "be sent north or outside the Federal lines."[12]

Imogene's father, John B. Jordan, traveled to St. Louis upon her incarceration there. On January 14, Jordan swore out an affidavit before a local notary public pleading his daughter's case. He said he had always supported the Union and had always opposed bushwhackers and guerrillas. He claimed Imogene was only sixteen years old when she ran away from home the previous fall. He asked Union authorities to show mercy in consideration of her youth and indiscretion. He fretted that banishing her to the South might lead her to "a life of infamy and disgrace." He begged for her to be banished to Canada, where he intended to take his family, "unless the charges against her are of such a serious nature as to prohibit such action."[13]

All these letters and affidavits landed in Imogene's file in the solicitor's office. Solicitor Samuel S. Boyd returned the file to the provost marshal general's office on or about January 16. He suggested banishing Imogene Brumfield to Canada "where she can be under the control of her father."

The provost marshal general's office passed the file and Boyd's recommendation on to assistant adjutant general J. F. Bennett. On January 18 Bennett returned the file with instructions from General Grenville M. Dodge to banish Mrs. Brumfield to Canada.[14]

Before such an order could be issued, however, Union authorities caught Imogene in the act of even more illicit conduct. Recently released Gratiot Street Prison inmate Martha Keeton sneaked back into the prison. She smuggled Imogene some furs for her trip north. Provost marshal general J. H. Baker promptly dispatched Peter Tallon, chief of US military police, to the prison to seize the furs from Imogene .[15]

Once the contraband was confiscated, Colonel Baker issued an order the next day, January 19, releasing Imogene Brumfield. He stipulated that she go immediately to Canada and not return to the United States during the war.[16]

Imogene was too much of a troublemaker to stay in the country. She journeyed back to Canada with her father.

By the time the Civil War ended, she must have changed her mind about never wanting to see the "accursed shores" of the US again.. On May 27, 1865, her brother-in-law, Byron Scoville, wrote to Colonel Baker from Chicago. He wanted a permit allowing Imogene Brumfield to return to the United States. Scoville said he was prompted to make such a request after seeing an order from the War Department releasing all persons under sentence of imprisonment "during the war."[17]

Baker replied to Scoville on May 31. He said the application could not be granted at present, but he would refer the request to the commanding general of the department. He said Scoville would be notified when an action had been taken on the matter. After waiting over a month with no word from St. Louis, Scoville again wrote to Baker on July 3 pressing his appeal. "The war having closed," he insisted, "and persons daily returning to Missouri who have been banished from that State 'during the war,' you will be kind enough to forward to me a permit that Mrs. Imogene E. Brumfield may return, she being banished from Missouri during the war by your direct order."[18]

A month passed. Still no word from Baker. Scoville grew impatient and wrote directly to General John Pope, who had replaced General Dodge as commander of the Department of the Missouri. In a letter dated August 7, Scoville recounted the facts of Imogene's case. He said she had been held prisoner without charges in St. Louis for three months. Colonel Baker would not even grant her a hearing, although petitioned to do so several times. The only satisfaction Scoville had gotten was an assurance that the commanding general would review his request. The war was over. Prison doors were thrown open.

Scoville assured the general that Imogene, who was born in New York, was not and never had been an enemy or traitor to her native land and had always been in favor of putting down secession. He asked, therefore, that Pope issue a permit for her to return to Missouri.[19]

Provost marshal Colonel James Baker was reluctant to allow Imogene Brumfield to return to Missouri, even after the war had ended. (Courtesy of Wikimedia.)

The Rest of the Story

Presumably Imogene Brumfield was eventually allowed to return to the United States. No record of such a permit survives.

Around 1870, Byron and Amelia Scoville were still living in Chicago with several other family members in the household. They included Imogene and Amelia's younger sister Ida.

What happened to Imogene in the years after the war remains a mystery.[20]

Chapter 11
Confederate Mail Handlers

When Federal soldiers raided Eliza Haynie's Saline County home in the late spring of 1864, a quick once-over through the house turned up a cache of possible stolen goods. But it wasn't the hidden merchandise that finally landed Eliza and her nineteen-year-old daughter in a Union military prison two hundred miles from home. It was something else the soldiers found when they came back for a closer look later the same day.

On June 13, 1864, Captain Wilson L. Parker of the Fourth Missouri State Militia Cavalry led a Federal scout through Saline County. One of his sergeants, W. M. Sapp, struck the track of what he assumed to be a party of guerrillas. He followed the trail a short distance, but he lost it. Wandering around in an effort to regain the trail, Sapp and his men came upon the home of Mrs. Eliza Haynie. The house was about a mile and a half above Miami, just south of the Missouri River.

While Sapp went to the front door to ask how to get back to Miami, some of his men rode around to the back yard. They caught young women carrying clothes and other articles from the house and hiding them outside. The men reported this suspicious activity to their sergeant. Sapp demanded to know what the women were hiding—and why.

The woman gave a flimsy excuse that they were afraid the soldiers would take their clothes and burn down the house.

Dissatisfied with this response, a couple of Sapp's men went into the house. They came back with two memorandum books that were later used to implicate the thirty-seven-year-old Eliza in disloyal activities. The exact contents of the books are unknown.

Meanwhile, some of Sapp's other men found two horses, saddled, bridled, and tethered not far from the Haynie home. One of the horses had a US bridle. Not far from where the horses were tied,

Sapp and his men discovered what appeared to be a guerrilla camp. It had been recently deserted. After a brief search for the guerrillas, the Federals returned to the main road.

Suddenly, the crack of gunshots filled the air.

Two bushwhackers fired upon the Union troops just three hundred yards from the Haynie home.[1]

What happened next is not clear.

When the smoke cleared, Sapp rendezvoused with Captain Parker. The Federals returned to search the Haynie residence. Parker found cloth, silverware, and other dry goods in a trunk inside. One of his men found shoes and boots in an upstairs room. In total, the goods in question were worth at least fifty dollars, a large sum at the time. The captain asked Eliza where she had gotten them. She had purchased part of the goods from two merchants in Miami. Her husband, Frederick Haynie, had bought some before he had left for the Confederate Army.

In addition, Sergeant Sapp found a pair of saddlebags containing letters written by Confederate soldiers, mostly members of General Mosby M. Parsons's brigade.[2]

Parker confiscated the goods. He took them—and Eliza—to the merchants in Miami from whom she said she had purchased them. Parker swore in the storekeepers. Under oath, they confirmed some of her story. They identified part of the items as having been purchased by Eliza or members of her family.

Then the Miami merchants' statements started working against Eliza. They weren't sure about some of the other merchandise. Part of it had not been sold, they said. The implication? The articles had been stolen.

Parker returned some dress patterns, some bed ticking, and one pair of shoes, amounting to about fifteen or twenty dollars' worth of goods, to Eliza.

Then he arrested her and her nineteen-year-old daughter, Rachel.

He took them and the rest of the merchandise to Sedalia, where he turned the prisoners and the suspect goods over to the assistant provost marshal.[3]

Eliza and her daughter were charged with disloyalty, harboring and feeding guerrillas under the command of a man named Campbell, aiding and abetting the enemies of the United States, and receiving stolen property. Union authorities escorted them to Jefferson City on July 26 for trial by military commission and paroled both of them to the limits of Jefferson City the same day. The parole stipulated they report to the provost marshal's office each day.[4]

Not all the women arrested in Missouri for aiding bushwhackers had the means or inclination to engage lawyers, but Eliza Haynie did. When her trial began on July 28, she introduced Ed Belch as her counsel and pleaded not guilty to all charges.

Captain Parker, the prosecution's first witness, was a mixed bag. He knew nothing of the accused harboring or otherwise aiding bushwhackers, only that his men had discovered what appeared to be a Rebel camp near her home. He did not know whether the merchandise he found on her premises was stolen, only that the Miami merchants said they had not sold part of it. His most damning testimony was that the saddlebags found on the Haynie premises contained Rebel mail.[5]

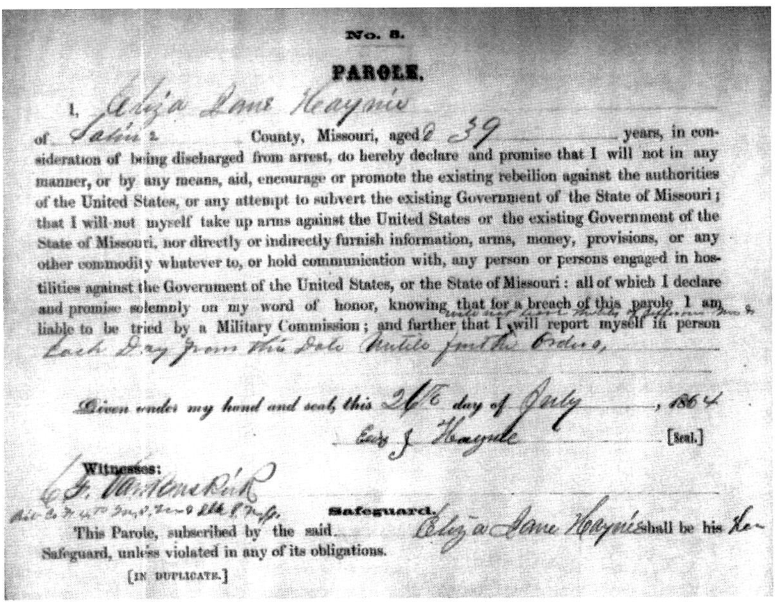

No. 8.

PAROLE.

I, Eliza Jane Haynie of Saline County, Missouri, aged 39 years, in consideration of being discharged from arrest, do hereby declare and promise that I will not in any manner, or by any means, aid, encourage or promote the existing rebellion against the authorities of the United States, or any attempt to subvert the existing Government of the State of Missouri; that I will not myself take up arms against the United States or the existing Government of the State of Missouri, nor directly or indirectly furnish information, arms, money, provisions, or any other commodity whatever to, or hold communication with, any person or persons engaged in hostilities against the Government of the United States, or the State of Missouri: all of which I declare and promise solemnly on my word of honor, knowing that for a breach of this parole I am liable to be tried by a Military Commission; and further that I will report myself in person each day from this date until further orders,

Given under my hand and seal, this 26th day of July, 1864.

Eliza J Haynie [Seal.]

Witnesses:

F. Van Vonnekirk

Safeguard.

This Parole, subscribed by the said Eliza Jane Haynie shall be his Safeguard, unless violated in any of its obligations.

[IN DUPLICATE.]

Eliza Haynie was paroled to the limits of Jefferson City on July 26, 1864. (From Union provost marshals' records.)

Sergeant Sapp's testimony largely reflected that of his commanding officer. He had no personal knowledge that Eliza had ever helped bushwhackers. He knew nothing about whether the goods found at her house were stolen.[6]

The prosecution's third and final witness was James C. Anderson, a clerk in the office of the provost marshal at Sedalia. James was not related to Bloody Bill Anderson. He confirmed Captain Parker had turned over to his office a lot of goods seized at Eliza's residence. He said two citizens from Frankfort, Missouri, later claimed part of the goods. The Frankfort residents identified the items as their belongings; bushwhackers stole them.[7]

In his rebuttal of the prosecution witnesses and in his closing argument, Belch suggested at least one of the incriminating memorandum books was not found on Eliza's premises. It was found at the camp two hundred yards away. He elicited an admission from Parker that Eliza had told him two strangers left the saddlebags, asking that she take care of them. She promised to do so, not knowing what was in them. Belch characterized as hearsay the accusation that anything found at the Haynie home was stolen.[8]

Eliza's trial concluded on August 3.

She was found not guilty of harboring and feeding guerrillas and not guilty of receiving stolen property.

She was found guilty of disloyalty and guilty of aiding and abetting the enemies of the US, but only on the single count of hiding Rebel mail.

She was sentenced to confinement for the duration of the war at a place to be designated by the commanding general.

General William Rosecrans, commanding the Department of the Missouri, approved the findings in mid-August. He ruled that Eliza be confined at the Alton Military Prison in Alton, Illinois. Sent to St. Louis shortly afterward, she was held initially at the Myrtle Street Prison and then transferred to the Gratiot Street Female Prison by September 7.[9]

On September 17, W. L. Brown, who lived in Eliza Haynie's neighborhood, wrote to General Rosecrans on her behalf. He said there were a number of able-bodied men in the same neighborhood equally guilty of the charges on which she had been convicted. They were still at large. Brown didn't say so, but perhaps he felt Eliza was being picked on because her husband was in the Confederate Army.

He asked the general to give careful consideration to her case "in the name of mercy and humanity." He said Eliza had several small children. Now, no one was caring for them. Her relatives were poor and her husband was in the Rebel army. The kids needed their mother, Brown argued, especially with winter coming on, or else they might suffer from lack of food and clothing. He begged for clemency. In a postscript, he assured the general the woman was no relation of his. "I certainly have no partiality for bushwhacking, having been robbed by them three times in the last two weeks," Brown added, but "there are some others in the neighborhood who should occupy her place."

Despite Brown's eloquent plea, Rosecrans decided it was too soon to consider a mitigation of her sentence.[10]

Rachel's trial was conducted about the same time as her mother's.

She, too, was found guilty and sentenced to imprisonment at Alton for the duration of the war. Union authorities forwarded her from Jefferson City to St. Louis on September 22 and admitted her to the Gratiot Street facility. They transferred her to Alton, just across the Mississippi River from St. Louis, on October 10. Her mother was presumably sent there at or near the same time.[11]

Although Rosecrans originally was reluctant to show leniency in late September in the case of Eliza Haynie, he softened his stance just a couple months later. On December 8, he commuted both women's sentences to six months' imprisonment.

It was not unusual during the Civil War for commanding generals to cancel or commute the sentences of military commissions. This was certainly true of St. Louis generals in their dealings with the bushwhacker belles of Missouri. Even three-fourths of the way through the Civil War, most high-ranking Union officers did not want to be seen as making war on women. Especially when the evidence against the women was shaky to begin with, as it was in the case of Eliza and Rachel Haynie.

Rachel's new sentence dated from August 19, 1864. Eliza's new sentence dated from August 23, 1864.

The two women were accordingly released in early 1865.[12]

The Rest of the Story

Both Eliza and her daughter returned to Saline County after their release.

The Haynie family was still living in the Miami vicinity around

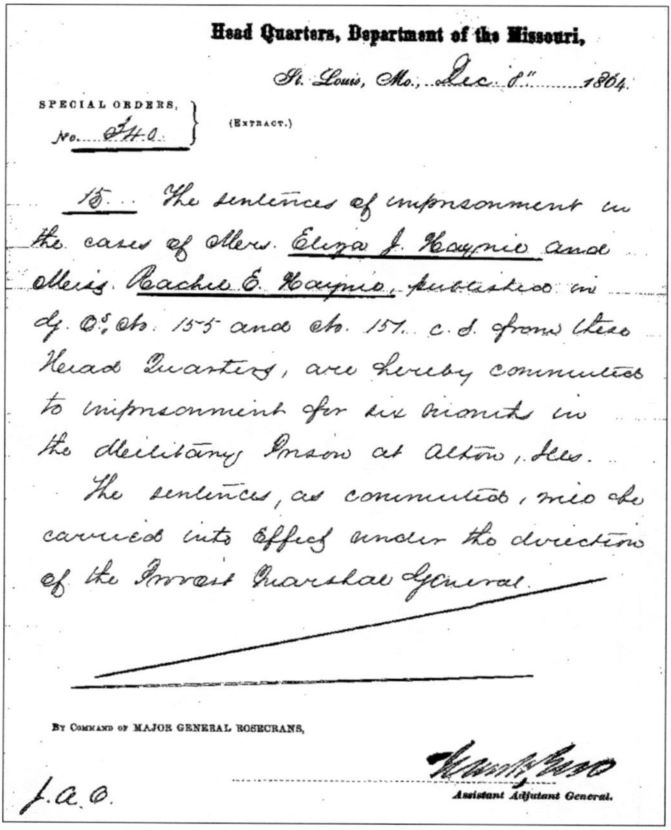
Head Quarters, Department of the Missouri,

St. Louis, Mo., Dec. 8th 1864.

SPECIAL ORDERS, No. 340. } (EXTRACT.)

15. The sentences of imprisonment in the cases of Mrs. Eliza J. Haynie and Miss Rachel E. Haynie, published in G. O. No. 155 and No. 151, c. s. from these Head Quarters, are hereby commuted to imprisonment for six months in the Military Prison at Alton, Ills.

The sentences, as commuted, will be carried into effect under the direction of the Provost Marshal General.

BY COMMAND OF MAJOR GENERAL ROSECRANS,

Assistant Adjutant General.

J. a. o.

The sentences of Eliza and Rachel Haynie were commuted from imprisonment for the duration of the war to imprisonment for six months. (From Union provost marshals' records.)

1870. Eliza was the head of household. Her husband was missing from the home, although it's not clear whether the couple had separated or he simply was not counted in the census. Rachel, twenty-six, was still living at home with eight younger siblings. Eliza died in 1876 and is buried at Miami Cemetery.

In 1880, Rachel was still single. She lived in Benton County with the family of her younger sister, Narcissa Proffitt. She later moved to Oregon with Narcissa's family. She died there in 1907, having never married. She is buried at Mt. Hope Cemetery in Baker County, Oregon.[13]

CHAPTER 12

Fannie Houx and the Excitement Surrounding Her Case

Whatever the players' opinions on slavery, Confederate and Union alike, the word of a slave was usually insufficient to land a white woman in jail during the Civil War.

Plus, in those days, if you belonged to a prominent family, that came with certain privileges.

Neither of these things kept Fannie Houx out of hot water.

In Fannie's trial, the world heard a slave's testimony that bushwhackers whipped and kicked him on Fannie's property while Fannie egged them on. By itself, the presence of a black witness on the stand was enough to make the case scandalous in some eyes. The slave did not mince words. He described the event in gruesome detail.

Fannie was the thirty-one-year-old mother of five small children, including an infant. She faced the task of overcoming a black man's testimony to win her freedom and ensure her baby didn't starve while she was locked up.

Fannie's case reaches to us across the years and shines a harsh limelight on the complex social intricacies of the period.

About the first of July, 1864 a black man named Jackson reported Fannie to Union authorities at Lexington for harboring bushwhackers. Jackson, like many slaves, did not have a surname and was described in Union records only as Jackson "a colored man." He was the property of Fannie's father-in-law, William Houx, who owned a farm several miles south of Lexington. Fannie and her kids also lived on the farm while her husband, George W. Houx, was away in the Confederate Army. After preliminary investigation of Jackson's charges, Union authorities assigned a military commission already in session in Jefferson City to hear Fannie's case.[1]

Lieutenant James M. Gavin, assistant provost marshal at Lexington, arrested Mrs. Houx in late July and sent her by steamboat to Jefferson City for trial. He also sent Jackson, as the primary witness against Fannie, to Jefferson City on the same steamer. Gavin warned judge advocate Major Douglas Dale, who'd been assigned to prosecute the case, that it had aroused "considerable excitement about Negro testimony."[2]

That was probably an understatement.

Fannie's trial got underway on August 6. Fannie was officially charged with "harboring and feeding guerrillas" and with "giving aid and comfort to the Rebel enemies of the United States Government." The specification in each case was that she had sheltered, fed, and otherwise entertained guerrillas and outlaw enemies of the US on or about June 27 at the William Houx farm. Fannie pleaded not guilty. At the outset of the trial, she asked to enter a statement into the record. She stressed her vulnerability; she was alone as the only adult white person on the William Houx farm. She pointed out that she had often helped Federal soldiers. Her statement was read to the court. Major Dale objected to its being entered into the record on the grounds that the statement was in the style of a closing argument, not an opening defense. The commission sustained the objection.[3]

Jackson the slave was then called by the prosecution as the first

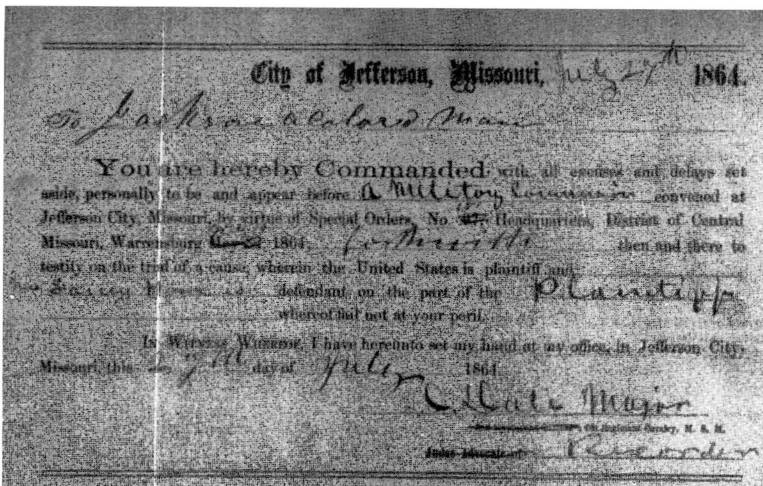

City of Jefferson, Missouri, July 27th 1864.

To Jackson a Colored Man

You are hereby Commanded with all excuses and delays set aside, personally to be and appear before a Military Commission convened at Jefferson City, Missouri, by virtue of Special Orders, No [illegible] Headquarters, District of Central Missouri, Warrensburg [illegible] 1864, [illegible] then and there to testify on the trial of a cause, wherein the United States is plaintiff and [illegible] defendant, on the part of the Plaintiff whereof fail not at your peril.

In Witness Whereof, I have hereunto set my hand at my office, in Jefferson City, Missouri, this 27th day of July 1864.

[illegible] Dale Major

[illegible] M. S. M.

[illegible] Recorder

Jackson, a slave, was subpoenaed to appear before a military commission in Jefferson City in the case of Fannie Houx. (From Union provost marshals' records.)

witness. He said that on Monday morning, June 27th, he was plowing in a field on the William Houx farm when he saw some men on horseback go to a well near the house. About an hour later he went to the house for breakfast. Near the well, he saw some wash pans and towels the men had used. He sat down in a chair near the kitchen door to wait for breakfast. Fannie came out and told him to go "watch for the Feds" because otherwise they might come and "get to fighting" and somebody might get killed.[4]

"I don't care if they do," Jackson replied.

Fannie threatened to tell the bushwhackers what he said when they came back, but Jackson replied that he didn't care.

Glancing toward a nearby apple orchard, Fannie said, "Yonder they come now."

"Let them come," the defiant Jackson said. "I don't care."

About twelve guerrillas rode up to the house. As soon as the first two dismounted, Fannie told them what Jackson had said.

The first one stepped up to Jackson, who was still seated in the chair, and said, "God damn your black soul, what do you mean talking that a way?"

The second bushwhacker asked his partner who he was talking about, and the first man said, "That old nigger sitting there. The lady says so."

The second man then pulled out his pistol, struck Jackson on the head with it, and threatened to blow his brains out.

Fannie sent a son up a nearby hill to watch for Federals. She had a son named William, who would have been 12, and another named Frank, who would have been 10. The record is not clear which son. She invited the guerrillas into the house for breakfast, and they trooped past Jackson into the dining room. Jackson was still sitting in the chair a few minutes later when they finished eating and came back outside.

Things turned violent.

The same two men who had abused him earlier went to the woods and came back with hickory switches, one of them a five- or six-foot-long hoop pole. They cursed Jackson and ordered him to come out into the yard. When he didn't respond quickly enough to suit them, one man grabbed Jackson by the shirt collar and jerked him up. Still spitting obscenities, the man kicked Jackson and hit him another lick with his pistol until he got Jackson into the middle of the yard.

There the two bushwhackers made him take off his shirt, and one of them started hitting him with the large hickory switch, using both hands to grip it. "He just tip-toed to it," Jackson recalled, "and came down on me the same as if he was beating an ox."[5]

Taking a breather from his ruthless attack, the man doing the whipping turned to the other bushwhackers and said, "Boys, you've got nothing to do but cut hickories and fetch them to me as fast as I can wear them out." The rest of the gang went to the woods and brought back five more hickory switches. When the man tired of whipping Jackson, he told him he could put his shirt back on. But as Jackson started toward the kitchen to put the shirt on, the same man picked up a clap board, a thin piece of lumber used for siding, and beat him with it until he reached the kitchen door. A second man then started cursing Jackson and ordered him back into the yard. He wore out another hickory on Jackson before the whippings stopped.[6]

Jackson's suffering wasn't done yet. The verbal abuse continued. The bushwhackers threatened to kill him if he reported them to the Federals. Finally a young man among the guerrillas named Tom Crawber, with whom Jackson and his wife were acquainted, came out of the house. He told the other bushwhackers they had done enough. At long last, Jackson was allowed to go into the kitchen for breakfast.[7]

The defense's primary strategy—rather than deny the events—was to impugn the integrity and reliability of the prosecution's witness. On cross-examination, Fannie's attorney, Allen Richardson, sought to show inconsistencies in Jackson's testimony. He also suggested that Jackson held a grudge against Fannie because she had intervened on behalf of his wife a few weeks earlier. That's when he and his wife had gotten into a violent argument and he had struck his wife.

Major Dale pointed out that the few inconsistencies Richardson found in Jackson's story concerned minor points that did not change the main facts of the case.

The only defense witness was Jacob Price, sheriff of Lafayette County. He said Mrs. Houx had often expressed opposition to bushwhacking. He maligned Jackson as untrustworthy, even though he was "a good boy to work." His testimony lost most of its weight when the prosecution asked him about his relationship to the accused and Price was forced to reveal that he was Fannie's brother.

Price had brought some depositions he took from citizens in Lexington impeaching the initial testimony Jackson had given to Lieutenant Gavin, and Richardson attempted to enter them into the record. Dale objected that the statements had been taken without notice to the prosecution and without his having a chance to cross examine the witnesses. The objection was sustained.

In her closing statement, Fannie claimed the bushwhackers came to her house without her consent or knowledge. In a new twist, she said Jackson's wife was already cooking for them before Fannie realized what was happening. The rest of her statement, like most of the defense's argument, was mainly an attempt to challenge the fine points of Jackson's testimony.[8]

On August 8, Fannie was found guilty and sentenced to be confined to the city limits of Lexington for the duration of the war. She remained in Jefferson City on parole pending the promulgation of her sentence. Meanwhile, no one seemed to care about the brutal beating of Jackson, the slave. No one was charged or brought to justice for that act.

The record of Fannie's trial was sent to the Department of the Missouri headquarters in St. Louis. On August 19, on behalf of department commander William Rosecrans, assistant adjutant general Frank Eno wrote to General Alfred Pleasonton, the Warrensburg district commander. Eno returned Fannie's record with a recommendation that her sentence, which he considered too lenient, be reconsidered. Eno said her case contained "some very anomalous features" when compared to cases of other women who had recently been tried on similar charges. He cited specifically the case of Saline County residents Eliza and Rachel Haynie, who had been found guilty at Jefferson City of harboring and feeding bushwhackers on "evidence less positive and direct" than in Fannie's case. They had been sentenced to confinement in Alton Military Prison for the duration of the war.

Fannie Houx, Eno added, did not attempt to disprove the charges against her except by impeaching the witness, "which attempt appears upon the record to have utterly failed." Captain Eno concluded that the lenient sentence could not be considered a punishment and would not deter others who might be tempted to commit similar offenses.[9]

Union authorities in the District of Central Missouri agreed to take a second look at Fannie's case. Her parole was revoked. She was returned to the military prison at Jefferson City to await the reconsideration of her sentence.[10]

Fannie pleaded for her freedom. On August 23, she wrote a letter to Lieutenant Frank Swap, assistant provost marshal at Jefferson City. She said she was "exceedingly anxious" to obtain a ten-day parole to go home to get her infant. Her other children could get by without her, but her baby needed a mother's care. Fannie was sure that, when Swap reflected on the matter, he would "deem it an act of charity" to grant her such a reasonable request. She could not believe he would refuse to do so.[11]

Fannie overestimated the magnanimity of Union authorities. On August 26, the military commission agreed with Eno and made her sentence even more stringent. The commission found that she should spend the rest of the war in a military prison instead of on parole in her hometown. Captain Richard L. Ferguson, district provost marshal, wrote to Swap from Warrensburg on September 1 with instructions that Fannie should remain in close confinement and not be paroled.[12]

Fannie's brother Jacob had a lot to say about what happened.

After staying in Jefferson City for his sister's trial, Jacob Price returned to Lexington. From there, the sheriff took up his pen on September 7, the same day that General Rosecrans confirmed Fannie's new sentence, to plead her case in a letter to Brigadier General Egbert B. Brown. Brown had recently been restored to command of the District of Central Missouri after the brief stay of General Pleasonton. Price lamented that the affidavits he had gathered at Lexington and carried to Jefferson City had not been allowed as evidence in his sister's case. Further, Major Dale had not kept his promise to allow time for Fannie or her lawyer to summon rebuttal witnesses from Lexington after Jackson's testimony was introduced.

After the trial concluded and the papers were forwarded up the chain of command, Sheriff Price waited in vain at Jefferson City with Major Dale's continued assurance that the papers would return soon and his sister would probably be able to accompany him home. After two weeks, Price finally tired of waiting and went home alone.[13]

Price painted Fannie as the mother of five small children who depended on her for food and clothing. He asked the general to do whatever he could to gain her release. He implored prompt action because he had been paying all her expenses since her arrest.[14]

As if to grease the wheel, Price went on to congratulate Brown, a Conservative Unionist, on his return to command of the district. Price said he and his fellow members of the Conservative Party of Lafayette County celebrated Brown's restoration as "a great victory over the Radical Party," the abolitionist wing of the Republican Party. The Radicals, Price said, "boasted and blowed" that they had gotten Brown removed. They were also proud that they had ousted Colonel McFerran, former commander of the sub-district of Lafayette County. They bragged that would have things their own way, which, Price admitted, was true for a while, until Brown reassumed command. Since Brown's return, Price said, the Radicals seemed to have "caved in."[15]

Perhaps Price's lobbying effort on behalf of his sister paid off. On September 12, General Brown issued an order granting her a parole on oath while awaiting the execution of her sentence. She signed the oath the next day and was released. She had permission to return to her home in Lafayette County on the conditions that she report to Lieutenant Gavin in Lexington on or before September 25 and that she return to Jefferson City and report to Lieutenant Swap when summoned. Effectively, the terms of the parole were even more lenient than her original one had been.[16]

In January 1865, Union authorities in St. Louis finally got around to inquiring about the disposition of the Fannie Houx case. Lieutenant Gavin said that Miss Houx was home on parole. Provost marshal general Colonel James H. Baker ordered that she be arrested and sent to his St. Louis office.

After over three months of relative freedom, Fannie's luck turned again. She was arrested. This time holding her child close, she was taken to Warrensburg. From there, the mother and child were forwarded to St. Louis on February 5, and the next day they were committed to Gratiot Street for "safe keeping until further orders."[17]

Shortly after Fannie and her child reached St. Louis, two men arrived in the city to lobby on her behalf: another of her brothers, James A. Price, and her stepbrother H. B. Branch. Price was a colonel in the Platte County Enrolled Missouri Militia. Branch was colonel in the Buchanan County militia and a prominent Republican politician in St. Joseph. In other words, both were important men.

> The Enrolled Missouri Militia was a state militia organization founded in Missouri in mid-1862. It was a part-time, mandatory force whose primary duty was to provide local defense, thereby freeing the full-time, federally funded Missouri State Militia volunteers for offensive operations throughout the state against guerrillas or Confederate raiding parties. The order creating the EMM required all men between 18 and 45 to declare their sympathies. Loyal men had to enlist, while anyone previously in arms against the Union or who declared himself in sympathy with the South was registered as disloyal. This requirement drove many Southern men into the brush as guerrillas or into Confederate service. Others reluctantly registered as loyal and joined the EMM—resulting in many dubious warriors within the ranks. Most members of the EMM, though, were entirely loyal.

On February 16, Price and Branch succeeded in getting Fannie paroled to Lexington on $3,000 bond. The parole required her to stay within the limits of Lexington and to report to Baker weekly by letter. She had to report in person whenever called.

Price stayed behind in St. Louis to press for a final and favorable disposition of his sister's case after Fannie and her child returned to Lexington. However, on February 28, he wrote to Baker saying he had been unable to do anything further to secure his sister's final release. He had been confined to his bed. He had just received a telegram summoning him to Lexington on an important matter. He asked Baker to let Fannie's case stand "in its present shape" until his health allowed him to return to St. Louis and once again give the matter his full attention.

Price hoped to have a personal interview with General Grenville M. Dodge, who had replaced General Rosecrans as the department commander. He felt sure of success if given an opportunity to properly state the facts of his sister's case. Price thanked Colonel Baker for the favor he had already shown him and Fannie.[18]

Fannie's supporters were smooth flatterers.

In Lexington, Fannie reported to Colonel Baker by letter each week. It was time to lobby on her own behalf. In her letter of March 31, 1865, she asked that the limits of her parole be extended to include all of Lafayette County so that she could return to her home in the countryside. By granting her request, Baker would be conferring "a great favor on an unfortunate being."[19]

Fannie reported to Baker again on April 6, and then the next day, April 7, she wrote directly to General Dodge. She had seen in the newspapers that Dodge released a large number of female prisoners. She wondered whether she might be released as well. She was willing to take an oath of allegiance. No one had testified against her at her trial "except a Negro man who was angry with me." She was not guilty of the charges against her of feeding and sheltering bushwhackers.

She asked again to be released from her parole. She lived just seven miles from Lexington and wanted to return to her own home and to her children, who needed her. If Dodge wished to know more about her, he could check with General R. C. Vaughn, commanding the Enrolled Missouri Militia in the Lafayette County district. She also gave the names of several other Union men as references.[20]

In her April 14 letter to Colonel Baker, Fannie reported that she was "still at this place," and she repeated that she would be glad if she could be released as other prisoners recently had been. "I am in hopes," she said, "as the war is so near over, I will be released immediately."[21]

By April 28, nothing had changed. Her letter showed her mounting frustration. She reported that she was still at Lexington, and she asked whether Baker thought it would be worthwhile for her "to get up a petition" for her release. "I can get plenty of Union men to sign it," she promised. She also repeated that she was willing to take the oath "or do anything to be released."[22]

Eventually all the letters paid off.

On May 11, in consideration of the "faithful service" of James A. Price and H. B. Branch Colonel Baker finally released Fannie from her bond. The limits of her parole were extended to the loyal Union states and territories. The conditions of the parole required her to continue reporting by letter to the provost marshal's office in St. Louis but on a monthly rather than weekly basis.

It wasn't a full release. "The circumstances of her case," Baker explained, "do not warrant her release from all restraint." Over the next few weeks, though, the war continued to wind down, even in

This home in Higginsville, Missouri, built by Fannie Houx and her husband after the war, is on the National Register of Historic Places. (Photo by the author.)

Missouri, where many partisan fighters held out to the bitter end. On June 5, General Dodge released Fannie from all restrictions of her parole.[23]

Despite having been convicted of what was considered a serious offense, Fannie ended up spending very little time in prison, mainly because of prominent family members lobbying on her behalf. It paid to have connections, even for the bushwhacker belles.

The Rest of the Story

After the war, Fannie and her husband, George Houx, continued living in Lafayette County.

By 1870 they lived in the southeast part of the county near present-day Aullville. They had six children living in the household.

Ten years later the couple lived in nearby Higginsville and still had four children at home.

The home that George Houx, a stonemason, built in Higginsville is on the National Register of Historic Places. One of George and Fannie's sons, Frank L. Houx, went on to become governor of Wyoming.

Fannie's husband died in 1898. She later moved to California, where she died in 1915.[24]

As for Jackson, the slave, he seems to have disappeared from the historical record after his testimony against Fannie Houx in the summer of 1864.

Chapter 13
Susanna Justice: Guerilla Spy

Twenty-four-year-old Susanna Justice was arrested in Platte County in July 1864 on suspicion of being a guerrilla spy. She was described as a person of "dangerous character." After keeping her jailed for over four months, Union authorities released her when they realized one of the primary witnesses against her was decidedly more dangerous and unsavory than she was.[1]

In 1859, Susanna journeyed to Missouri from Tennessee with her two small children and her husband, A. S. Justice, and settled in the Parkville area of Platte County. A few months later, Susanna gave birth to another child. In November 1861, her husband joined General Sterling Price's Missouri State Guard and then followed Price into the Confederate Army. She was left at home with three small children, one of whom soon died. With almost no financial support from her husband, Susanna made a living through sewing, spinning, and other similar odd jobs. In February 1863, she moved to Weston, about twenty miles northwest of Parkville and just across the Missouri River from Fort Leavenworth.[2]

Around July 22, 1864, three and a half years after her husband left for combat, Susanna met a man in Weston. The man wanted her to help him locate John C. Calhoun "Coon" Thornton, a Confederate recruiting officer then operating in the Platte County area.

The man's identity? According to Susanna, she knew he was a Federal detective from Fort Leavenworth but did not know his name. The detective claimed that he represented himself as a major in the Confederate Army who was on guerrilla duty.

In either case, Susanna guided the man to New Market in northern Platte County and then to Union Mills near the

Buchanan-Clinton county line. There, the pair turned back. They had gone about a half mile when they were captured by some men who called themselves wolf hunters. Susanna took them to be Federal militia. The "wolf hunters" escorted Susanna to Cameron in northeastern Clinton County and turned her over to post commander E. C. Catherwood. He arrested her and the men who brought her in left. Susanna did not know what happened to the man she had been piloting.[3]

Charged with being a guerrilla spy, Susanna was shipped from Cameron thirty five miles to St. Joseph, headquarters of the District of North Missouri.

Henry M. Herman, the US scout who had sought Susanna's help in locating Thornton, also turned up in St. Joseph. He gave a statement on July 30 to district provost marshal J. M. Bassett. Calling himself "Chief Scout, Department of Kansas," Herman said Susanna was personally acquainted with three-quarters of Coon Thornton's men and with the main Rebel sympathizers in Platte County. She was a prominent Rebel, and she professed to be an "ardent guerrilla spy." Herman went on, "I consider her as a dangerous woman to be allowed north of and inside our lines."

There was no suitable place to keep this dangerous woman in St. Joseph. On August 5, district commander General Clinton B. Fisk sent Susanna, along with the evidence against her, to St. Louis for safekeeping.[4]

Housed initially at Myrtle Street Prison, Susanna was called before provost marshal examiner Frank E. Brownell. She gave a deposition on August 13.

What of her husband? She had received only three letters from her husband since he left in November 1861, the first one in April 1862 and the last one in June 1863. The only money he had ever sent home was $10, delivered to her by Henry Broadhurst, a soldier in her husband's regiment.

Did she support her husband? When her husband left, she told him not to bother coming back if he joined the Rebel army because she wouldn't live with him. Would she live with him now if he came home? No, she would not.

Lynch's Slave Pen in St. Louis, circa 1856. During the war, it was converted to Myrtle Street Prison, where Susanna Justice and several other women in this book were imprisoned at least briefly. (Courtesy of the Missouri Historical Museum.)

What of the man seeking Coon Thornton? She had never acted as a guide for anyone other than the man who wanted her to help him find Coon Thornton. This man had not represented himself to her as a Rebel officer. He had shown her a pass, but she did not examine it closely.

Had she ever guided bushwhackers? She did not even know Coon Thornton or any of his command. Further, she did not know any bushwhackers. Would she willingly act as a guide in the future? No, she would not, because she had no relatives in the area. She admitted she had known some men from Platte County who had joined the Rebel service, but she did not know their present whereabouts.

Where did her loyalties lie? She was not a Southern sympathizer. She wished to see the South put down and the Union restored.

Had she carried Confederate mail? She knew of no mail

carrying operations and had not received mail from the South or sent any to the South other than the three letters her husband had sent her and one she had sent him in January 1863.[5]

Lieutenant Brownell turned the transcription of his interview with Susanna over to examiner George W. Shinn, who sent it to chief examiner Gustavus Cohn. Shinn observed Brownell's examination had been very thorough, but he did not think Susanna's testimony was reliable. Cases such as this one, with one party affirming and the other denying the facts, were very difficult to investigate. He recommended that Mrs. Justice be held, pending expected additional evidence.[6]

Cohn, in turn, wrote to the provost marshal's office at St. Joseph on September 6 requesting further evidence. He agreed that the case, with two contradictory witnesses, was difficult to investigate. Around the same day that Cohn wrote his letter, Susanna was moved from Myrtle Street Prison to the Gratiot Street Female Prison.[7]

On September 8, acting district provost marshal A. J. Harding wrote to Major H. H. Heath, provost marshal general of the Department of Kansas. Henry Herman, the scout who had made the arrest, was from Heath's department. Harding asked Heath to forward any other testimony he might have in Mrs. Justice's case.[8]

No additional evidence was forthcoming. The case was referred back to St. Louis sometime in the fall of 1864. On November 26, solicitor J. Warren Bell wrote to Joseph Darr, Jr., acting provost marshal general. Bell suggested that there was no evidence in Susan Justice's case "sufficient to convict." He opined that "her statement, if true, should entitle her to release" upon whatever terms the commanding general saw fit. Darr referred the case to judge advocate Lucien Eaton.[9]

On December 5, Major Eaton forwarded the case to assistant adjutant general Frank Eno. "I see no justified reason for holding this woman," Eaton said. "The only witness against her is Harry Truman. She should be released on oath."

Harry Truman was the most common alias of Jacob W. Terman,

a notorious Federal scout and spy. Terman had been convicted in August at St. Joseph of murdering Southern-sympathizing citizens in Chariton County in June 1864. He had been sentenced to death only days before Eaton's communication to Eno. (The sentence was immediately commuted to imprisonment, and Terman was soon afterwards released altogether.)

Although Terman was a man of many aliases, Harry Truman and Henry Herman, the scout who arrested Susanna Justice, were clearly not the same person. At the time of Susanna's arrest, Truman was behind bars and involved in his court martial proceedings at St. Joseph. However, it's possible that Harry Truman was the source for some, if not all, of Herman's accusations of disloyalty against Mrs. Justice. Truman had previously operated as a scout and spy in her home territory along the Kansas-Missouri border.

When Herman arrived in St. Joseph in late July to give his statement against Susanna, Truman was already there as a prisoner. It's likely the two men might have talked prior to Herman's deposition.

The only other plausible explanation is that Eaton might have simply confused Harry Truman and Henry Herman.[10]

On December 6, the day after Eaton's letter to Captain Eno, the captain wrote to Colonel Darr. By order of commanding general William S. Rosecrans, he instructed Darr to release Susanna Justice upon taking an oath of allegiance, as recommended by the judge advocate. Darr had General Rosecrans's order drawn up the same day, and Susanna was released from Gratiot Street Prison.[11]

Like a number of bushwhacker belles, Susanna had been arrested on shaky evidence. She had been accused, or so Union authorities in St. Louis believed, by a man whose reputation was far worse than her own. Herman's testimony might have been influenced by Terman. If so, it was worthless. Terman had a notorious reputation, even in Union circles, for his cruel and unyielding treatment of anyone he suspected of being a Southern sympathizer.

The Rest of the Story

Did Susanna separate from her unreliable husband when he returned from the Rebel army, as she'd sworn to do? Perhaps. Her movements after the war have not been traced.

A. S. Justice, though, was living in Texas at the time of the 1870 census with a new wife.[12]

CHAPTER 14

Professors of the Christian Religion

Sometimes bushwhacker belles faced vague charges. Despite flimsy evidence, they ended up in jail. In the case of the Kincheloe sisters, Union officers mucked up their orders so often and did such a slipshod job of collecting evidence that eventually the sisters earned their freedom from a frustrated Federal general.

It's hard to say whether they were guilty as charged. The reader can decide. Here is their story.

The record tells us that soldiers of the First Missouri State Militia Cavalry caught sixty-three-year-old Louis Kincheloe feeding guerrillas in late July 1864. This was at his home in Lafayette County about fifteen miles south of Lexington. On August 2, 1864, regimental commander Lieutenant-Colonel B. F. Lazear sent some of his soldiers back out to arrest Kincheloe's two daughters, Miss Mary Kincheloe and Mrs. Elizabeth "Lizzie" Stone, instead of the aging Kincheloe. He must have felt "the old man" bore little blame for guerrillas using his home as their resort.

In reporting his action to district headquarters at Warrensburg, Lazear stressed that Lizzie Stone was married to Confederate soldier David W. Stone. Was that why she and her sister were arrested?

The two sisters were in their early twenties. Both stood just a hair over four and a half feet tall, Lizzie with her dark hair and dark eyes, and Mary with her light hair and blue eyes. Were they really bushwhacker belles? Lazear thought so. He was sure they helped bushwhackers throughout Lafayette County.

David Stone had received a furlough pass from the Missouri State Guard in the fall of 1861. Lazear's men confiscated this from the Kincheloe home, and Lazear submitted it as contraband to reinforce his argument. He did not want to allow the two women to return to Lafayette County "for the present," even if the commanding general did not think it necessary to send them south.[1]

Although the two young women lived with their father, they were not there at the time the Federals found guerrillas at the Kincheloe residence. They weren't even in the same county. The sisters were in Johnson County at a "protracted meeting," a type of extended religious camp meeting common during the 1800s. They were arrested there on August 4. Taken a short distance to Warrensburg, they were held there while Union authorities gathered evidence against them.[2]

Lieutenant James M. Gavin, assistant provost marshal at Lexington, took statements about the Kincheloe sisters from twenty-six-year-old Lafayette County resident E. A. Eddy on August 12. The witness said he knew both women and considered both of them disloyal. He didn't personally know if they fed or harbored bushwhackers; he had only heard of such activity through the reports of others.[3]

The next day, a Lexington resident named L. A. Neill testified that he knew Lizzie and considered her a Rebel. As with Eddy, his knowledge of her sheltering bushwhackers came only from hearsay.

Neill referred Lieutenant Gavin to John Green of Wellington as a man who might know more about Lizzie Stone. If Gavin ever interviewed Green, no record of the examination survives.[4]

On August 16, Lizzie Stone and Mary Kincheloe were transported under guard from Warrensburg to department headquarters in St. Louis.[5]

Even though the evidence against them was flimsy at best, the Kincheloe sisters were committed to the Gratiot Female Prison. Both women decided to make themselves younger, a common ploy of the bushwhacker belles. Lizzie gave her age as twenty-four, when she was at least twenty-five. Mary, who was about twenty-one or twenty-two, reported hers as nineteen.[6]

On or about August 22, several Union citizens of Lafayette County, including John A. Brown, penned a letter to the military headquarters at St. Louis saying they were personally acquainted with Lizzie Stone and Mary Kincheloe. All of them said they had no knowledge the young women ever fed bushwhackers. Brown and his fellow petitioners occasionally passed the Kincheloe residence and had never seen bushwhackers at the house. The young women could not have been prominent players in supplying bushwhackers because their means were limited. The father also had scant resources. The petitioners had heard Mr. Kincheloe express himself against bushwhackers. If the sisters were released, "we hope their lives will correspond to their profession as professors of the Christian religion." Brigadier-General R. C. Vaughn, commander of the Fifth District of the Enrolled Missouri Militia, which covered Lafayette County, endorsed the letter. He said he knew the petitioners to be strictly loyal men.[7]

Lizzie Stone gave a deposition in St. Louis on August 29. She told her examiner, W. A. Owesney, that she moved in with her father when her husband went into the Confederate Army in 1862. She had been outside Lafayette County only twice since then. She took a trip to St. Clair County, seventy miles to the south, in April 1864 to bring her sister home from an extended visit with relatives. Jim Lane's Kansas jayhawkers had invaded St. Clair and burned the county seat of Osceola in 1861, because of the town's Southern leanings, but the area was loyal in comparison to Lizzie's home territory. The only other time Lizzie had left Lafayette was when she and Mary were captured in adjoining Johnson County at the religious gathering.

Had she seen any Confederate soldiers at the meeting? She had not. She had taken dinner with about thirty Federal soldiers, some from Colonel Jennison's Seventh Kansas and some from the First Missouri State Militia Cavalry. No bushwhackers had visited her father's house lately, but they had called several times during the summer of 1863, usually in squads of about ten.

Did she and her family feed the guerrillas willingly? "They would just ride up to the house and demand what they wanted in so many minutes."

Did she ever refuse to feed them? Sometimes, yes, when they came during the night.

Was the South justified in fighting the war? Lizzie did not know. "I know nothing about politics," she added. Her husband didn't breathe a word to her about joining the Confederate Army until the day he left; she tried to dissuade him. She had never helped soldiers of the Confederate Army, never received any letters from her husband, and never sent any to him. She did not belong to or know of any secret Southern society.[8]

Lizzie's sister also gave a statement on the 29th. Mary's testimony largely reflected that of her older sister. Lizzie had not heard directly from David Stone, but his father, Wyatt Stone, shared news from some of Shelby's men. David was dead.

Bushwhackers had not visited her father's house since the summer of 1863, when they came about six times. They generally got something to eat, but, if they got any feed for their horses, "they stole it."

Had Mary ever refused to feed the guerrillas? "I have refused to cook for them as a matter of convenience. I also disbelieve in that way of getting along. I think guerrilla warfare is dishonorable. Always did."

She had one brother and several cousins in the Confederate Army. She had not seen her brother since he left home in August 1862, but the family had heard indirectly from him the previous spring.

Did she want to see the South succeed in the war? Mary was "not particular" and didn't care which side won. She added that she would willingly live under the US government.[9]

After his interviews with Lizzie and Mary, Owesney turned the transcripts of his examinations over to Gustavus Cohn, chief of the examining bureau. Cohn thought Lizzie was "a good Rebel woman" who would do all in her power to help bushwhackers if she were allowed to return home. He thought Mary was "a very good Rebel."[10]

Ironically, though, on the same day of the Kincheloe sisters' interviews, Colonel J. P. Sanderson, provost marshal of the Department of the Missouri, issued a general order that was perhaps prompted in part by the shallow evidence in their cases. Directed to district and assistant provost marshals, the order reiterated the need to follow established regulations in the arrest and forwarding of prisoners. He warned that the provost marshals themselves would be disciplined if they continued to send prisoners to department headquarters unaccompanied by sufficient testimony against the accused parties.[11]

Flimsy evidence wouldn't fly on his watch.

Lizzie and Mary retained the St. Louis law firm of Doniphan & Field to represent them. This move belied the assertion of John

Brown and his fellow petitioners that the Kincheloe family lacked means. On September 6, an agent of the firm wrote to Colonel Sanderson. Lizzie Stone and Mary Kincheloe were "amply able to give bail for their appearance before such tribunal as you may indicate"—he wanted parole until such time.[12]

St. Louis Union authorities felt the case against Mary Kincheloe was especially weak. On September 17, solicitor J. Warren Bell wrote the provost marshal general's office in reference to her case. There was "not the slightest evidence against the accused"—he recommended her release at once.

Instead, the provost marshal general sought more evidence. He referred the case back to Captain Richard L. Ferguson, district provost marshal at Warrensburg. On September 27, Ferguson contacted Major Henry Neill, Lazear's successor in command of the First Missouri Cavalry. He asked for a list of Neill's men who might know whether Mary Kincheloe aided guerrillas. "Miss Kincheloe, I suppose, is well known to some of your regiment," Ferguson said.[13]

The next day, Ferguson also replied to the provost marshal general's office in St. Louis. "The disturbed state of the country and the excessive duties required of the soldiers" in his district made it difficult for an examining officer to obtain the necessary escort to travel and procure testimony. Ferguson would, however, immediately contact Lieutenant Gavin at Lexington, calling his attention to the matter and instructing him to forward any additional evidence as soon as possible. "Miss Kincheloe," Ferguson concluded, "is said to have often been seen in company with a band of bushwhackers of which her brother is a member."[14]

Meanwhile, Lizzie Stone languished in prison. She wrote on September 27 to St. Louis attorney U. L. Boyce pleading her and her sister's cases. She and Mary had been "imprisoned through a malicious falsehood of another and not through anything we ever did." They were "perfectly innocent of ever having did the slightest thing in either word, act or mind that would have been in the slightest calculated to injure our country." Lizzie continued her impassioned plea,

> I can say with all candor and sincerity that we have ever lived strictly loyal. And though they may keep us here and punish us for

> nothing, yet will they never change me, for I shall ever love that dear old Union which our Forefathers fought, bled & died to establish & never would I so disgrace and bemean myself as to do ought that would be in the slightest calculated to injure that glorious cause.
>
> And then, Mr. Boice, would it not look strange—Nay! very unreasonable to suppose that we would be disloyal to our country when our Father & Mother were strictly loyal and ever teaching their children to strictly regard the laws of their country and to honor that glorious old flag that bears the Stars & Stripes.

Their imprisonment, Lizzie said, had been a "heart-rending trial" for their parents; it was for their sake that she earnestly asked for release. Both she and Mary had been in delicate health since their imprisonment. Mary, in particular, had been very ill almost the whole time. "I cannot, for the life of me," Lizzie added, "see why it is those in command do not have something done with our cases. I feel confident that if our cases were brought up that we most assuredly would be released." Lizzie earnestly called Mr. Boice's attention to the sisters' "unhappy & sorrowful condition" and beseeched him to consider their case.[15]

Boice turned Lizzie's letter over to the provost marshal general's office. He was the third official to request parole for the Kincheloe sisters. He had made security arrangements.

However, the young women were still held, pending the arrival of the additional evidence promised by Ferguson.[16]

On October 8, authorities in St. Louis still awaited additional proof in the Kincheloe sisters' cases. But the promised evidence never arrived. On October 21, Colonel Bell, the departmental solicitor, forwarded the two cases to judge advocate Lucien Eaton. In his opinion, the evidence was "too light" for conviction. He requested Eaton to render his judgment on the cases. After examining Mary Kincheloe's case on October 22, Eaton concluded, "There is no evidence in these papers to warrant the detention of Miss Kincheloe, presuming that all available evidence against her has been secured. I therefore recommend her release on oath, calling attention to my remark in the case of Mrs. Stone."[17]

This remark, directed to assistant adjutant general Frank Eno, was basically that she and her sister should never have been sent to

St. Louis in the first place.

Eaton concurred with Colonel Bell's opinion; there was not enough evidence to detain Lizzie. He wanted to make her take an oath and release her. Further, measures should be implemented to prevent the arrest and forwarding of prisoners "without documentary evidence to establish guilt *prima facie*." Much needless expense was incurred "by the arrest of persons on base rumor and vague suspicions." The arrest and forwarding of such prisoners was in violation of Paragraph 8 of Special Orders #23 issued in 1862. The order specified that documentary proof must accompany prisoners sent to St. Louis. Eaton wanted the order republished for the information of district and subordinate officers.[18]

After receiving Eaton's recommendation, Eno, by order of department commander General William Rosecrans, referred the cases of Lizzie and Mary back to the provost marshal general's office with instructions that they would be released on their oaths. Paragraph 8 of Special Orders #23 should be republished as Eaton suggested.

An order for Mary's release upon taking the oath went out on October 24. She was turned loose the next day.[19]

The same day, Lizzie, too, finally got her order of release. Mary requested permission to remain at the female prison with her sister until Lizzie took her oath and earned her freedom. The request was granted. Mary returned to the Gratiot Street Female Prison.

The next day, she and Lizzie walked out of the prison together, ending their three-month ordeal.[20]

The Rest of the Story

Joseph Darr, Jr., took over as acting provost marshal general after Sanderson's death in mid-October. On October 26, the sisters' acquittal day, Darr responded to Major Eaton's suggestion that Paragraph 8 of Special Orders #23 be republished. Colonel Darr told the major he would republish the order if he thought it would do any good. But instructions about the arrest and forwarding of prisoners had been so blatantly and repeatedly violated in the past that only the arrest and punishment of offenders would get the message across. To emphasize his point, Darr enclosed a copy of the

General William Rosecrans intervened in the case of the Kincheloe sisters, and they were released on their oaths. (Courtesy of the Library of Congress.)

order Colonel Sanderson had issued back on August 29, the day the Kincheloe sisters were examined by Lieutenant Owesney. He cited it as an example of instructions that had been previously ignored.[21]

Was Colonel Darr's suggestion that officers should be punished for forwarding prisoners to St. Louis on insufficient evidence ever implemented? If so, there is little evidence of the fact. Under pressure to drive out guerrillas, district provost marshals continued throughout the war to arrest the guerrillas' female associates on sometimes scant evidence and send them to department headquarters. Few, if any, of the officers ever faced disciplinary action for their overzealousness.

In 1870, Lizzie Stone and Mary Kincheloe's parents still lived in Lafayette County in the Concordia vicinity.

Two or three of their brothers lived the rest of their lives there.

What happened to the sisters after their Civil War troubles has not been traced.[22]

Chapter 15
The Handsome and Fascinating Mollie Goggin

Some bushwhacker belles were women of equal parts sass and loveliness. Mollie Goggin was one.

By all accounts a great beauty, Mollie was full of spunk. Cheeky to a fault, she never hesitated to speak her mind. When her fiery words got her arrested, she employed charm, rather than reason, to get out of trouble.

This is how it happened.

On March 16, 1864, Union authorities apprehended a bushwhacker named James Murray near Pisgah in Cooper County. He wore a Rebel badge with the phrase "Victory or Death" and the name "Mollie Goggin" inscribed on it in needlework. He went to jail at Tipton in neighboring Moniteau County.

A month later around April 18th, Union authorities at Tipton summoned eighteen-year-old Mollie from her Pisgah home. Lieutenant Franklin Swap, assistant provost marshal, asked her about the embroidered patch. The sassy Mollie didn't just admit she had made the badge. She became defiant. She was a Rebel and always had been, she proclaimed. She had helped Rebels and would continue to do so. She never had and never would take an oath of allegiance to the Union. She would consider it a pleasure to be sent south.[1]

For some reason, Lieutenant Swap allowed Mollie to go home, but he did report the girl's statements to the District of Central Missouri headquarters at Warrensburg. Another two months passed. On June 18, Colonel T. A. Switzler, provost marshal of the district, sent instructions. Swap was to take Mollie into custody for disloyalty and send her to Jefferson City for trial by military commission. Mollie was arrested that very day and taken to Jefferson City. The commission convened in her case on June 20, and she pleaded guilty to "uttering disloyal sentiments."[2]

The next day, she was released on parole in the town of Jefferson City to await her sentence. The condition? She must report to the assistant provost marshal each day at 9:00 a.m. Tentatively decided in late June or early July, the terms of her sentence called for Mollie's confinement at a military prison in St. Louis for the duration of the war. The papers in her case made their way to department headquarters.

On July 6, however, Major James F. Dwight, acting judge advocate of the department, wrote to General Egbert B. Brown, commanding the District of Central Missouri. Dwight said William Rosecrans, commanding general of the department, had instructed him to return Mollie's file with a recommendation that her sentence be reconsidered. Although Brown had at first been told Mollie could go to St. Louis, Dwight explained that there was no room for her in any of the military prisons in the area. She could perhaps be confined at the Missouri State Prison in Jefferson City instead.[3]

Meanwhile, Mollie had the run of Jefferson City. She got to know

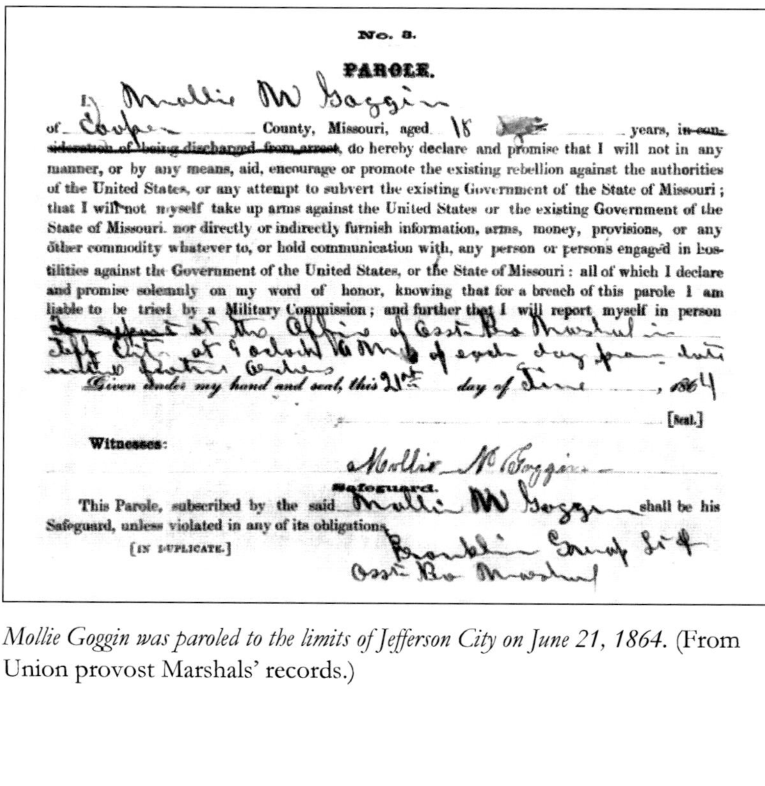

No. 3.

PAROLE.

I, Mollie M Goggin of Cooper County, Missouri, aged 18 years, ~~in consideration of being discharged from arrest~~, do hereby declare and promise that I will not in any manner, or by any means, aid, encourage or promote the existing rebellion against the authorities of the United States, or any attempt to subvert the existing Government of the State of Missouri; that I will not myself take up arms against the United States or the existing Government of the State of Missouri, nor directly or indirectly furnish information, arms, money, provisions, or any other commodity whatever to, or hold communication with, any person or persons engaged in hostilities against the Government of the United States, or the State of Missouri: all of which I declare and promise solemnly on my word of honor, knowing that for a breach of this parole I am liable to be tried by a Military Commission; and further that I will report myself in person at the Office of Asst. Pro Marshal in Jeff City at 9 o'clock A.M. of each day from date until further orders

Given under my hand and seal, this 21st *day of* June, 1864

[Seal.]

Witnesses:

Mollie M Goggin

Safeguard.

This Parole, subscribed by the said Mollie M Goggin shall be his Safeguard, unless violated in any of its obligations.

[IN DUPLICATE.]

Asst. Pro Marshal

Mollie Goggin was paroled to the limits of Jefferson City on June 21, 1864. (From Union provost Marshals' records.)

several Union officers, charming them with her beauty and feminine wiles. But Mollie soon tired of the uncertainty of her situation. On August 16, she wrote to Major General Alfred Pleasonton, who had replaced General Brown in command of the district. She wanted him to expedite her case. Since she was on parole, she was on her own expenses and, therefore, in a "very unpleasant situation." Mollie appealed to the general that she would "be very glad, if consistent with right and the public service," to receive her sentence as soon as possible.[4]

The next day, General Pleasonton asked his judge advocate, Captain A. R. Conklin, for a report on Mollie's case. Conklin told Pleasonton that Mollie had been convicted of disloyalty and sentenced to prison. Conklin said her sentence had been forwarded to St. Louis for confirmation —but failed to mention that General Rosecrans had rebuffed a previous attempt to send Mollie there. Meanwhile, she was on parole in Jefferson City. On the 19th, Pleasonton sent a note to Captain Richard L. Ferguson, who had replaced Switzler as provost marshal. He demanded to know by what authority Mollie had been released on parole.[5]

Presumably the general's indignation stemmed from Mollie's rebellious conduct while on parole. Despite her temporary release on a promise of loyalty, she had proved unrepentant in her Southern sympathies. She was not bashful about expressing them, all the while continuing to beguile the Union officers with her charm and good looks. Her continued presence in Jefferson City had become a nuisance to Union authorities there in the state capital.[6]

If General Pleasonton did not already know about Mollie's misconduct prior to his inquiry to Captain Ferguson, he soon learned about it. On August 20, Lieutenant Swap wrote to Ferguson earnestly recommending Mollie be confined at St. Louis until her sentence was approved or disapproved. After all, this would be consistent with the treatment other bushwhacker belles received for lesser crimes. Swap said Mollie had "persisted in her sympathies for the enemies of the government." But there was no suitable place in Jefferson City to incarcerate her. Mollie took "particular pains to display in public the colors of the Southern Confederacy and refuse[d] all advice to be more consistent in her conversation and dress."

Captain Ferguson forwarded the letter to General Pleasonton on the 23rd. He also replied to Pleasonton's inquiry concerning the authority by which Mollie had been released. He told his commanding officer he didn't know for sure who had authorized the parole—but he (correctly) guessed Lieutenant Swap was probably the officer who had released her.[7]

At least one unfavorable report about Mollie's conduct also reached St. Louis about the same time as Swap's letter to Warrensburg. Peter Tallon, chief of US detectives in St. Louis, made a trip to Jefferson City on August 21. Upon his return two days later, he reported what he had witnessed to Colonel J. P. Sanderson, provost marshal of the Department of the Missouri.

Lieutenant Swap had informed Tallon of Mollie's brazen disloyalty when he first reached Jefferson City. Shortly after her arrest, Mollie had even slapped General Brown in the face while he was arguing with her and trying to get her to take the oath.

Tallon took it upon himself to visit Mollie. He "was astonished to find her the object of… attention" of a party of six or eight Federal officers who were "boarding in the same house." Presumably this meant they were staying at the same house where Mollie was living. "She is handsome and fascinating in appearance," Tallon continued, "which is the only way I can account for her being treated in the way she is by all the officers, all of whom pet her very much."[8]

The detective decided to remonstrate with the young lady himself. He told Mollie he was going to try to get her removed to "a place of safety" when he returned to St. Louis.

If he meant it as a threat, though, it hardly took on Mollie. "Anything for a change," she replied dismissively. She would consider transfer a personal favor. She was tired of the monotony of her present situation. During this conversation, Tallon later fumed, "A Federal officer was at the time sitting by her side."[9]

In response to instructions from Colonel Sanderson, Lieutenant Swap sent Mollie to St. Louis on August 25. She was held temporarily at either Myrtle Street Prison of Gratiot Street Prison. For the next month, Union officials shuffled the paperwork in her case back and forth trying to clear up a technicality in her case. Finally, near the end of September, Mollie was shipped to the Alton Military Prison in Alton, Illinois, across the Mississippi River from St. Louis. There she was supposed to serve out her sentence for the duration of the war.[11]

The authorities who pronounced the sentence probably didn't count on the power of Mollie's feminine charm to alter its terms—but that's what happened. After her arrival at Alton, the Union officials at the prison soon fawned over the mesmerizing Mollie the same way the officers back in Jefferson City had.

Mary Pitman, a fellow prisoner at the Alton facility, gave a statement on December 3 exposing corruption at the prison. Pitman was a captured Confederate soldier and spy who had defected to the Union to mitigate her punishment. Federal authorities probably sent her to the Alton prison as an informant. Her accusations were racy to say the least. One of her main complaints was the preferential treatment that Mollie Goggin and another young lady, Florence Lundy, received. Below are her allegations against the prison inspector, Lieutenant L. W. Danforth, and other Union officers there.

When she first arrived, Mollie was sick. Danforth "was in her

Wartime photo of Alton, Illinois, with the Alton Military Prison, where Mollie Goggin was incarcerated, in the foreground. (Courtesy of the Missouri History Museum.)

room every evening till pretty late." He also went to her room the first thing each morning as soon as he got dressed. "Miss Goggins had everything she wanted in the way of food and delicacies" by Danforth's orders. Often the lieutenant went out and brought back oranges, lemons, and similar treats for her.[12]

After Mollie got well, one time Mary saw Lieutenant Danforth standing beside her near her room with his arm around her waist. When he saw Mary, he quickly drew away. He continued, however, to go to Mollie's room every day and "stay till called to meals," and then he went back after dinner and tarried until bedtime. The lieutenant, when he was not on duty, was always in either Mollie's room or Florence's room, "but Miss Goggins was his favorite."

Once, Mary saw Danforth sitting beside Mollie on her bed with his head on her shoulder and his arm around her. Most of the time he shut the door when he went to her room.

Alton Military Prison was a former Illinois state prison that had been reopened as a military prison in 1861. Overcrowding and disease were constant problems throughout the war, but Mollie and her fellow female prisoners were obviously accorded special treatment. Their cells were more like individual rooms with a certain amount of privacy for the prisoners—and their visitors.

Another time, Mary saw Danforth take Mollie out of the prison for a walk. Sometimes he even let her and Florence go out into town on their parole of honor. The lieutenant said he thought Mollie and Florence were in prison unjustly and he did not believe in putting women in prison anyway.[13]

Mollie expressed a wish to have a room next door to Florence, but the room was occupied by servants. Prison officials kicked the servants out and put them in "a cold room upstairs" so Mollie could have the room she wanted. The room was then "painted and fixed up in nice style" for the new occupant.[14]

Mary's accusations were risqué. For a young woman during the Civil War era, charges of sexual impropriety would have been particularly scandalous. But if Mollie's reputation suffered because of her intimate relations with Lieutenant Danforth, the record does not show it.

Captain Griffin Frost, a prisoner who kept a journal of his prison experiences at the Alton facility, also implied that Mollie, Florence, and two or three other young, female prisoners might have received special favor from the Union authorities at Alton. Frost felt that the lenient treatment of the pretty female prisoners was part of an overall pattern of lax enforcement. Even male prisoners, particularly officers, received privileges they had not previously enjoyed.

Less than a week after his arrival, for instance, Frost and some of the other Southern officers stood beneath the windows of the rooms where Mollie Goggin, Florence Lundy, and two other women were housed and serenaded "the fair ones." There was no reprimand. They were allowed to visit the young women in their rooms; Frost was impressed by the comfort and attractiveness of the rooms. The day after Christmas, the Southern officers were treated to a holiday feast in the women's rooms. The hostesses all seemed to be in good spirits and health except Mollie Goggin, who had been sick for several days. A few days later Mollie became so ill it was feared she might die, but by January 1, 1865, she had begun a rapid recovery.[15]

On January 5, 1865, four officers who had been on duty at the Alton prison since Mollie's arrival wrote to General Grenville M. Dodge, commanding the Department of the Missouri. They petitioned for the young lady's immediate release. By now Lieutenant Danforth had left the Alton prison. So the petitioners included the current prison inspector and assistant prison inspector. Mollie was only seventeen, they said, "a mere child in appearance and manner." (Mollie was actually eighteen.) They felt she had been imprisoned long enough. Since her incarceration, she had won the esteem and respect of all the officers there by her uniformly good and ladylike conduct.[16]

Perhaps Mollie had indeed behaved well since her incarceration. It was not unusual for the bushwhacker belles to soften their attitude in the face of harsh punishment. But what the prison officials didn't say was that Mollie's beauty and charm almost certainly quickened their impassioned plea.

The petitioners said Mollie was an only child who had likely been spoiled by her parents. According to the prison officials, Mollie "little thought when she said she was a Rebel that she would be taken from home and imprisoned for it, because she declares that she is not a Rebel and only said so to be 'contrary.'"[17]

The officers felt sure that, if Mollie were released, she would remain home quietly and utter no more disloyal sentiments, "for however foolish she may have been, we think she has learned a good, if perhaps a very, very hard lesson." The letter called upon the general, trusting to his well-known kindness of heart, to release Mollie immediately so that she could escape the adverse circumstances of the prison and reunite with her parents.[18]

A week later, on January 12, General Dodge granted the men's petition and issued an order remitting the sentence of the military commission that had tried Mollie. He directed that she be immediately released "in consideration of her youth and good behavior" and contingent upon her "loyalty and good conduct in the future." She took the loyalty oath and walked free on the morning of the 19th.

Mollie had been held in St. Louis for a month and jailed at Alton another three and a half. Her charm and good looks might have afforded her special treatment during her incarceration, but the length of her sentence was at least as long as the average bushwhacker belle sent to prison.

The Rest of the Story

Mollie's family members have proven tough to track down. The best candidates for Mollie's parents are George and Frances Goggin, who had a fifteen-year-old daughter named Mary in 1860. This Mary is the only Mary or Mollie Goggin in Missouri anywhere near the right age to be the correct Mollie. Contrary to the petition that said she was an only child, this Mary had one sister. However, it's possible that girl died prior to 1864—or else Mollie merely led the prison officials to believe she was an only child.

Captain Frost stated that, according to "Madam Rumor," Mollie had gotten engaged to a Federal lieutenant. This man had used his influence to get her out from behind bars. This was no doubt a reference to Lieutenant Danforth. Whether the couple ever married and enjoyed the loving and lasting peace that Frost hoped for them is unknown.

In fact, what happened to Mollie after her release is even less certain than her origins before the war.[19]

CHAPTER 16
The Very Bad Bond Women

Unraveling the bushwhacker belles' stories can be daunting. When two young ladies say they are "as loyal as anybody can be," yet others say they are "very bad women, and Rebels," neither the judge at the time nor the judge of history can say for sure which is true.

Like so many of our belles, twenty-two-year old Ruth Bond and her sister, eighteen-year-old Sarah Bond, stood accused of feeding and harboring bushwhackers. They'd previously been arrested on the same charge then turned loose for lack of evidence. This time, several of their neighbors swore out affidavits against them. The sisters claimed absolute innocence; they said they didn't even know why they were arrested. Perhaps the truth lay somewhere in the middle, as is often the case when disparate stories collide.

Around April 1, Federal authorities re-arrested these Miller County sisters and hauled them off to Jefferson City. The Bond girls and their case made it all the way to St. Louis before they found someone to take their side in the argument.[1]

After the Bond sisters were escorted to Jefferson City in early April 1864, the provost marshal of the Jefferson City sub-district, Lieutenant James M. Gavin, began gathering evidence against them. At first, he found three neighbors to testify.

Fifty-four-year-old Henry Jenkins was a close neighbor of the Bonds in Jim Henry Township northeast of the Miller County seat of Tuscumbia. His own brother Harrison had been arrested for helping bushwhackers earlier in the war. On the 11th, he testified that he had heard the young women say they had fed bushwhackers. They would do it again "in spite of hell." The Bond women openly claimed to be Rebels. They frequently stayed away from home, and he had ascertained that they often did not stay where they said they did. The implication, of course, was that they either stayed with bushwhackers or stayed where they could more readily help bushwhackers.[2]

Hannah Jenkins, Henry's daughter-in-law, was deposed on the same day. She said the Bonds always claimed to be in favor of the South. She did not know of any disloyal acts on their part.[3]

On April 22, Gavin interviewed Madison Carrendon, a man whom Henry Jenkins had recommended as knowledgeable about the Bond sisters. Echoing Jenkins, Carrendon said only that he had heard the young women say they'd fed bushwhackers and would do so again. They had the reputation of being Southern-sympathizers.[4]

On the evidence of these three statements, Lieutenant Gavin held the women in prison at Jefferson City. He sent the paperwork to Warrensburg, headquarters of the District of Central Missouri, on April 23. Thus began a long chain of officials reviewing, commenting on, and passing the file around like a hot potato.

First, Colonel T. A. Switzler, the district provost marshal, punted the file to General Egbert B. Brown, commanding general of the district. His notation: "...These women are loose characters and were arrested last summer upon the same charges. Evidence could not be obtained sufficient to convict them. The neighborhood in which they live has been infested with Bushwhackers whenever there was any in the country. The interests of the country would be promoted by sending them away."

On April 28, General Brown sent the file to department headquarters at St. Louis and suggested banishment for the Bond girls. An appropriate sentence—if the charges could be proved.[5]

The file was scant. Colonel J. P. Sanderson, provost marshal of the department, sent the papers back to Colonel Switzler. The message? Send more testimony, then return the file along with the defendants themselves.

Switzler remanded the case to Lieutenant Gavin, who once again started taking depositions nearly a month later.

On May 16, Jobe Wood testified that he could not say positively the Bond women fed and harbored bushwhackers. It was "generally believed that they are bushwhacker feeders, very bad women, and Rebels."

General Egbert B. Brown had the Bond sisters arrested and sent to St. Louis on charges of aiding guerrillas. Egbert Benson Brown, #31447, in the collection of Wilson's Creek Battlefield. (Courtesy of the National Park Service.)

Lydia Jenkins was either a sister-in-law or niece of the first witness, Henry Jenkins. In her interview on the 16th, she stated that one of the Bond sisters had always told her she was in favor of the South. Neighborhood folks believed the Bonds helped bushwhackers, but she did not know for sure that they had.[6]

The Bond sisters and the five weak testimonies against them were forwarded to St. Louis on May 17. Sanderson wasn't satisfied. The next day, he returned the papers to Switzler with a request that the depositions of the Bond sisters be added to the file. "This case in its present shape," he declared, "is wanting in material upon which to found even an opinion."[7]

Ruth and Sarah Bond were jailed in the Myrtle Street Prison. They languished there between two and three weeks without being examined or tried. They wrote to Colonel Sanderson in early June beseeching him to intervene on their behalf. They had no one in St. Louis to speak for them because their brother was in the Union Army, their father was dead, and their mother, who was not in good health, was home with the younger kids. "Please you will look over our case," they concluded.[8]

It is uncertain whether the Bond sisters had even given depositions in Jefferson City, as Colonel Sanderson believed. After appealing directly to Sanderson, the young women were promptly interviewed in St. Louis.

Here is what Ruth said in her June 6 deposition with her examiner, W. F. Dewey.

She lived in Miller County five miles from Tuscumbia and was twenty years old. This was a lie because she was at least twenty-three. She also did not reveal she had been previously married. In the late 1850s, she'd wed Lewis Hill. He soon left her and took custody of their baby girl. After their divorce, Hill remarried, and Ruth reassumed her maiden name. She no doubt wanted Dewey to think her innocent not just of the charges against her but also innocent in life.

She told Dewey her brother John was in Company A of the Sixth

Missouri State Militia Cavalry (which records confirm). Her father, who had died about a year earlier, had always been a loyal Union man. She had no relatives in the Confederate Army or in the brush. All of her connections were Union. She had always been for the Union. "I am as loyal as anybody can be," she said, "and so is my sister and mother."[9]

There had never been any bushwhackers or Rebels of any kind fed at her house. If they did come, she wouldn't feed them. She had seen bushwhackers pass by two or three times but never knew of any of them stopping at the house—except one time early in the war when they came and stole a horse and a gun from her father. A man named Crabtree was the captain of the gang that robbed her father. She named four other men from her neighborhood (Mike Clark, James Revis, and John and Wiley Shoemake) who had joined bushwhacking gangs. She had not seen any of them since they left the area. She belonged to no secret organization and did not know of any such organization.[10]

She did not know why she and her sister were arrested. She thought it might have come about because of something Hannah Jenkins had said about them. Hannah's husband, William Jenkins, had formerly served in the Confederate Army but had flipped sides. He was now a member of the same Union company as Sarah and Ruth's brother John. Hannah had been with her husband in the field but was forced to leave by the captain. When she returned to the neighborhood, she got mad at Sarah for some reason and reported the sisters to Federal authorities. Ruth didn't know why Hannah was angry.[11]

Sarah parroted much of her sister's testimony in her June 6 deposition.

Aside from repetitive information her sister had already shared, Sarah explained her occasional absences from home; she sometimes stayed with a married sister—a reference to Mahala Bond Curty. This sister's husband—David Curty—was a member of the Enrolled Missouri Militia.

Sarah had never carried any letters to send beyond the Union lines or for any other purpose.[12]

The game of hot potato began again.

After deposing the Bond sisters, Captain Dewey turned their

statements over to Colonel Sanderson. He felt if the statements constituted the only evidence in their case, "there is nothing to convict them of any disloyal act."

Colonel Sanderson, in turn, wrote to Colonel Switzler asking where the papers in their case were. The tone of his letter suggests that Sanderson was unaware of the charges against the Bond girls or of any previous testimony in the case, despite the fact that their file had been sent back to Warrensburg from his office only three weeks earlier.

On June 9, Colonel Switzler referred the matter to Lieutenant Gavin at Jefferson City. He instructed Gavin to send copies of the papers in the Bond case to the provost marshal general directly with whatever recommendation he felt the case warranted.

Gavin forwarded the file to St. Louis on or about June 13th. His recommendation? Send the Bond women out of the state.

Sanderson reviewed the papers and referred the case on June 14 to General William Rosecrans, commanding the Department of the Missouri. Sanderson did not think the evidence in the case justified conviction and banishment. He, therefore, did not agree with Lieutenant Gavin's recommendation that the young women be exiled. "It seems to me they have already been sufficiently punished," he added.

On the 17th, Rosecrans ordered the women released on bond, and four days later they were freed on $500 bond each.[13]

In total, they were stuck in Union jails almost three months—based entirely on the hearsay testimony of their neighbors.

The Rest of the Story

Ruth and Sarah Bond returned to their home territory. They still lived in the Miller County area after the war.

In 1869, Ruth remarried, this time to Reuben Rader in neighboring Cole County. There is no trace of the couple after their marriage.

In 1870, Sarah was still single and lived with her sister Mahala and the rest of the David Curty family in northern Miller County not far from the Bonds' old home.

In 1872, she married Elias Swalen, and in 1880 the couple lived in Tuscumbia with no children in the household.[14]

CHAPTER 17
The Post Oak "Prostitutes"

One of the vilest accusations against a woman in the 1860s was that she was a prostitute. So when a Federal captain made the implausible claim that he had found a bevy of bawdy bushwhacker belles, it was worth further investigation.

For the women of Post Oak, the choice to support the South translated to putting their characters in the crosshairs. Accusers bandied about nasty terms—prostitute, woman of ill fame, murderer, thief, and gambler—with abandon.

On June 17, 1864, Captain Joseph A. Peak complained about twenty-four females living in the area of Post Oak, at the southern edge of Johnson County. They were "active Rebels, aiders and abettors of the Southern Confederacy, and harborers of Bushwhackers, some the wives of Bushwhackers." Peak served in Company A of the Seventh Missouri State Militia Cavalry in Warrensburg. In his letter to his regimental commander, Colonel John F. Phillips, Peak said the women fed the outlaw bushwhackers and gave them all the information they needed to evade Union troops. What's more, he claimed to have proof. As though to stress his point, Peak added, "At least two-thirds of these females are of the worst class of prostitutes."[1]

Really? At least sixteen prostitutes plying their trade in and around a tiny, rural community in Johnson County, Missouri?

Peak, who hailed from the Post Oak vicinity, detailed all the names of these rebellious and supposedly lewd women. The list would come in handy when Union authorities investigated his shocking assertion. Nearly all of the women were arrested or at least investigated by Union authorities. Ten of them are of particular interest here, because their cases can be partially documented by primary sources.

Let us look a little closer at the stories of Miss Jane Ward, Mrs.

Eliza Spencer, Miss Mary Spencer, Miss Harriet Spencer, Miss Jennie Spencer, Mrs. Wealthy Robertson, Miss Clara Little, Miss Fannie Little, Miss Missouri Cull, and Miss Mary Cull. Were they as treacherous and dissolute as Peak wanted his commander to believe?[2]

First, here is what we know about these women from census records and other sources. All of their families except the Littles had lived in the Post Oak area for many years. All had come to Missouri from the upper South. In all but the Ward family, the father or husband was dead or otherwise absent from the home. The Little family had been prosperous at one time, but the death of John Little, the father, had left them in financial difficulty.[3]

Colonel Phillips turned Peak's letter over to General Egbert B. Brown, commanding the District of Central Missouri. On June 19, Brown forwarded it to departmental commander William Rosecrans in St. Louis.

Brown noted that, although the women mentioned all resided within the same ten-mile-square tract of land, they were "a fair representation of that class who are harboring and feeding bushwhackers in all other tracts of this district." Echoing the allegation contained in Peak's letter, Brown went on to characterize the women as "prostitutes who are supported by the bushwhackers and with whom they divide their plunder in the same manner as the thieves and gamblers support the same class in the larger cities."

Those are some pretty heavy statements for the time.

General Rosecrans instructed Brown to carefully investigate the women's cases and not sent them to St. Louis until he was "perfectly satisfied of the bad character of the women."[4]

Before any further action could be taken, though, a detachment of soldiers from Phillips's regiment went out on a scout into Post Oak and had a run-in with the Spencer women. On the morning of July 1, Eliza Spencer and her daughters were at breakfast when six or eight soldiers of Company K arrived at their home and asked for some bread. According to company commander William B. Ballew, the Spencer women told his men they couldn't part with any bread because their dogs needed it. The women boasted that they "would feed no Black Republicans"—Radical abolitionists. They had fed bushwhackers, the women said, and would do so again whenever they wanted to. They even dared Ballew's men to molest anything on their premises. The women said they would report the soldiers to Warrensburg if they did.[5]

Shortly after this incident, Lieutenant John H. Smith, assistant provost marshal of the district, began gathering evidence to use against the women named in Peak's letter.

Here are some of the injurious things others said about these bushwhacker belles.

July 12, 1864, was a busy evidence-gathering day for Lieutenant Smith. William Day and Thomas Williams, both of the same company in the local Enrolled Missouri Militia, were eager to cooperate. Both men gave statements that day against Eliza Spencer. They also testified against Emily Cull, who was investigated along with her older sisters even though Peak had left her off his list.

William Day said he had overheard Emily talking at the Cornelia post office on or about the first of September of the previous year. She said she had fed bushwhackers in the past and would do it again if she got the chance because "she considered them her friends." She later said essentially the same thing several other times. Day accused Miss Cull of being "a girl of ill fame" whom he had reason to believe had "cohabited with the bushwhackers." [6]

Thomas W. Williams swore out an affidavit against Emily Cull. Williams had heard Miss Cull say at the Cornelia post office on or about September 1, 1863, that she had fed bushwhackers and would do it again. He heard her make similar statements after that date.[7]

A. J. Cecil gave a statement indicting Emily's sister, Mary Cull. On or about September 15, 1862, partisan leader Bill Stewart and a band of about twenty bushwhackers robbed his house in Cornelia. A few days later, he and a party of Union men were pursuing Stewart when the Federals discovered Mary Cull at the residence of Douglas Wright.

Mary had some of the items Stewart had taken from Cecil's house. Mary said the items had been given to her by a man named Hackler (very likely Crud Hackler), a notorious bushwhacker and member of Stewart's gang. "Mary Cull gives information to bushwhackers and is a woman of ill fame," Cecil concluded. "In about nine months from the time she had my goods, she brought forth a young heir."[8]

Day said that on or about September 1, 1863, while he was acting as captain of an independent Union company, he and about thirty men went to the home of Mrs. Spencer. There they saw four bushwhackers flee at their approach. Day and his men discovered that Eliza had prepared dinner for the Rebels. She was also known to have fed them on various prior occasions throughout the summer of 1863. Since Eliza's husband had left to join the Southern army in 1862, her home had become "a regular bushwhacker camp." Thomas Williams repeated Day's allegations.[9]

The next slew of witnesses testified on July 14.

Lieutenant George Chiles of Captain Peak's company said that on or about June 20, 1863, he and about twenty of his men went to the house of old Mary McGowan. Eighteen-year-old Jane Ward and her younger brother lived there at the time. When Chiles asked Jane whether she had seen any bushwhackers, she was defiant. She asked him why he posed such a question to her because she wouldn't tell him even if she had seen any guerrillas. She said she would feed them, too, because they were her friends. If she were a man, she would be a bushwhacker herself and fight the Federals "as long as she had breath." Chiles threatened to burn her house if she did not stop her "fancy talk." Jane dared him to. If he did, she promised to burn the house of every Union man in the county.[10]

James Todd, another member of Peak's company, swore he had known Jane for about nine years. She had been "a violent Rebel ever since the war broke out." Todd, who lived in Jane's neighborhood and was home on furlough at the time, heard her say on or about March 1, 1864, she would feed bushwhackers every chance she got. In addition, he confirmed Chiles's account of the events that transpired at Mary McGowan's house because he was had been present. Bushwhackers were continually at Mrs. McGowan's house to see Jane whenever any of them were in the county. He concluded

Jane was "a woman of ill fame."[11]

Todd also testified against twenty-seven-year-old Wealthy Robertson. Her husband was a bushwhacker. She helped bushwhackers. Specifically, on or about June 1, 1864, she said she fed bushwhackers and would do so again.[12]

During the Civil War, blood wasn't always thicker than water. Wealthy's brother, William Austin, spoke against her. She wrote him a letter on or about May 10, 1863, stating that she intended to hold to her husband's Rebel principles as long as she lived. Her husband had been a bushwhacker since the beginning of the war.[13]

Nearly a month passed before Lieutenant Smith took the next spate of depositions on August 11 and 12.

Mrs. Margaret Burk had been living with Mrs. McGowan around 1860. She had lived in the same neighborhood as the Spencer family for twelve years. She was illiterate and signed her statement with a mark.

She said Mary Spencer had been a violent Rebel since the outbreak of the war. Mary had fed and harbored bushwhackers ever since there had been any in the county. Around the 20th of September, 1863, Mary Spencer, Hattie Spencer, Jennie Spencer, Clara Little, and Fannie Little bought nine or ten pairs of boots and seven hats in Sedalia. Upon returning to Johnson County, they delivered the supplies to bushwhackers on Blackwater Creek.

Margaret swore out similar but separate affidavits against Hattie Spencer, Jennie Spencer, Clara Little, and Fannie Little. She did not testify against Wealthy Robertson, who had lived with her at Mrs. McGowan's a few years earlier.[14]

James Todd, the soldier who had testified against Jane Ward and Wealthy Robertson, came back at this time and swore out separate depositions against Clara Little and Fannie Little. He said they were both violent Rebels. Around June 20, 1864—the same time Peak's outraged letter started the investigation—he had met Clara and Fannie driving a two-horse wagon on the road near Warrensburg. He asked them about any bushwhackers in their part of the county. They challenged him to come into their neighborhood and see for himself whether there were any guerrillas. He told them that he suspected they fed bushwhackers. They admitted not only that they fed bushwhackers but also that they would keep at it as long as there were any to feed.[15]

On August 13, Lieutenant Smith took a statement from Barton Oliphant, a nearby neighbor of the Spencer family. He was a nephew by marriage of Margaret Oliphant, another of the women named in Peak's letter.

Oliphant had known Mary Spencer since childhood. She had been a violent Rebel since the outset of the war. He saw bushwhackers run from Mrs. Spencer's house in the summer of 1862. Right after that, he heard Mary say she had fed bushwhackers and would do so again. Around October 1, 1863, she made a similar statement. She also told some Federal soldiers that she intended to raise bushwhackers to fight them. Mary's general character was "that of a woman of ill fame."

The same day, Oliphant swore testimony against Hattie and Jennie Spencer that was almost identical to what he said against their older sister.[16]

Oliphant was a member of the local Enrolled Missouri Militia, and he came back a few days later on August 16. He gave depositions against the Cull sisters. They, too, were very similar to his statement against Mary Spencer. Missouri and Mary Cull were both violent Rebels and women of ill fame who helped bushwhackers every chance they got. Further, on or about June 1, 1864, a detachment of his militia unit came under fire from bushwhackers from a house where the Cull sisters resided.[17]

The same day, August 16, Lieutenant Smith turned over to district provost marshal Richard L. Ferguson all the evidence he had thus far collected in the cases of the women named in Peak's letter. He would keep a list of the women's names and try to obtain more information.[18]

On August 20, Captain Ferguson forwarded the papers to General Alfred Pleasonton, who had replaced Egbert Brown as commanding general of the district. Ferguson's comment? Banish virtually all the women his office had investigated. Ferguson had a particularly low opinion of Jane Ward, whom he considered "a notoriously bad, bad woman."

In a surprise move, Pleasonton dropped or deferred the cases against Jennie Spencer, Missouri Cull, and Emily Cull for unknown reasons. On August 20, he ordered the arrest of the remaining eight women against whom evidence had been gathered during the previous two months. They were to be sent to department headquarters in St. Louis for the disposition of their cases.

Eliza Spencer, Mary Spencer, Hattie Spencer, Mary Cull, Clara Little, Fannie Little, Jane Ward, and Wealthy Robertson (along with two other women) were rounded up on August 23 and August 24 and sent to St. Louis.[19]

The women arrived there on August 26th. At first they went to the notorious female prison on St. Charles Street. They must have been moved almost immediately, though, because the next day one of them won her temporary freedom from the Myrtle Street Prison. On August 27th, Hattie Spencer gave bond of $500 and was released on parole in the city of St. Louis with a promise to appear for trial when called. She wasted little time getting in trouble again, however. Within a few days of her release, she was charged with complicity in the robbery of two revolvers from a US soldier. Re-arrested, she returned to prison.[20]

Hattie Spencer wasn't the only one of the Johnson County females who had resources to tap during her time of hardship. Despite the supposed financial straits in which John Little's death had left his family, the Little sisters still had influential friends, if not abundant monetary assets. They called upon these connections in their need. On August 29, St. Louis businessman Edward Stafford wrote to Colonel J. P. Sanderson, provost marshal of the department, beseeching him to show leniency in the case of Clara and Fannie Little. Stafford wanted their order of banishment to the South modified so the young women could remain in St. Louis under the care of their relatives or go to any Union-loyal state where they might have the protection of loved ones. He had been assured that the accusations against the Little sisters resulted from false information and misrepresentation. Banishment to the South would be "an act of great injustice." Stafford concluded, "Any reasonable bond for the future good conduct of the ladies will be given by parties of unquestionable loyalty in this city. And to save them from a possible fate that would be worse than death they appeal to you in confidence."[21]

We finally hear from the impugned women themselves on September 2, when Union authorities deposed them.

Clara Little said she was a Southern sympathizer. But she was willing to take an oath of allegiance, and she would like to see the authority of the United States government "restored as it once was." The only time she or her family had helped bushwhackers was in June 1864 when a party of about eighty or ninety men wearing Federal uniforms stopped at her mother's house. The impostors demanded supper. Mrs. Little initially refused to fix them anything, but they threatened to burn her house. She relented. The men, whom Clara surmised were guerrillas, left as soon as they ate. Neither she nor any member of her family gave them information or extra provisions.

The only other time any Rebels had stopped at the Little home was once during the fall of 1861 when a party of regular Southern soldiers took supper there.

Clara said she knew a couple of men whom she had heard were bushwhackers. But she never had any communication with them or any other guerrillas. She had a brother in the regular Confederate Army. He had sent her two or three letters, and she had sent one to him. This was her only communication with Rebels. (The brother she referred to was likely Tom Little, who apparently was indeed in the Confederate Army at this time but who earlier had been a Quantrill guerrilla. After the war, Little was hanged by a mob at Warrensburg on suspicion of robbery.)

Clara admitted that she and Fannie accompanied the Spencer sisters to Sedalia in early September 1863 when the boots and hats were purchased. But she herself had not made the transaction. She knew nothing about the disposition of the goods.[22]

Fannie largely corroborated her older sister. In fact, their responses to the examiner's questions were so similar that they either were telling the truth or had rehearsed their answers. Fannie added only two points to Clara's testimony. About the same time the regular Southern soldiers took supper at the Little home in the fall of 1861, Fannie encountered a few other men she thought to be Southern partisans near her house. They asked directions to Blackwater River. Secondly, the Spencer sisters purchased the boots and hats. They planned to give them to their bushwhacker friends. She didn't know which Spencer girl made the actual purchase.[23]

Mary Spencer told the examiner she had helped Rebels only twice.

In the fall of 1861, she made three or four shirts for her brother and his comrades, who were then in General Sterling Price's army. She saw no Rebels during all of 1862 and 1863, but during May of 1864, about one hundred bushwhackers came into her neighborhood. Approximately thirty ate dinner at her house, but she did not give them information or help them in any other way. (This was probably the same band that Clara Little remembered as having visited the neighborhood in June of 1864.)

Mary admitted she was a Southern sympathizer who would consider it her duty to help regular Southern soldiers if she met any. She wished to see the authority of the US government restored only if it were done under "the old constitution"—the constitution that protected the institution of slavery. She had never willingly helped guerrillas because she did "not approve of their warfare." About the boots and hats, she and her sister, Hattie, had indeed bought them, actually seven pairs of boots and three or four hats, not nine pairs of boots and seven hats. She bought the supplies for three families in her neighborhood who were preparing to go south, not for guerrillas.

Concerning the other specific charge against her—the open declaration that she had fed bushwhackers and would do so again—Mary admitted that she had made such a statement. But she did so only because Federals soldiers were accusing her, swearing at her, and abusing her at the time. She lashed out in anger at them.[24]

Hattie Spencer's testimony generally followed the pattern of her sister's, although not as closely as Fannie Little's had followed Clara Little's. Hattie was more specific in describing the the gear purchased in Sedalia. Her father got one of the hats and one pair of boots, and she named five other males from her neighborhood who received the rest of the hats and boots. All five were mere boys from twelve to seventeen years old. They were going south with their mothers, carrying passes from Union authorities to make such a trip.

Yes, a party of about one hundred men visited her neighborhood in May 1864 and her family had fed about thirty of them. The sisters' stories diverged slightly here; unlike Mary, Hattie claimed they were regular Confederate soldiers, just not in uniform.

What about the occasion when Captain Day had driven several bushwhackers from her mother's home around September 1, 1863?

Hattie had not even seen the men before they were chased off. Her younger brother later said the men had merely asked for a drink of water. Hattie had never told anyone that she did or would feed bushwhackers

Union authorities had arrested Hattie once previously, in the fall of 1862. Colonel E. C. Catherwood had charged her with verbally abusing one of his soldiers. Hattie said she never even saw or spoke to the man who brought the charge. She never took the oath before her release. Her father had been driven out of Johnson County by threats on his life.[25]

Eliza Spencer's turn. Like her daughter Hattie, Eliza said that during April 1862 she had fed a company who called themselves Confederate soldiers. She fed them only because they threatened to burn her house. The men whom Captain Day had driven from her place in September 1863 were not at her house but in a grove nearby; they had only asked for a drink of water. On a couple other occasions she had given men water, she said, but she had not fed them or helped them in any other way. The only time any Southern soldiers had actually stayed at her house was in February 1863 when her son came home and spent one night there. (Killed sometime during the summer following his February visit, Eliza's son David served in the Missouri State Guard. But he was not a regular Confederate soldier in 1863 as Mrs. Spencer believed—or at least wanted the Federals to believe.)

The fifty-six-year-old Eliza had perhaps done less in deed to support the Rebel cause than her daughters. But her sympathies for the South were even stronger than Mary's and Hattie's. Or maybe she was just less intimidated by the examiner—and more willing to state her true feelings. Did she sympathize with the South? "Of course, I do."

Did she wish to see the South win its independence? "Of course, I want the South to gain, but I would prefer the government as it was."

Was she was willing to take an oath of allegiance to the US? "Not unless I was allowed to go home as soon as I took it."[26]

Next it was time to hear the stories of the Cull women.

Twenty-three-year-old Mary Cull said she had previously lived in Johnson County with her sisters Missouri and Emily. But for the past five months, she and Emily had been living by themselves in neighboring Henry County. They made their living by weaving, knitting, and sewing for other people. She gave Missouri's age correctly as thirty-one. She cited her younger sister's age as seventeen when Emily, in fact, was twenty-one. Perhaps Mary purposely understated Emily's age in hopes that Union authorities might go easy on her.

Mary gave the names of six bushwhackers she knew. Included among the group were Johnson County partisans Bill Stewart and Crud Hackler and Cooper County guerrilla Frank Parker. She also mentioned two other bushwhackers she knew who had been killed within the past year or so, one of whom was Eliza Spencer's son David. The bushwhackers stopped to visit at her place "quite often;" they stayed anywhere from five minutes to half a day, and yes, she regularly fed them.

Mary's examiner, Frank Brownell, must have wondered why she entertained bushwhackers on such a regular basis. Was she a prostitute as Captain Peak reported? Lieutenant Brownell meant to get at the truth.

Did she run a boarding house or a tavern, he asked. She did not. The men never stayed all night. The men never paid her for what they ate. She fed them only because they had threatened to burn her house if she didn't.

She acknowledged that Hackler had given her a pair of shoes and one of the other bushwhackers had given her a gold locket. She did not know the items had been stolen from A. J. Cecil.

Mary admitted having a baby out of wedlock. She had been engaged to Frank Parker in the fall of 1861, and the couple had a fourteen-month-old child. She would not be willing to marry him now "because he has ruined me and become a bushwhacker and a bad man." Then, to clarify the circumstances of her pregnancy, she added an afterthought: "He never used force."

Mary had no sympathy for bushwhacking and was entirely opposed to it. Indeed, in the summer of 1862, she gave information to Federal soldiers concerning the whereabouts of guerrillas. She had always told them when asked. Mary was willing to take the oath of allegiance "or any other oath if they would permit me to go home."[27]

If any of the young women were as unabashedly staunch in her

Southern sympathies as Eliza Spencer, it was Jane Ward. Jane told her story to examiner Lieutenant Isaac Ruth.

Jane went to stay at the Mary McGowan farm on February 14, 1864, because her fourteen-year-old brother, Thomas, had already been working there for about a year. Three and a half months later, around June 1, a party of Federals came to the farm. Among them were the two men who had done so much denouncing—James Todd and Barton Oliphant—and their leader, a Lieutenant Houts (probably William S. Houts).

Lieutenant Houts tried to make Thomas Ward tell him whether there were any bushwhackers in the area and where they might be camped. Houts started cursing the boy when he wouldn't cooperate. "I took my brother's part" and "told the lieutenant he was acting very ungentlemanly toward my brother." Later, she and Thomas led the soldiers to a nearby bushwhacker camp, but the partisans had left before they arrived. Houts accused Jane of feeding bushwhackers. She denied the charge. If her older brother Larson, a recently discharged Confederate soldier, were in the area, she would feed him and consider it the right thing to do.

What of a second confrontation with some of these same Federal soldiers about June 15? Jane didn't recall the incident. Federal soldiers visited her so often she could not remember each time. She never told Federal soldiers the bushwhackers were her friends and that she would do all she could for them. But "The Federal soldiers abuse me and, of course, I abuse them."

Did she know Lieutenant Chiles? Jane did not, although the name sounded familiar.

What about the June 20th incident in which Lieutenant Chiles came to her house? Jane remembered that a party of five or six Federal soldiers who had been watching the road in front of the house came inside and helped themselves to some food that she had prepared. The soldiers asked whether she had seen any bushwhackers, and Jane told them that, even if she had seen any, the soldiers "would be none the wiser." The Federals demanded to know whether she fed bushwhackers. She answered that she would feed her friends but that, as it was now, she had nothing left to feed them. She didn't specify who her friends were. The soldiers, riled by her sassy reply, said they wished she were a man. Jane retorted that "it was fine thing on their part I was not." The soldiers threatened to burn her house, and she told them that if they did, there would be "smokes all around." Jane did not know where any bushwhackers were during this conversation, but she would not have told even if she had known. It was wrong to tell on either party. "I don't want to be the cause of anyone's life being taken."

She knew several bushwhackers, but refused to give names. Jane avowed herself a Southern sympathizer "and a Rebel" but had never engaged in spying or mail carrying.[28]

Finally, it was Wealthy Robertson's turn to testify.

Although she was a Southern sympathizer, Wealthy was willing to take an oath of allegiance to the Union. Her husband was in the Rebel army in Shelby's command, but she had no other relatives in the Confederate Army and none in the brush. A party of Southern soldiers did indeed come to her house about the first of June 1864. The captain told her he needed dinner for twenty-five men, but Wealthy replied she could not accommodate that many. When he insisted, she fixed dinner for seven. The band ate and left. Wealthy gave them no information or other provisions.

On three separate occasions during July 1863, Wealthy fed squads of Southern soldiers. One squad consisted of fourteen men, and the other two had eight men each. The men told her they were in the Confederate Army. She did not report them because she "had no man about the house." Yes, she knew a few bushwhackers, but she had not seen them since they had taken up bushwhacking. If her husband was a bushwhacker, she did not know it. The last time she saw her husband was about three months ago—the fourth Sunday of the previous May. He had stayed home one night, and when he left, he had told her he was headed to Texas on an errand.

She denied James Todd's accusation that she had said she had fed bushwhackers and would do so again. Some guerrillas camped about a quarter of a mile from her house one time, but she did not know about it until after they were gone. Also, a man came to her gate one time and was shot by Federal soldiers as a bushwhacker. Wealthy did not know he was a bushwhacker until after he was killed and did not know why he was coming to her house. She did not approve of bushwhacking and had never written to bushwhackers, received letters from them, or helped them in any way.[29]

On the evening of September 2, the same day they had been examined, the Post Oak women and three or four other women were moved from the Myrtle Street Prison to the Gratiot Street Prison. Griffin Frost, a male prisoner, saw them when they were first brought in, and he noted in his journal that they were nearly all dressed in black. All but two of the women were young, he said. Of these two, one had a child with her, and the other was very old and feeble, hardly able to walk. (The woman with a child was probably Wealthy Robertson, and the feeble, old woman was no doubt Eliza Spencer.) The women were treated to supper in the officers' dining room before being led across the street to the female quarters.[30]

The women were usually not housed in cells as such, with iron bars. In fact, at least a couple of the prisons were just homes that had been converted to prisons.

Although Hattie Spencer had gotten into trouble for helping a robbery when she was paroled shortly after her arrival in St. Louis, her difficulties did not dampen the efforts of those working on her behalf. In early September, St. Louis attorney and Missouri state representative Charles P. Johnson asked the Department of the Missouri headquarters to allow Hattie to leave St. Louis for one month with the promise that she would return at the end of that time to fully answer the charges against her. Johnson said that Miss Spencer wanted a speedy trial. She felt sure she could "prove her entire innocence of any charges that may be presented against her." On September 7, Hattie's parole was extended for thirty days, her application for permission to leave the city was granted, and she presumably left.[31]

The friends of the Little sisters still worked on their behalf as well. On September 7, Thomas Garrett wrote to Colonel Sanderson saying that "a man of the highest respectability" had asked him to intervene on behalf of Clara and Fannie Little. He also said the young women's aunt, a Mrs. Crane of St. Louis, had assured him that the charge of aiding bushwhackers against Clara and Fannie was "entirely without foundation and that it proceeds upon the mistake or malice of the person accusing them." (Their Johnson County neighbor Margaret

Burk made the accusations.) Garrett asked that the Littles be paroled on their oath and bond and a pledge to remain in St. Louis County. They had no desire, Garrett explained, to return to Johnson County "so long as matters continue in the present unsettled condition."[32]

When they heard they were to be banished to the South, Clara and Fannie Little dispensed with intermediaries and wrote directly to General Rosecrans on September 20th. They beseeched him to commute the sentence to a parole within St. Louis County on bond and oath. They continued:

> We feel satisfied there has been some misunderstanding or misrepresentation in our cases and think it possible they have been confounded with others. We pledge you our honor as ladies that we have not harbored Bushwhackers or given... encouragement to Rebels in arms against the US government and feel sorry that such representations have been made against us. Trusting in your kindness and goodness which ever prompts the acts of the brave and generous, we remain your petitioners.
> Respectfully,
> Fannie H. Little
> Clara E. Little.[33]

Rosecrans sent for the papers in the cases of Clara and Fannie Little. He got them on September 21. After reviewing the paperwork, he made it known that he planned to commute the banishment decrees against the two young women. Learning of the general's intent the next day, Thomas Garrett again wrote to Rosecrans that he was gratified. He was confident the Little women would "so conduct themselves in future that you will consider the clemency extended to them well bestowed." Garrett went on to urge Rosecrans to expedite the official order releasing Clara and Fannie on parole because "they have already been more than a month in the most close and dreary confinement and their health has given way under it and the anxiety they have suffered." This might have been an exaggeration, but the health of many of the women held in St. Louis prisons did deteriorate during their imprisonment. Although life at the Gratiot Street Female Prison was tolerable by Civil War prison standards, overcrowding still led to unsanitary conditions and disease.

The official order releasing Clara and Fannie Little was issued that very day. They were paroled to St. Louis County on a bond of $3,000 each. This was fairly steep. Most bonds during the Civil War, were in the $1,000 range.[34]

The rest of the Post Oak women did not get off as lightly. Facing a variety of charges from "harboring and feeding bushwhackers" to "using disloyal language," they were held for court martial (except Wealthy Robertson, whose trial was postponed so that witnesses could be subpoenaed).

General Rosecrans intervened in the cases of Eliza Spencer, Mary Spencer, Hattie Spencer, Mary Cull, and Jane Ward prior to their trial. On October 17, 1864, he issued Special Orders No. 288 banishing them to the free states north and east of Springfield, Illinois—instead of Southern states as originally planned. According to the decree, Rosecrans took such an action "because the time of the military courts is occupied with a more respectable class of prisoners, and he is not without hope that, removed from temptation, and deprived of the opportunity of indulging their taste for the society of murderers, thieves, and guerrillas, they may become, if not loyal and good citizens, at least more creditable specimens of their sex." The women were sent to their places of exile the next day.[35]

In other words, he chose leniency not because they were innocent, but they were too depraved for him to bother with them.

Perhaps it would not surprise Rosecrans that not all of the women obeyed the terms of their release.

In late December, Jane Ward found her way back into Johnson County and was promptly re-arrested. Captain Ferguson wired St. Louis asking what to do with the recalcitrant Miss Ward. Judge advocate Lucien Eaton, who had been part of the military commission appointed to try the Post Oak females, recommended to provost marshal James H. Baker that Jane be tried for violating the special order of banishment. "Otherwise," he concluded, "all the parties banished will swarm back upon us." On January 8, 1865, Jane, whom Eaton had earlier called a woman of "doubtful fame and undoubted disloyalty," was accordingly sent to St. Louis under guard. She was banished south on January 19, at the same time as Bill Anderson's sisters.[36]

Meanwhile, Wealthy Robertson's trial, was postponed a second time and rescheduled for January 1865. In the end, however, Wealthy

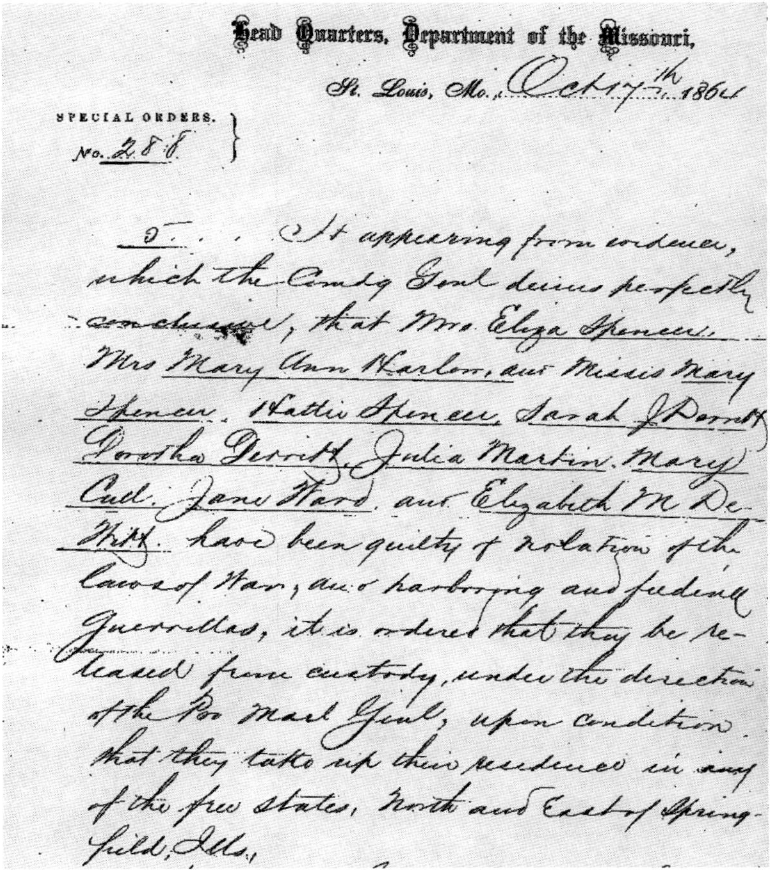

Head Quarters, Department of the Missouri,
St. Louis, Mo., Oct 17th 1864

SPECIAL ORDERS.
No. 288

5. . It appearing from evidence, which the Comdg Genl deems perfectly conclusive, that Mrs. Eliza Spencer, Mrs Mary Ann Harlow, and Misses Mary Spencer, Hattie Spencer, Sarah J Derritt, Dorotha Derritt, Julia Martin, Mary Cull, Jane Ward, and Elizabeth M DeWitt, have been guilty of violation of the laws of War, and harboring and feeding Guerrillas, it is ordered that they be released from custody, under the direction of the Pro Marl Genl, upon condition that they take up their residence in any of the free states, North and East of Springfield, Ills,

Order banishing the Post Oak women to the free states north and east of Springfield, Illinois. (From Union provost marshals' records.)

Back in Johnson County, Jennie Spencer, who did not travel to St. Louis with her mother and sisters, was re-arrested in early January. It's not clear whether her apprehension stemmed solely from the previous charges against her or if she was accused of some new offense. At any rate, while she was still a prisoner at Warrensburg, her case was examined at St. Louis in mid-February. She was found guilty of "aiding and giving comfort to the Rebel enemies of the United States; feeding, harboring, and encouraging Bushwhackers and Guerrilla bands; and neglecting to report such outlaws to the Federal authorities." An order of banishment to go to Ohio for the remainder of the war was issued on February 19. Presumably she had requested such a dispensation, perhaps because that is where her mother and sisters had gone. On or after February 22, Jennie was escorted to St. Louis. The quartermaster department transported her to Ohio.[38]

Arrested for helping guerrillas, the Post Oak women were called prostitutes, women of ill fame, and similar vile names. But there is scant evidence any of them actually sold their bodies for financial gain, either during the war, as Captain Peak alleged, or after it—not unless they once again made the unlikely choice of setting up shop in the sparsely populated backwoods of Johnson County.

The Rest of the Story

Nearly all, if not all, of the women from Post Oak who were arrested for disloyalty in the summer 1864 returned to their home territory after the war.

In 1870, Eliza Spencer lived in Madison Township in the west-central part of the county. Mary, Hattie, and Jennie lived there; all were unmarried.

We don't know what happened to Mary and Emily Cull. Their older sister Missouri moved to Chilhowee Township south of Madison Township.

Margaret Little also lived in Chilhowee Township in 1870, and both Clara and Fannie were single and living with her.

Fannie Little wed Asa Hyatt on December 20, 1872, in Johnson County. However, the union did not last long. She was back living with her mother by 1880; Asa was also back with his own family.

Jane Ward married Simon Bennett in Johnson County on December 2, 1872. The couple disappears from the record after that.[39]

CHAPTER 18
Notorious and Active Rebels

Bushwhacker belles were arrested for a variety of reasons. Some were caught in the act of helping guerrillas. Some were accused by their Union neighbors. And some were indicted by their own words.

Such was the case with Julia Martin and Dortha Durrett.

Both Julia and Dortha lived in Johnson County south and southwest of Warrensburg in the general vicinity where the Post Oak females resided. They were arrested about the same time the Post Oak women were taken into custody.

But they were not named in Captain Peak's letter and were not labeled as prostitutes. Instead, they were apprehended as active rebels after letters they wrote to friends or family fell into the wrong hands.[1]

Here is their story.

Twenty-two-year-old Julia Martin lived just south of Post Oak in Henry County. She first came under intense Federal scrutiny in late May 1864. She wrote a letter to a Southern-sympathizing girlfriend, twenty-year-old Sena Bell, who lived across the county line in Post Oak Township. The letter fell into the hands of Union authorities.

Julia began the letter with a mundane topic—the weather. But she wrote in what seems to be more metaphorical than literal terms. She said rains and dark clouds had hovered over her area in recent days. Now, she said, "Brite day has again spread her silvery mantle over our land and every thing looks well in our gardens." Julia had learned Thomas Cramer was not dead as she and Sena had feared. She was sure Sena would rejoice at the news "of the return of that one dear dear friend, dearest of all your friends." Julia also informed Sena that a company of Missouri partisans had recently "got in from Rebeldom" (i.e. the South).[2]

Julia had blue eyes and light hair and stood only five feet tall, but her fiery attitude belied her diminutive stature. Speaking of the newly arrived guerrillas, she said, "I do hope they will come in, one to every bush, and kill every devil of militia that they can catch. I do wish some of them would give Clinton a call." (Clinton, the seat of Henry County, was occupied by Federal soldiers at the time of Julia's letter.) Julia's epistle cautioned Sena, "Don't let anyone see this badly written letter."[3]

After gaining possession of the incriminating letter, Lieutenant Stephen M. Williams, the assistant provost marshal at Clinton, began to gather evidence against Julia. He took four testimonies on June 17. Here is what they said.

Jonathan Eshew, a fifty-four-year-old resident of Clinton, said it was "the impression of the loyal citizens" that Julia Martin had been carrying dispatches to bushwhackers ever since the outbreak of the war. Sometimes, when he was not home, Julia would pass his house and threaten his family with taunts that she was going to get the bushwhackers to drive off the family's horses. We don't know why. Julia made a pair of pants for one of General Sterling Price's men when he was on his way to Lexington.[4]

Twenty-one-year-old Bernard Greenlee said Julia Martin was a Rebel. She and two bushwhackers had come to his father's house in the fall 1862. While Julia and one of the men hung back about three hundred yards from the house, the other man came to the Greenlee barn and stole a horse.[5]

Twenty-one-year-old Jonathan Brown swore Julia was a "notorious rebel." During the year 1862, she led bushwhackers to several Union men's homes so that the men could be "robbed of everything in their houses and of their horses." Julia acted as a courier for the guerrillas, and she would "ride day and night carrying messages."[6]

Twenty-eight-year-old William Weaver owned a hotel in Clinton and was a captain in the local Enrolled Missouri Militia. He reiterated some of the same accusations as the others and then added that at different times when he was scouting through the countryside he had met Julia Martin "traveling unusual fast and her excuse was not sufficient for doing so." Several men Julia had mentioned in her letter were, in fact, notorious guerrillas, although he did not know Tom Cramer.[7]

Lieutenant Williams took two more statements on June 18.

Garrett Freeman, a twenty-four-year-old captain in a local home guard unit, said he led a scouting party to Julia's stepfather's house in the fall 1862. While there, he heard Julia threaten to have two sisters of Union leanings "taken to the brush by the bushwhackers." Like Weaver, Freeman knew for sure that some of the men mentioned in Julia's letter were bushwhackers. There were rumors Cramer was, too.[8]

Thirty-nine-year-old George Murray followed the pattern of the others. In addition, he frequently saw Julia out on the high prairie on horseback letting her horse graze. He was "of the impression from her actions that she was standing picket for the bushwhackers."[9]

Despite the sentiments Julia expressed in her letter and the several witnesses against her, the investigation into her alleged disloyalty suddenly stalled.

But two months later something happened to revive it.

In mid-August, a letter twenty-four-year-old Dortha Durrett wrote to her father fell into Union hands. Dortha's home was in southern Johnson County, west of Post Oak, but her father, Benjamin Durrett, was temporarily living in St. Charles County. Dortha's letter was dated August 12, 1864. After scrawling that the family was all well, she told her dad about two recent skirmishes in the Durrett neighborhood between bushwhackers and "the Feds," as she called the Union troops. She talked about a lad called "Ed"—apparently one of her younger brothers or another close relative. Ed's horse took a bullet during one of the melees. Then he killed a sergeant and mortally wounded another Federal soldier. "He is given up to be one of the bravest boys that ever drew a pistol," Dortha bragged. Although her mother and the whole family would like to see him, Dortha "would not advise [her father] to come back home."[10]

Dortha's missive was intercepted soon after she wrote it. Unlike in Julia's case, Union authorities did not wait to gather more evidence before apprehending the letter writer. Dortha was taken into custody at her home on August 15th by Captain Melville U. Foster. For good measure, Foster also arrested Dortha's twenty-one-year-old sister,

Sarah. Both sisters, like Julia, stood five feet tall and had blue eyes and light hair. They were taken at first to nearby Holden and then on to Warrensburg eighteen miles away.[11]

The arrest of the Durrett sisters must have awakened authorities to the fact that Julia Martin's very similar case was languishing at Clinton. Julia was arrested on August 20 and taken to Warrensburg to join the Durrett sisters in the guardhouse.[12]

Meanwhile, the provost marshal's office started gathering evidence against the Durretts to supplement Dortha's confiscated letter.

On August 31st, William Sheek, a private in the Seventh Missouri State Militia Cavalry, testified. He visited Dortha's home the summer of 1864. He heard one of the sisters say that she had fed bushwhackers and would do so again. The other sister said essentially the same thing after she had been arrested and brought to Holden.

The next day, fifty-four-year-old Rezin Lotspeich, who lived in the Durrett neighborhood, stated that Dortha and Sarah were "active Rebels." The home of Mrs. Durrett was, in his opinion, "a place of resort for bushwhackers."[13]

Dortha Durrett gave her own statement on or about September 1st. Here is what she said.

She had one brother and several other relatives in the Rebel army. She considered herself a true friend of the Southern cause. Southern troops had frequently eaten at her family's house. She always treated them kindly, and if she were released and allowed to go home, she would still treat them with respect. She had several bushwhacker friends whom she had known since before the war began. Squads of bushwhackers had visited her home on several occasions during the present summer.

About two weeks ago a detachment of Federal troops attacked some bushwhackers at her home, killing one of the guerrillas. Dortha could not in good conscience take the oath of allegiance to the US government; it would be in direct conflict with the obligation of an organization to which she belonged. She considered that obligation paramount to the oath of allegiance.[14]

On September 16, the Durrett sisters and Julia Martin were escorted to St. Louis on charges of giving aid and information to

Photographed circa 1868, this building served during the war as Gratiot Street Prison, where Julia Martin and a number of other women in this book were received before being taken to the female facility across the street. (Courtesy of the Missouri History Museum.)

bushwhackers, with a recommendation that they be sent out of the state. They were received at Gratiot Street Prison.[15]

When Dortha Durrett was interviewed on September 20, she changed the words of the tune she had sung three weeks earlier.

Although she was a Southern sympathizer, she was willing to take the oath of allegiance to the US. She was not a member of the KGC (Knights of the Golden Circle), the OAK (Order of American Knights), or any other secret organization, and she did not know anyone who was. She had never fed or assisted bushwhackers. She did not approve of guerrilla warfare. She had one brother who had been in General Price's army, but he was now a prisoner. She had no other relatives in the Southern army. She did not look upon bushwhackers the same as Confederate soldiers. She personally knew only one bushwhacker, William Scott.

Then, after having just claimed she had never helped bushwhackers, she admitted that parties of guerrillas visited her home from time to time, including at least a couple of occasions when they had identified themselves as "Yager's men." (This was a reference to partisan leader Dick Yeager, who marauded in the counties just south of the Missouri River in the early summer of 1864.) At least one squad who visited said they were Shelby's men, Dortha added.

Had Federals and bushwhackers ever skirmished near her home? She spoke of a time about a month earlier when one bushwhacker had been killed by Federal troops under Captain Melville Foster. (This was no doubt a reference to the skirmish Dortha had mentioned in the letter to her father.)

Why was her father not living at home? He had left the previous March because there was no work and her brother-in-law had asked her father to come and work with him.[16]

Sarah Durrett's testimony the same day largely mirrored that of her older sister.

Besides the brother Dortha had mentioned, Sarah brought up two uncles in the Southern army. Unlike Dortha, Sarah said she did not personally know any bushwhackers. Although her family had fed bushwhackers two or three times, it was only because the guerrillas had forced her mother to prepare food for them. The most recent visit bushwhackers had paid to the Durrett home, Sarah said, was about six weeks ago when a party of six or seven guerrillas calling themselves Colorado men had stopped at the house. They later said they were Shelby's men. Only after they left did Sarah learn they were actually Yeager's men. (This was the same occasion on which Captain Foster skirmished with the bushwhackers.) Her family gave these men no information. The Durrett home was not a resort for "men of this character."[17]

Julia Martin also finally got a chance to tell her story on September 20.

Was Julia acquainted with any bushwhackers? She knew Tom Cramer by sight but knew nothing about him. She had never helped bushwhackers in any way. Bushwhackers had been in her neighborhood only twice that she was aware of. On one specific occasion in 1862 or 1863, Federal soldiers and bushwhackers fought near her house. A bushwhacker was killed. She was not home when the skirmish occurred and only met the bushwhackers when she returned to her house after the fight because they had returned there, too, to check on their dead comrade. The guerrillas merely looked at the dead bushwhacker and departed, leaving the burial to the neighborhood people. Julia had not seen or communicated with any of the bushwhackers prior to the fight.

What of the incident in which Julia helped two bushwhackers in the theft of a horse from Mr. Greenlee? She was merely out one morning looking for a bridle she had lost the evening before. She ran into two men near the Greenlee place. One of them rode up to her and asked her what she was doing. He accused her of being a spy and demanded to know where she lived. When she answered, he told her to go home. She obeyed and had nothing more to do with the man.

What about the incident in which she threatened to have the two young women of loyal Union sentiments taken to the brush? Yes, she did say those things. But she did so only in anger; their brother had come to her house and accused her of complicity in the theft of the Greenlee horse and otherwise abused her.

Julia never made pants for the soldier in Price's army.

Yes, she was a Rebel sympathizer, but she did not approve of bushwhacking. She would report the hideouts of bushwhackers to Federal authorities if she knew about them.[18]

Charged with harboring, feeding, and giving information to bushwhackers, Julia Martin and the Durrett sisters were held for court martial after their respective statements. On October 3, judge advocate Lucien Eaton examined Julia's case. Citing the expense of procuring the necessary witnesses and the lack of definiteness in their statements, he joined Captain Ferguson in recommending that she be sent to live in the northern free states. A week later he made a similar recommendation in the cases of Dortha and Sarah Durrett. He felt sure they were disloyal but evidence was lacking to convict them on any specific offense. All three women were included in Special Orders #288, dated October 17, the same order of banishment by which the Post Oak women were required to reside in the free states north and east of Springfield, Illinois.[19]

Exactly where Julia Martin went to live during her exile is not known. The Durrett sisters landed in Mount Sterling, Illinois, on October 22. They were still there in June 1865 when they applied to B. F. Westlake, the local provost marshal, to revoke their banishment and provide them transportation to return home. They told Westlake they had been "thrown among strangers" and were without means. Writing to St. Louis, Westlake recommended the request be granted, "the rebellion having now been crushed." (The war had officially ended in April.) He added that the sisters had "faithfully observed their parole" and "conducted themselves with circumspection" during their stay in Mount Sterling.[20]

When the bushwhacker belles' disloyal statements were written down in black and white, it was hard for them to deny their true sentiments. Sometimes the best they could hope for was to mitigate their punishment. Facing court martial and possible imprisonment for the rest of the war, Julia Martin and the Durrett sisters got off with banishment from the state.

But it probably didn't feel like a victory.

The Rest of the Story

Was the Durrett sisters' request for transportation granted? We don't know. Either way, they did return to Missouri. It's hard to say whether they went back to their old home in Johnson County and, if so, how long they stayed.

Both young women married shortly after the war in nearby Cooper County. Sarah wed James Marshall in September 1866. Dortha married Edwin Marshall two months later.

Sarah and her husband moved to Kansas in the early 1870s, and in 1880 they lived in Montgomery County. They had six children. Sarah died there in 1917.

What happened to Dortha in later life is not known.[21]

After the war, Julia Martin returned to her old stomping grounds of Henry County. In 1867, she married George W. Glasgow, a former Missouri State Guard and Confederate soldier. By 1870, the couple still lived in Henry County and had two infant children. The family moved to Texas in the mid to late 1870s. By 1880, the household included seven children. Julia died in Texas in 1909.[22]

Chapter 19
Four-Time Jailbird "Lizzie" Dewitt

Bushwhacker belles wrote too many letters for their own good. Elizabeth "Lizzie" DeWitt expressed her Southern sentiments in a letter. It fell into Union hands. She became yet another target of the Union roundup of Southern-sympathizing young women in the Johnson County area in August 1864. Being a bushwhacker belle was turning into a dangerous business.

A Union man who testified against Lizzie after her arrest was shot dead a few days later. Speaking out against the belles could be even more dangerous.

A native of Alabama, Lizzie had moved with her family to eastern Kansas about 1859 when she was fifteen. Sometime near the beginning of the Civil War, the family moved across the Missouri border to Cass County. Lizzie was a blue-eyed, light-haired girl who stood just five feet tall. But she was full of spunk. She clashed with Union authorities in Cass County and, according to her accusers, spent a couple of brief stints in the guardhouse at Harrisonville. Perhaps in search of a more hospitable environment, Lizzie and her parents moved east again in March of 1863 to neighboring Johnson County about nine miles northwest of Holden.[1]

Now, Lizzie was in trouble again. Her incriminating letter was addressed to a young woman in Saline County. It was intercepted at Marshall by Lieutenant-Colonel B. F. Lazear. On August 10th he forwarded it to Captain James H. Steger, assistant adjutant general of the District of Central Missouri at Warrensburg, to be used as evidence against Lizzie.[2]

Lazear informed Steger that the letter in question was the second communication of hers expressing disloyal sentiments that he had. The first had been found in Cass County in April 1863 among some silverware. Lazear recommended that Lizzie should "certainly be sent to Dixie as soon as possible."[3]

Captain Steger turned the matter over to provost marshal Captain Richard L. Ferguson, whose investigation turned up two previous letters written by Lizzie, not just one. The three letters do not survive today, so we don't know their exact contents. A Federal paraphrasing suggests that one of the incriminating remarks Lizzie wrote was that three of her acquaintances (Parson, Henry, and Bud) had gone south with Quantrill's raiders after they sacked Lawrence.

Lizzie was taken into custody on August 15 by Captain Melville U. Foster. The same officer arrested the Durrett sisters the same day.[4]

Lizzie's father and mother, William and Elizabeth DeWitt, were also arrested at or near the same time. Captain Ferguson gathered additional evidence to make his case against the family. Here is the testimony against them.

Deposed at Holden on August 29, John Windsor said he knew nothing about the DeWitts except from hearsay. They had a reputation for feeding and harboring bushwhackers. He once saw a man whom he took to be a bushwhacker go to the DeWitt home and seemingly come away with provisions. He wasn't close enough to see who the man was or how he was treated by the DeWitt family. Windsor claimed Lizzie had been arrested three times previously for disloyal activity and held briefly at Harrisonville in Cass County each time.[5]

Also interviewed at on the 29th, a man named Crat Dean said he, too, knew nothing definite against the DeWitts, but then he proceeded to give some fairly specific evidence. He had once seen some Union men go to the DeWitt home pretending to be bushwhackers. The family appeared to be "glad to see them until they saw their mistake." Dean was not at the house at the time but in a cornfield nearby where he "could see their manners." When Lieutenant James Couch of the First Missouri State Militia was killed by bushwhackers the previous spring, "Old Mr. DeWitt appeared to be very much elated over it and said that the bushwhackers would make these black Republicans all leave the state of Missouri before another year." Had he ever heard of Lizzie DeWitt being arrested and put in the guardhouse at Harrisonville for harboring bushwhackers? Yes, Dean had.[6]

On September 7, Crat Dean was, in the words of Captain Ferguson, "most brutally murdered." Ferguson said he believed the killing was for "no other cause than giving evidence" against the DeWitts."[7]

On September 12, Ferguson referred the case against the DeWitts to General Egbert B. Brown, commanding the District of Central Missouri. Ferguson recommended sending them to St. Louis to be dealt with as authorities there saw fit. But the charges against the father and mother were dropped the next day. Brown apparently decided the individual cases against the father and mother were not strong enough to pursue.[8]

The case against their daughter went forward. Charges were officially filed against her, accusing her of aiding and encouraging bushwhackers. The statement of charges specified that she had fed and harbored bushwhackers. She had also written letters expressing her love for Rebels, calling them her "gallant friends," stating her opinion that they had a right to be in Missouri, and making use of "many other wicked and disloyal expressions." Lizzie was shipped to St. Louis on September 16 with Julia Martin, Dortha Durrett, and Sarah Durrett. In Lizzie's transfer papers, Ferguson cited as evidence the letters she had written, her three previous incarcerations for disloyal activity, and the statements of Windsor and Dean. Also, Lizzie had admitted her sympathies were with the South and she would consider any Rebels who came to her house friends. Lizzie had refused to take an oath of allegiance to the US. "Owing to the distracted state of affairs in the section of country where the DeWitt family resides," Ferguson concluded, "better or more complete evidence could not be obtained."[9]

Upon her arrival in St. Louis, Lizzie was housed at Gratiot Street Prison. She gave her age as only seventeen (three years younger than the truth). She was interviewed by assistant examiner Isaac Ruth on September 20. Here's what she said.

Yes, Lizzie did write the three letters Ruth now possessed. The one found in the silverware in Cass County she had written to her brother urging him to remain in the Confederate States Army. The one recently intercepted by Lieutenant Colonel Lazear she had written to a female acquaintance named Sallie in Saline County. The third one she had written to Nannie Thomas of Pleasant Hill.

No, Lizzie had never been arrested or put in the guardhouse at Harrisonville.

Yes, she was acquainted with a few bushwhackers, including some of Quantrill's guerrillas, but she did not consider Quantrill's men bushwhackers. Besides, she had never helped any of them in any way except one time about two years ago. That's when some Southern partisans had come to her house and demanded something to eat and she had given it to them. She was a Confederate sympathizer but was willing to take an oath of allegiance to the Union.

Although she had initially told Captain Ferguson at Warrensburg that she would not take such an oath, she had changed her mind—but he would not let her take it at that point.

And no, she had never assisted in carrying mail for Rebels.[10]

After questioning Lizzie, Ruth turned her case over to Captain Gustavus Cohn, chief of the examining bureau. He in turn referred it to the provost marshal general's office with a recommendation that Lizzie DeWitt be sent out of the state.

Lizzie was included in General Rosecrans's banishment decree, dated October 17, 1864. That order also exiled the Durrett sisters, Julia Martin, the Spencer women, Mary Cull, and Jane Ward. Ordered to live in the free states east of the Mississippi, Lizzie took up residence, along with the Durrett sisters, in Mount Sterling, Illinois, arriving on October 22. She was still with the Durrett sisters in June 1865, when the three women applied to Federal authorities for transportation home.[11]

Captain Ferguson thought bushwhackers had killed Crat Dean for no other reason than his speaking out against Lizzie and her parents. That might have been part of the reason, but General Brown thought it had more to do with Dean having acted as a guide for Federal troops sent out from Holden in search of guerrillas. Bushwhackers gunned Dean down for his trouble, and two nights later a detachment of soldiers from Holden killed four Rebel sympathizers in retaliation.

One thing was sure. "This infernal guerrilla warfare," as Brown called it, was becoming increasingly perilous for all parties, including the bushwhacker belles.

Notorious guerrilla leader William Quantrill, whom Lizzie DeWitt did not consider a bushwhacker. (Author's collection.)

The Rest of the Story

Whether the transportation home that Lizzie requested was provided is uncertain. She did, in all likelihood, return to Johnson County at the end of the war.

Her parents were still living there in 1870. John Windsor, one of the men who testified against the DeWitts, lived in the same neighborhood. Lizzie's whereabouts at the time and in succeeding years are unknown.[12]

Chapter 20
Dancing with a Rebel Flag

Susan "Sue" Bryant was arrested in August 1864 shortly after a letter she had written fell into the hands of Lieutenant-Colonel B. F. Lazear at Marshall. The outcome of her case, largely because of the intervention of her father's influential friends, was considerably different from Lizzie DeWitt's. Young women arrested in Missouri for disloyal activity during the Civil War were treated more leniently by Union authorities if they came from prominent families than if they came from humble backgrounds. Perhaps no case better illustrates this truism than Sue Bryant's.[1]

Sue grew up in Marshall, seat of Saline County. Her father, John W. Bryant, was the circuit attorney. In October 1863, the family moved to Boonville in neighboring Cooper County, and John Bryant returned to private law practice. About February or March of 1864, Sue enrolled in the Boonville Female Seminary, an exclusive school run by James D. Hurst. As part of the school's year-end closing ceremony in June, a calisthenics class of which Sue was a member gave a public exhibition. Half the girls wore white dresses trimmed with blue, and the other half, including Sue, wore white dresses trimmed with red.[2]

After school was dismissed for the summer, eighteen-year-old Sue remained at home throughout most of June and July. About the first of August she visited her old hometown of Marshall, staying with the family of John Sheridan, clerk of the circuit court. Sue had recently corresponded with Sheridan's stepdaughter, Susan Isaacs, about the women's seminary in Boonville. She brought along the red and white dress to show her friend. On the evening she arrived, she put the dress on and went through the movements she had learned in calisthenics class in front of Mrs. Sheridan, two of her daughters, and a family servant.[3]

On August 5, guerrilla leader Bill Jackson (son of former Missouri governor Claiborne F. Jackson) and his band of about ten men came into Marshall. They burned the courthouse. During the bushwhackers' brief stay in town, Sue was seen at the gate of the Sheridan home greeting and shaking hands with John Piper, a friend of hers who had recently joined the guerrillas.[4]

The next day, Lieutenant-Colonel Lazear occupied Marshall with a detachment of Union troops and began rounding up Southern sympathizers in response to Jackson's raid on the town. The Sheridan family's black servant girl told some local Union ladies about Sue's calisthenics exhibition. Construing the performance as "dancing with a Rebel flag" around her, they reported it to Lazear. News of her brief encounter with John Piper was also relayed to the Federal officer.

Sue had left town before Lazear's takeover to spend the weekend with a friend who lived in the country, but she was arrested at the friend's house and brought back to Marshall. Union soldiers rifled through her trunk at the Sheridan house and found a letter that a young woman named Lou Mayfield had written to her from Pleasant Green, Cooper County. They also seized the suspect dress, which Sue described years later as "red, white, and red with the immortal thirteen red buttons down the front of the waist." A letter Sue had written from Marshall expressing her sympathy for the Southern cause was intercepted or confiscated about this time as well. It was addressed to a Miss Knox, a young woman who had been Sue's classmate.

Sue refused to take an oath of allegiance to the US, as some of the other Southern sympathizers arrested during the roundup did. She was held at Marshall until August 17th, when Lazear sent her and the evidence against her to district headquarters at Warrensburg. Lazear declared that Sue had the reputation of being "a most notorious rebel and in full fellowship with the guerrillas."[5]

On August 22, district commander General Alfred Pleasonton turned Sue's case over to Captain Richard L. Ferguson, district provost marshal, with an order that she be escorted to St. Louis. Two days later, Ferguson sent Sue under guard to Colonel J. P. Sanderson, provost marshal of the department.[6]

General Alfred Pleasonton had Sue Bryant arrested and forwarded to St. Louis. (Courtesy of the Library of Congress.)

Sue told her family and friends or let them assume that she had been arrested primarily for wearing the red and white dress. Outraged, they bombarded Union authorities with letters of support for Sue.

On August 26, James Hurst, principal of the Boonville Female Seminary, wrote to provisional governor Willard P. Hall. Sue had worn the dress as part of an exhibition, he said, meant as a celebration of the national colors. He had no idea the dress would be construed as a secessionist garment. Hurst beseeched Hall to use his "personal and official influence in relieving the young lady from the extremely disagreeable condition in which she is placed." Several other citizens of Boonville added their signatures to the document as a testament to Hurst's trustworthiness.[7]

The next day, E. B. McPherson, one of the men who had signed his name to Hurst's letter, wrote his own letter to Hall. A hotel keeper in Boonville, McPherson said Sue Bryant was arrested merely for wearing a uniform prescribed by her school. She was guilty of no offense, as far as he knew. Her parents were "among the most esteemed citizens" of Boonville. If the governor would intercede on Sue's behalf, it would "endear (him) to her estimable family and gratify everyone here who has an impulse of humanity in his heart."[8]

The same day, August 27, J. H. Wright of Boonville called at the governor's mansion in Jefferson City bearing several letters from other citizens of Boonville, which he meant to deliver to Colonel Sanderson in St. Louis. Hall fired off a missive to Sanderson for Wright to take with him as a letter of introduction vouching for his loyalty and truthfulness.[9]

On the 28th, Boonville merchant D. C. Lionberger, another of the men who endorsed Hurst's letter, also wrote directly to Governor Hall. Sue Bryant was under arrest, as he understood the charge, principally for wearing a white and red dress. He, like Hurst, explained that her dress was part of a public exhibition that included about twenty-five girls and which was attended by over 600 people. Concerning any other charges, Lionberger knew nothing. He asked that she be given a trial as soon as possible so that, if innocent, she could be released to come home. Lionberger allowed that the girl may have been "a little impudent," but he thought "youthful indiscrepancies should sometimes be overlooked." Sue's father, he reminded the governor, was a lawyer in Boonville and "an honorable gentleman."[10]

Two other prominent citizens of Boonville, J. L. Stephens and William E. Burr, traveled to St. Louis in late August. While there, they wrote to Colonel Sanderson asking that Sue be released on parole pending the outcome of her case. They told the colonel that Sue was "a reputable young girl, aged about sixteen." (She was, in fact, eighteen.) The men called Sanderson's attention to the previous letters written by other citizens of Boonville attesting to the girl's "high character." They were willing to put up a bond for her release until her case was settled or until her father could arrange to furnish a bond.[11]

Perhaps Union authorities soon realized on their own that they had erred in construing Sue Bryant's wearing of the red and white dress as a flaunting of Rebel colors. If not, they were surely convinced by the avalanche of letters attesting to her innocence of the charge. However, they were little swayed to drop the proceedings against her, because they still had the incriminating letters, which constituted the strongest evidence against the young woman.

Although the letter Sue wrote to Miss Knox is extant, the writing is so dim as to be virtually indecipherable. However, the legible parts of the letter and Union summaries of its contents reveal that one of the most damning passages was a request Sue made. If Miss Knox saw the bushwhackers, she should "give them [Sue's] undying love, and say to them, 'God bless them in all their wise undertakings.'"[12]

Lou Mayfield's letter to Sue, dated August 2, is fully legible. It reveals that, when Sue first started for Saline County in late July, she was intercepted by Captain Joseph Parks of the Fourth Missouri State Militia. She was brought back to Boonville. Lou was of the opinion that Parks "should have some kind of emetic administered in the form of a pistol shot." Lou joked that Sue's mistake was starting off in "bad company" and that, if she had taken along "your humble servant," she would have had no problem. Lou had heard that "the Feds caught H—l [hell] on the other side of the river the other day." She asked Sue whether it was true—and then said she hoped it was. "The bushwhackers have been cutting up some around here," Lou continued, "and I think so much about them that I have forgotten how to spell or do anything else."

She said that, if the bushwhackers came over on her side of the river, someone had better warn the Federals not to send any "flying Dutchmen out this way, for if you do, they will catch the devil soon enough." ("Dutchmen" or simply "the Dutch" was a derogatory name that Southerners gave Germans, particularly German soldiers in the Union Army, during the Civil War. "Dutch" was a corruption of Deutsch, the German word for German.) Some Federal soldiers had been in Lou's neighborhood recently foraging for corn and they had "served their Union friends pretty badly" by stealing every chicken and turkey the Union people had and had even eaten an old gobbler and the hens that were setting. "As all varmints do," Lou opined, "I suppose they suck the rotten eggs, too." After relating some of the latest gossip about a few of the "Rebel Boys" she and Sue knew, Lou closed her letter "Your true friend, Rebel."[13]

When Sue arrived in St. Louis, she was initially jailed at the St. Charles Street Prison, which was notorious for its mistreatment of prisoners. Late in life, Sue remembered the short time she spent there as the worst experience of her life. About the first of September, she was moved to the Female Military Prison across the street from the Gratiot Street Prison, where conditions were much better. She recalled years later that the Federal officers there were the first ones she had encountered since her arrest who treated her well or behaved like gentlemen.[14]

She was interviewed at the female prison on September 2. Here is her side of the story.

How did she come to be wearing the red and white dress? She repeated much the same story Hurst and others had told in their letters to Governor Hall.

She was shown the two letters that had fallen into Union hands. Yes, she had written one, and Lou Mayfield had written the other one to her.

Did she know any bushwhackers? Yes, but only two: Dick Derrick, who had been killed about three weeks earlier in Saline County, and John Piper, the young man she had spoken to at Marshall. ("Dick Derrick" was probably a mistranscription of Dick Durrett, a member of Bill Jackson's band who had been executed by Lazear's troops not long after the Marshall raid.) Sue had known Piper about five years and had been "intimately acquainted" with him, but when she saw him in Marshall, she barely spoke to him. Were they boyfriend-girlfriend? Lovers? Or just good friends? The record is not clear. It was the first time she had seen him since he had taken to the brush, she said, but she merely asked him about his health and exchanged a brief handshake.

Sue had never helped bushwhackers. Piper was the only one she had ever even seen. She did not sympathize with bushwhacking and, if given a chance, would not give information to or otherwise help guerrillas but that she was "perfectly willing to give any information to soldiers belonging to the Confederate Army or do anything that would benefit the Southern cause." Despite her willingness to aid Confederate soldiers, she said she had never done so.

Yes, she had written letters to Southern soldiers held in Union prisons. But she had always complied with the regulations pertaining to prison correspondence.

She was indeed a Southern sympathizer and did not wish to see the South put down or the authority of the Union established over the country.[15]

The stream of letters from influential citizens on Sue's behalf hardly slowed after she was shipped to St. Louis. On September 5, Thomas L. Price, a former lieutenant governor of Missouri, wrote to General Egbert B. Brown, who had reassumed charge of the District of Central Missouri after Pleasonton's temporary command. Like the letter writers who had petitioned Governor Hall, Price explained that Sue's wearing of the questionable dress was part of a public ceremony. His daughter had attended the ceremony, so he knew the accusation that she had worn it as a display of "Secesh" (secessionist) colors was "positively false." Price dismissed the allegedly disloyal letters as "just such as unoffending and innocent young ladies are often in the practice of writing without knowing the effect or the bad results and with no intention of doing harm to the peace of the country." Price knew the Bryant family and, even if Sue, a young lady of "high moral worth," were guilty of this indiscretion, he would be inclined to forgive her "on her promise of better and more prudent conduct in the future." He asked for Brown's "kind consideration" in the matter.[16]

Celeste B. Price, daughter of Thomas Price, also wrote to General Brown on September 5. She confirmed what her father had said—she was present in Boonville when Sue Bryant had worn the red and white dress. The exhibition was a gymnastics exercise Professor Hurst took from his books, the same books "used in all Northern schools." The letter found in Sue's trunk was "an uninteresting schoolgirl's note written without any disloyal intention." Celeste was apparently not aware of the letter Sue had written, nor was she aware that Sue was no longer being held at Warrensburg. Appealing to General Brown "as a husband, father, and as a citizen," she asked that Sue be immediately released, and she closed by apologizing that she would not be able to visit the general and his wife in person the following evening at a social function that was planned to honor a number of ladies.[17]

On September 9, Sue Bryant's case was referred back to Captain Ferguson at Warrensburg, although the reason is not clear. Perhaps a document was missing from her file or departmental headquarters merely wanted clarification of the allegations against her. At any rate, Ferguson replied the same day, saying he had forwarded the evidence against Sue on August 24th. He detailed the conversations he had with her while she was in his custody. "I would respectfully state that I have never talked with a more violent rebel than Miss Bryant." When he talked to her about the bushwhackers, "she spoke of them as Southern troops." Although she did not openly endorse their crimes, he got the impression that "such were her real feelings and sentiments."[18]

Back in St. Louis, Sue's file, including Captain Ferguson's statement, was turned over to General Rosecrans in mid-September. Meanwhile, Sue finally consented to take the oath of allegiance. On September 18, despite Captain Ferguson's negative opinion of her, Rosecrans issued Special Orders #259 mitigating her sentence. He said her sympathy for bushwhackers was clear. Any statements she might make to the contrary were "unworthy of credence," because she had deliberately allowed her friends and family to believe she was arrested merely for "displaying colors."[19]

However, "in consideration of her youth, sex, and the worth of her friends, who wish to save her from ruin, on the high road to which she has so evidently and early entered," Miss Bryant would be paroled and "permitted to return to her friends upon her oath and adequate security for her future good behavior." Rosecrans further directed that the letters of both Sue Bryant and Lou Mayfield be published "to warn thoughtful parents and teachers . . . of the fearful downward course of the youth of our state, when educated girls of respectable parents write such letters and express sympathy with outlaws, thieves, and murderers more degraded then the savages who murder the inhabitants of our frontier settlements."[20]

Friends of Sue's father posted her bond in the amount of $3,000, and Mr. Bryant was there to take her home when she signed the oath of allegiance and was released on October 10.

She was in custody just under two months. It paid off to have friends and family in high places.

The Rest of the Story

Returning to the Saline County area, Sue was married in 1866 to John R. Cason, a former Confederate soldier. By 1870, they were living in the county with two young children. The couple went on to have several more children.

Cason was twice elected sheriff of Saline County. Later, he became a Secret Service agent, and the family moved to Washington, DC.

In 1905, Sue wrote an article about her prison experiences during the Civil War that appeared in the *Confederate Veteran*. The only part of the ordeal she recalled with any fondness was her time at the Female Military Prison, where she made many friends and learned to cook and do other domestic chores.

Still defiantly sympathetic to the South, Sue claimed she had only submitted to the humiliation of taking the oath because friends of the Bryant family had tricked her. They'd made her think she was needed at home to care for her sick father, and she only learned of the ruse when he arrived to take her home.[21]

Perhaps that's true—but it's just as likely her memory was colored by the stories the guerrillas and their bushwhacker belles told each other after the war. Their leaders may have signed treaties officially ending the war, but the guerrillas held out to the very end. The Union invaders may have overwhelmed them with superior numbers and firepower, but they could never crush their soul or discredit their noble cause.

Chapter 21
To Be Hung by the Neck Until Dead

When Mary Surratt was hanged in July 1865 for conspiracy to assassinate President Abraham Lincoln, she became the first woman ever executed by the US government. Only Sarah Jane Smith's fragile health and dubious mental capacity kept her from beating that mark by almost a year. Union authorities were loath to impose death sentences on women during the Civil War—and even more loath to carry them out.

Here is Sarah Jane's story.

Sarah Jane left her home in Washington County, Arkansas, in 1862, when she was just sixteen years old. She traveled to the Union-held town of Springfield, Missouri, in company with a family seeking refuge from the bitter partisan warfare that raged in northern Arkansas and southern Missouri. Sarah's mother had died three years earlier, and her father was away from home, having joined the Confederate Army under Sterling Price. Unmoored, Sarah Jane drifted back and forth between Missouri and Arkansas.

In late 1863, she left Springfield and went back home to see her kinfolk. After a two-month visit, she returned to Springfield. She stayed there about three months before starting back toward Arkansas in the spring of 1864. She got as far as Cassville, where she met three of her male cousins, whom she knew to be bushwhackers.[1]

The young men were headed to Springfield. Sarah Jane turned around and started back with them. When the foursome got to within about ten miles of Springfield, they set up camp in the woods. They stayed there about two weeks, getting provisions from citizens in the area. Sometime in May the four cousins cut down four or five miles of telegraph lines along the Wire Road that ran between Springfield and Cassville. Caught in the act of cutting down the poles with an ax, they were arrested and taken to Springfield as prisoners.[2]

Sarah Jane was kept in Springfield several weeks and was then sent to Rolla. Although cutting telegraph wires, a common guerrilla tactic, was a serious offense in the eyes of Union officials, she was soon turned loose without a trial. She hung around Rolla until about the first of September and then started back toward Springfield, walking part of the way and hitching a ride with a wagon train part of the way. Not long after the trip began, she fell in with a lawyer from Rolla and a sergeant of the Forty-eighth Missouri Volunteers. She learned they were members of a secret Southern society of which she was also a member (probably the Order of American Knights). The lawyer, who was about forty-five years old, said his name was Williams and that he had a wife and five kids. The sergeant told her he had formerly been a Rebel soldier and that he would desert and go back to the Southern army if he was ever called upon to fight as a Federal.

Secret Southern Societies

Several secret societies that promoted the interests of the South were active in the northern and border states during the Civil War. The Knights of the Golden Circle, perhaps the best known of these groups, was established prior to the war with an original goal of colonizing a "golden circle" of territories from Mexico, Central America, and the Caribbean as US slave states. After the Civil War started, the group focused on supporting the Confederacy. Many of its members were Peace Democrats, or Copperheads, as Radical Republicans called members of the Democratic Party who opposed the war. The KGC collapsed about 1863, and the Order of American Knights (OAK), which also had its origins before the war, rose on the ruins of the former group. The Order of American Knights was particularly active in Missouri, or at least rumors to that effect were prevalent. In 1864, provost marshal general Colonel John P. Sanderson and his detectives uncovered evidence of the group in the St. Louis area. Near the end of the war, as the OAK began to disintegrate like its predecessor, the Sons of Liberty was organized, but it never gained significant influence.

The men each offered to pay her five dollars if she would go back up the road toward Rolla and cut the telegraph wires on the Springfield Road. She accepted the bargain, probably little realizing

General Henry Halleck, whose Special Orders No. 32 led to the sentence of death pronounced on Sarah Jane Smith. (Courtesy of the Library of Congress.)

that she was agreeing to commit a crime that was punishable by death. In December of 1861, General Henry Halleck, then commanding the Department of the Missouri, had issued Special Orders No. 32 to that effect in response to the destruction of bridges, railroads, and telegraph wires in northern Missouri.[3]

Williams had left an ax hidden alongside the road about six miles from Rolla. Sarah Jane went back and retrieved it. She chopped the wires as she had been hired to do, hid the ax, and then started back down the road toward Lebanon. However, Williams and the sergeant were nowhere to be found, and she was never paid for her dirty deed. Instead, she was arrested and taken to Rolla on September 7.

The next day she gave a full confession detailing her movements over the past two years. She told of helping her cousins cut down the wires near Springfield and described how she had been hired to cut the wires near Rolla. Although the sergeant had apparently double-crossed her or at least reneged on paying her, she refused to reveal his name, and she also would not identify her cousins by name.[4]

Sarah Jane was sent to St. Louis on October 22 and committed to Gratiot Street Female Prison the next day. On November 7, a military commission that had convened in St. Louis three weeks earlier heard her case.

The trial was short and, from Sarah Jane's standpoint, not at all sweet. The statement she had given at Rolla was read, and she admitted that it accurately reflected the facts of the case. Her only defense was that she "didn't know it was wrong to cut the wires at the time [she] did it." She complained that Williams and the sergeant didn't pay her the money they promised her and that she never saw them again.

Charged with violating Special Orders No. 32, she was found guilty and sentenced to be "hung by the neck till dead." Three days later, Major General William S. Rosecrans, commanding the Department of the Missouri, approved the findings of the commission and ordered that the execution be carried out on November 25.[5]

On November 10, the same day that Rosecrans approved Sarah Jane's sentence, acting provost marshal general Joseph Darr, Jr. informed her by letter of the general's verdict. "Madame," the grim missive began, "it becomes my duty to inform you of the following

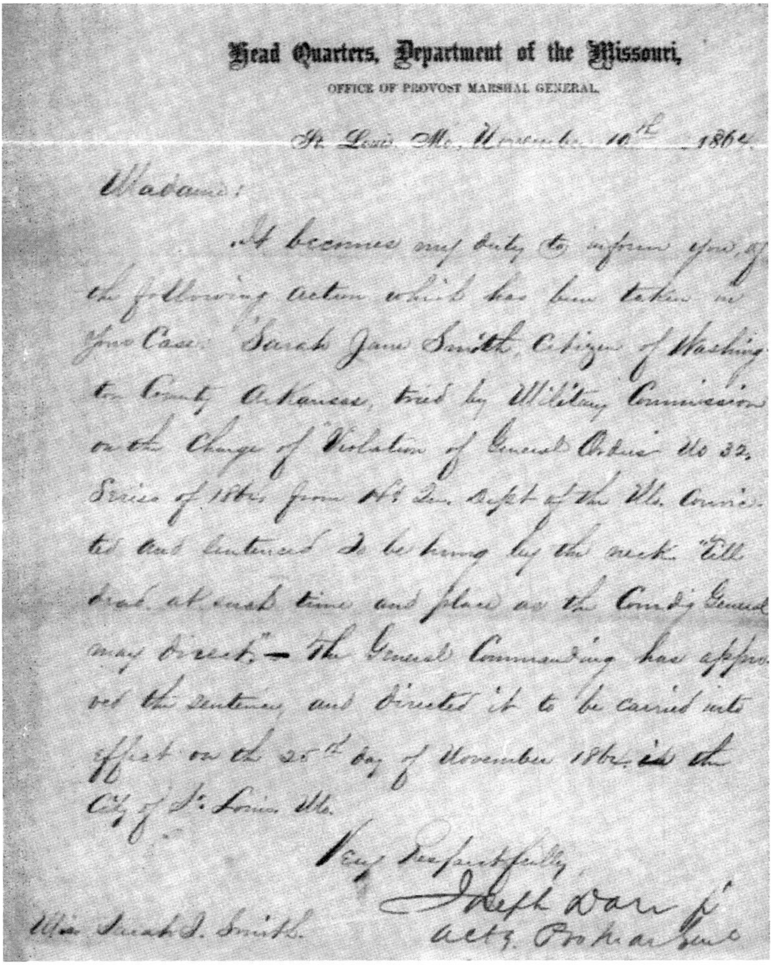

Head Quarters, Department of the Missouri,
OFFICE OF PROVOST MARSHAL GENERAL.

St. Louis Mo., November 10th 1864.

Madame:

It becomes my duty to inform you of the following action which has been taken in your Case: Sarah Jane Smith, Citizen of Washington County Arkansas, tried by Military Commission on the Charge of Violation of General Orders No 32, Series of 1864, from Hd Qrs Dept of the Mo. Convicted and sentenced "to be hung by the neck till dead at such time and place as the Comdg General may direct." — The General Commanding has approved the sentence and directed it to be carried into effect on the 25th day of November 1864 in the City of St. Louis Mo.

Very Respectfully,

Joseph Darr Jr
Actg. Pro Mar Genl

Miss Sarah J. Smith.

Letter to Sarah Jane Smith informing her that she was to be executed. (From Union provost marshals' records.)

action which has been taken in your case." Citing the judgment of the military commission that she was to be hanged by the neck until dead, Darr went on, "The General Commanding has approved the sentence and directed it to be carried into effect on the 25th day of November, 1864, in the city of St. Louis, Mo."[6]

Fortunately for Sarah Jane, not all the Union officers she met were as blind and unyielding as the military justice system under which she was convicted. A couple of surgeons and other officers helped change her capital sentence.

After examining her on November 15, surgeon George Rex, in charge of the military prison hospital in St. Louis, concluded that she was "subject to periodical paroxysms of unconsciousness simulating epilepsy, and although viciously inclined, does not seem to be possessed of a degree of mental capacity to have realized the character of the offenses committed by her." Rex added that he felt Sarah Jane was "not a perfectly responsible creature."[7]

Another surgeon also examined Sarah Jane, and he echoed Rex's opinion. "I do not believe that this woman possesses sufficient mental capacity to fully appreciate the crimes which she has committed," the second surgeon said, "nor do I regard her as an entirely responsible person."[8]

On or near the same date that the surgeons examined Sarah Jane, six members of the military commission that had sentenced her also joined the campaign for clemency in her case. In a letter to Rosecrans, the officers asked that the general give "merciful consideration" to her case and mitigate her sentence "if consistent with the public justice." They believed Sarah Jane to be "an ignorant country woman entirely unaware of the enormity of the offense which she committed, willful and stubborn in her ignorance." Sarah Jane was alone and unrepresented at her trial, and they had sentenced her to death only because they felt, based on the scant evidence presented at the trial, there was no other course open to them. The dictates of General Halleck's 1861 special order prescribing the death sentence for anyone convicted of destroying telegraph wires had left the commission little choice.[9]

Responding to the pleas for mercy, General Rosecrans issued an order on November 17 commuting Sara Jane's sentence to confinement at the Alton Military Prison in Alton, Illinois, for the duration of the war. On November 25, she was transferred from Gratiot Street Prison across the Mississippi River to the Alton prison.[10]

Like a lot of prisoners closely confined in unsanitary Civil War prisons, Sarah Jane Smith became deathly ill after a few months at Alton. On March 31, 1865, James T. Cooper, assistant prison inspector, wrote a letter recommending a medical examination for Sarah Jane. "Since her confinement here," Cooper reported, "she has labored under a severe and protracted illness, and there is every indication that her disease is permanent and will result in her early or at least premature death." He said the young woman desired to take the oath of allegiance and be released and allowed within the Union lines for the duration of the rebellion. Cooper felt her removal from the prison would be an act of humanity that would "result in no evil for the country."[11]

Lieutenant-Colonel John H. Kuhn, commanding the military station at the prison, asked the prison's head surgeon, M. B. Cochran, to examine the prisoner. Major Cochran reported on April 3 that Sarah Jane "is subject to epilepsy, which is very severe, and in my opinion her mind is so impaired that she could do no probable injury to the Government and that a release is necessary to prevent her from becoming a troublesome charge." General Grenville Dodge, who had replaced Rosecrans in command of the Department of the Missouri, reviewed Sarah Jane's case on April 8 and directed that she be released on account of her health. The provost marshal general's office issued an order on April 12 directing that the prisoner be released, and Colonel Kuhn issued his own order the next day effecting Sarah Jane's release.[12]

The Rest of the Story

Sarah Jane was spared the death penalty, but for her the damage had already been done. She was released only because the illness she contracted had made her a "troublesome charge." No doubt the illness contributed to an early death, as prison inspector Cooper predicted, because Sarah Jane vanished entirely from the record after her release.

CHAPTER 22
Rebel Arms Supplier

Four months after the Fannie Houx case, another bushwhacker belle was arrested when her former slave turned against her. At Nancy Kemp's trial in early 1865, as in Fannie's case, the primary defense was to attack the witness on the basis of race. The strategy didn't work for Fannie Houx.

Would Nancy Kemp fare any better?

Sometime in the winter of 1862-1863, Lieutenant James McIntire of Company E, Sixty-seventh Enrolled Missouri Militia, was leading a scout through northeast Callaway County when he saw a black man running through an orchard on the property of Nancy Kemp. The soldiers overtook the man and interrogated him. His name was Henry, and he belonged to the Widow Kemp. (He might have been known as Henry Kemp, since slaves often took their owner's last name.) Nancy had sent him to warn some bushwhackers camped at a neighbor's house about Federal soldiers approaching. Henry led the soldiers to the neighbor's house. There McIntire captured three bushwhackers and also took the homeowner, Thomas Martin, and his son Nathan into custody.

Sometime in the summer of 1863, McIntire was again sent out on a scout trip to the Kemp home because of intelligence that Mrs. Kemp had stashed arms on her farm for guerrillas. The lieutenant found three shotguns and a rifle hidden in a stack of corn inside the barn, and he confiscated the weapons.[1]

Over a year later, Henry ran away from the Kemp farm and went to Wellsville in nearby Montgomery County. The Southern cause in Missouri was in disarray in the fall of 1864. General Price, to whom Southerners had looked for deliverance, had been driven from the state. Prospects for a Confederate victory were growing dim. In this atmosphere of turmoil, more and more slaves were leaving their owners.

At Wellsville, located about fifty miles east of Columbia, Henry began relating his former mistress's disloyal activities, and Union authorities started building a case against the forty-four-year-old Nancy Kemp.

Deposed on November 19, Henry said bushwhackers frequently camped about two hundred yards from Mrs. Kemp's house. She had supplied food and clothes to them on several occasions during 1863 and 1864. She sometimes ordered "her black woman" to cook for them, and sometimes compelled him to carry messages to bushwhackers concerning the whereabouts of Federal troops.[2]

On November 21, assistant provost marshal Isaac Garnett deposed Lieutenant McIntire at Mexico, seat of neighboring Audrain County. McIntire related the incident at the Kemp farm when he and his men had intercepted Henry running through the orchard. He also described the time he had seized the weapons hidden at the farm. When McIntire first arrived, Nancy Kemp denied there were any arms stashed on her place, but Henry took him to the barn where they were hidden. McIntire showed them to Mrs. Kemp, who "made no reply but turned away indifferently."[3]

Word of Mrs. Kemp's alleged misconduct reached St. Louis. Acting provost marshal general Joseph Darr, Jr. sent arrest orders to Mexico on November 25. Darr wanted any testimony about her. Lieutenant Garnett sent the evidence that had thus far been gathered, but Mrs. Kemp herself couldn't be found.[4]

On December 8, Lieutenant H. B. Sayre, who had replaced Garnett as assistant provost marshal at Mexico, detailed a sergeant to go out to Mrs. Kemp's residence and arrest her. But she was not found at home. He was having trouble promptly carrying out Darr's arrest order. Sayre passed along the order to the assistant provost marshal at Fulton, because the latter town was closer to Mrs. Kemp's residence than Mexico. On December 15, however, Mrs. Kemp came into Mexico on her own, and Sayre "was lucky enough to catch her here in town."[5]

Sayre took a statement from Mrs. Kemp on the day he arrested her. Here is what she said. Several Rebels, including Ammon Kemp, "a distant relative of mine," ate at her residence sometime the previous September or October, but she said she was in Fulton and not home at the time. She had made a Confederate uniform for her son, George W. Kemp, and he had left with Ammon Kemp. She also made some clothes for a Confederate soldier named Alonzo Garner the previous August and sent them to him in Indiana, where he was being held prisoner. She had otherwise never corresponded with any Confederate soldiers or officers. She had not seen her son since he left in September or October to join the Confederate Army. She concluded by saying she was a Southern woman. She wanted the South to win the war.[6]

On December 16, the day after she was arrested, Nancy was sent to St. Louis by rail and received at Gratiot Street Prison. Her trial on a charge of "disloyal practices" began on January 20, 1865, in St. Louis. One specification was that she had furnished Ammon Kemp and other "rebel enemies of the United States" with clothes and other provisions on or about August 5, 1864. The second specification was that she had concealed arms for guerrillas and warned them of the approach of Federal troops at various times during 1863 and 1864.

During the opening session of the trial, Nancy introduced attorney Peacock Cornwell as her counsel. She pleaded not guilty.[7]

Lieutenant McIntire, the first witness called by the prosecution, proved rather unconvincing. What did he know of Mrs. Kemp providing clothes and other supplies to Ammon Kemp and his guerrilla friends on or about August 5, 1864? He had seen the accused at her farm sometime in August or September of 1864—but could not be sure even of the month. He knew nothing personally about her furnishing supplies to guerrillas. He did know she had secreted weapons on her property sometime during 1863, but he couldn't say for sure the arms were for Rebels.[8]

After McIntire's testimony, the judge advocate asked for a continuance to procure other witnesses. The trial resumed on February 2. Nancy Kemp's former slave Henry stood as the next prosecution witness. Henry repeated the accusations he had leveled about Nancy regularly giving food, clothing, and information to Rebels. Much of his testimony centered on the arms she'd hidden on her property. Henry and Mrs. Kemp's son George had hidden the weapons in the barn after Mrs. Kemp told George to get them away from the house. Henry was sure she knew where they were hidden because she later saw him and George take the guns out of the corn stack and then put them back. When Lieutenant McIntire came to the farm shortly afterwards, the arms were still in the barn, and Mrs. Kemp denied there were any weapons at her place.[9]

On cross-examination, Cornwell got Henry to admit that Ammon Kemp's visits to the Nancy Kemp place were nothing more than "family visits" and that it was not unusual for travelers to stop at the Kemp place to eat. The attorney also tried to get Henry to admit that Nancy might have wanted the guns hidden to keep bushwhackers from stealing them. But Henry insisted she wanted them hidden so Federals could not get them.[10]

After the judge advocate announced that the prosecution case was closed, the defense read a deposition by Nancy's daughter Elizabeth Collins to the commission. Elizabeth, who had lived at her mother's residence the past two years, had no knowledge of her mother ever having furnished clothes or other provisions to Ammon Kemp or any other Rebels. The weapons hidden in the barn were four old shotguns and rifles that had been on the farm for some time. Elizabeth had hidden guns in the barn herself in 1862 to keep them out of the hands of bushwhackers, because guerrillas had previously called at the farm and demanded arms. She denied that her mother even knew the whereabouts of the weapons. She tried to implicate Henry by saying that he told the Federal soldiers, when they first found the weapons, that he didn't know anything about them.[11]

On February 4, the defense read its closing statement. Cornwell's main strategy, like that of Fannie Houx's lawyer, was to attack the prosecution's star witness on the basis of his race. Henry was "a negro, a slave formerly of defendant, belonging to a race steeped in ignorance and having no moral checks, whose race is noted for two prominent propensities, one stealing, the other lying." Further, Henry, by his own admission, had played a vital role in carrying out the crimes his former mistress was now charged with. Because of his own involvement in the crime and because of his race, Henry was not a fit or a convincing witness to testify against Nancy Kemp.[12]

The judge advocate rebutted Elizabeth Collins's deposition and the defense's closing statement. He pointed out that Elizabeth's admitted

General Grenville M. Dodge approved Nancy Kemp's sentence of imprisonment at the Missouri State Penitentiary for the duration of the war. (Courtesy of the Library of Congress.)

the time when this crime is alleged to have been committed." The implication? Even if Elizabeth were telling the truth about initially hiding the weapons herself, Nancy could easily have hidden them again later or ordered her son and Henry to do so. The defense's suggestion that Henry was an accomplice to the crime was nonsense; a person acting under coercion was a mere instrument of another and not an accomplice at all. Pointing to military law, the judge advocate added that, even if Henry were an accomplice, his involvement in the deed would not prevent him from being a valid witness.[13]

After a short deliberation, the verdict came back: guilty. Nancy was sentenced to prison for the duration of the war. General Grenville Dodge approved the finding and sentence on February 6 and directed that Nancy serve her sentence at the Missouri State Penitentiary.

She was committed to the Jefferson City facility shortly thereafter. As the Civil War wound down and Federal authorities emptied out their military prisons as a cost-cutting step, the state prison became overcrowded and even more inhospitable than normal. Fortunately for Nancy, her stay there was relatively brief. Lee surrendered to Grant on April 9, 1865, and Nancy was released on bond and oath ten days later.

Whether she ever saw Henry again is unknown. If she did, one can only imagine what she might have said to him. For a former slaveholder, being sent to prison on the word of a black man was a bitter pill to swallow.

The Rest of the Story

Nancy returned to Callaway County and was remarried there in May 1870 to George Thomas. In 1870, the couple lived in Callaway County with two of Nancy's daughters, Martha and Sarah, also in the household.

Ten years later, Nancy was a widow for the second time. She lived with Sarah and her husband in Callaway. She died in 1901 and is buried at Mount Carmel Cemetery in Fulton.[14]

Chapter 23
The Rebel Vixens of Chariton County

Forty-two-year-old Isabella Fox was arrested in Chariton County in January of 1865. She told local Union authorities that she was loyal and always had been. A few days later in St. Louis, she fine-tuned her statement, admitting that she had originally been a Southern sympathizer but had been loyal to the Union for the past year. As was the case with Mary Vaughn, considering the grief Mrs. Fox suffered at the hands of Union soldiers and citizens, the wonder is that she was not openly defiant in her Southern sympathies. Perhaps she feared banishment, but after examining her case, one might reasonably ask why she even cared.[1]

Several significant events led up to Isabella's supposed crime and trial.

In 1860, Isabella and her husband, fifty-year-old Peter, lived near Keytesville with five children in the household, including eighteen-year-old America and her thirteen-year-old sister, Melissa. Not long after, America married Giles Rice. When the war came on, Rice left home to join General Price's army in time for the Battle of Lexington. Claiming later that she had heard Rice was dead, America soon married or took up with Henry Jennings, who also had been a Southern soldier—while she was still married to Rice. When Rice returned home in 1863 very much alive, America remained the consort of Henry Jennings. Whether she and Rice ever officially divorced or she and Jennings ever officially married is not known.[2]

In early June 1864, guerrilla leader Clifton Holtzclaw raided Keytesville, a mile and a half west of the Fox home. A few days later, notorious Federal scout and detective Jacob W. Terman (alias Harry Truman) invaded the Keytesville area bent on revenge. Pretending to be Confederate guerrillas, the drunken Terman and his men plundered the neighborhood. Then they identified a number of active Southern supporters before announcing their true identity and purpose. Claiming Federal authority but acting beyond the scope of that authority, "Captain Truman," as Terman called himself, hanged a Southern sympathizer in front of a hotel in Keytesville on June 9. Then he dispatched squads into the surrounding countryside to kill or capture other Rebel sympathizers.

On June 10, four of Truman's so-called "scouts," led by a local Union man named Ephraim Clark, stopped at the Fox home and called for Henry Jennings and Peter Fox. They found Fox working in a nearby field, and Jennings emerged after rising from his sickbed in an upstairs room. The assassins took the two men to the woods behind the barn and opened fire on the unarmed pair. Hearing the shots, America Jennings ran to the scene in time to see her husband still alive and writhing speechless on the ground. Ephraim Clark stepped up and put another bullet through the dying man's head in America's presence.[3]

Later that day, Truman told America Jennings that he had ordered her husband's killing. He said Henry Jennings was a "mean man" who should have been killed long ago. He suggested that Giles Rice was somehow behind the killing, insinuating that Jennings had been killed because he had taken America as his wife while she was still married to Rice. Shortly after the murders Truman also spoke to her mother. He admitted ordering the death of Henry Jennings. He told Isabella he had not ordered the killing of her husband, Peter Fox. "My boys went a little over my orders here," he said.[4]

Both Isabella Fox and America Jennings testified against J. W. Terman at his trial by military commission at St. Joseph in July and August of 1864. At one point during the proceedings, Terman accused America of having left Giles Rice because he had joined the Union Army. America denied the charge. At least in this detail, she was telling the truth; Rice was a Southern soldier.

Terman was convicted of murder and other charges and sentenced to be hanged. But the punishment was immediately commuted to hard labor, and in early 1865 the prisoner was pardoned altogether and released.[5]

Upon Isabella Fox's return to Chariton County after she testified against Terman, her home became a stopping place for bushwhackers.

It was several months before her family's disloyal acts drew sufficient notice to stir Union officials to action. On January 9, 1865, Isabella and her daughter Melissa were finally arrested in Keytesville by US detective James Pickett on suspicion of harboring and aiding bushwhackers. They were transported to the Union post at nearby Brunswick. Federal officials began gathering evidence against them. America Huckshorn, a sister of Peter Fox, and her daughter Josephine were also arrested at the same time.[6]

Here are all the statements made against Isabella and Melissa.

On January 16, Catalina Dewey, a resident of Keytesville, swore out an affidavit. She had often seen Isabella's daughters riding about town with bushwhackers, "sometimes riding on the same horse with the Rebels and sometimes riding horses to themselves, going to and coming from Mrs. Huckshorn's."[7]

A week later, on January 23, Marilla Carman, another Keytesville resident, said she saw Isabella Fox riding out of town one time with bushwhackers. The general information around Keytesville was that the Fox family frequently harbored and fed bushwhackers.[8]

Also on the 23rd, D. B. Kellogg, a Keytesville merchant, said that not only did people believe the Fox family fed and clothed bushwhackers but he had even heard bushwhackers themselves say that such was the case. "There is no one in all the county who has a worse reputation than they have."[9]

On January 25, John S. Dewey, Chariton County public administrator and surveyor, stated that he knew Isabella Fox "to have the reputation of being a strong rebel, an aider, abettor & harborer of bushwhackers, of keeping a house of ill fame, of giving dances to bushwhackers & of being an inveterate hater of Union men, Federal soldiers & the Federal Government." Dewey didn't know Mrs. Fox's daughter Melissa well, but she had a reputation of being "a lewd woman" who was in sympathy with the rebellion. She gave aid and comfort to the bushwhackers. She even played the violin for their dances.[10]

Martha Hurt, yet another Keytesville resident, was deposed the same day as John Dewey. She saw Isabella Fox on the streets of the town in intimate association with bushwhackers during Price's raid. (General Sterling Price, who lived at Keytesville before the war, invaded Missouri on September 19, 1864, but he did not reach the Missouri River in the vicinity of Chariton County until mid-October. Guerrilla activity picked up throughout the summer and early fall of 1864. Mrs. Hurt's statement might have been a reference to partisan leader John Thrailkill's raid on Keytesville on September 20, 1864.) As evidence of the intimate relationship between Isabella Fox and the bushwhackers, Mrs. Hurt said she saw Isabella receiving gifts from them. She also knew Mrs. Fox to be a strong Southern sympathizer. She had the reputation of "keeping a house of ill fame" and "giving dances to Bushwhackers." Martha Hurt had heard Isabella Fox talk with great hatred for Union men and Federal soldiers.

Like John Dewey, Mrs. Hurt also gave a statement about Melissa Fox. She shared Dewey's opinion that Melissa was a lewd woman. She saw the young woman on the street with the bushwhackers the day they occupied Keytesville. Melissa went into stores and took out goods to give to the guerrillas, claiming the merchandise was contraband that was eligible to be seized by the Southerners. Martha also heard Melissa Fox say, when the bushwhackers first arrived, that she was glad to see them, that their time had come, and that "the abolitionists would have to go, for their time was out."[11]

The Fox women spoke for themselves on January 23.

Isabella Fox said the first time bushwhackers were ever at her house was the previous September when three of Holtzclaw's men ate breakfast. About a week later, seven or eight of the same gang came and ate supper. Then, near the middle of October, eight or nine of Jim Jackson's outfit, including the leader, came to her house. They stayed only about fifteen minutes. She "did not give him [Jackson] much encouragement" and he called her "a damned Radical." Those were the only instances that any guerrillas were at her house. However, five of them rode home from Mrs. Huckshorn's house with her and her daughter Melissa about the same time as Jackson's visit.

Isabella said she had never made clothing for the guerrillas or done anything disloyal, and she declared that she was loyal and always had been.[12]

Melissa Fox, gave a very similar statement to her mother's. The first time she ever saw any bushwhackers was about May 1864. They first came to the Fox home the following September. She mentioned specifically the two visits by Holtzclaw and the single visit by Jackson that Isabella had detailed. Holtzclaw's men had visited three or four times in total.

She had ridden through Keytesville on horseback behind a guerrilla named Samuel Coppidge.

She had made two shirts for two of Holtzclaw's men, for which she was paid twelve dollars, but she said this was all she had ever had to do with bushwhackers.

She was loyal and always had been loyal.[13]

On January 25, Isabella Fox and her daughter, along with America Huckshorn and her daughter, were sent to St. Louis and lodged in the Gratiot Street Prison. On January 28, both Isabella and Melissa gave additional statements to Federal authorities.[14]

Expanding on her earlier testimony, Isabella said that during the previous fall, when bushwhackers had visited her home a few times, the whole countryside around Keytesville swarmed with guerrillas. When Holtzclaw's men first came to her house and demanded breakfast, she told them the family scarcely had enough for itself. The men insisted, so she fed them because she feared they would steal her horses if she didn't. Holtzclaw's men had passed her house several times and stopped at her fence two or three times for water in addition to the two times she had fed them.

Clarifying the episode in which her daughter rode on horseback behind a bushwhacker, Mrs. Fox said it occurred the day Jim Jackson and his men had visited her house. The guerrillas had called in the morning and stayed only a few minutes. Later in the day, Isabella went to America Huckshorn's house, where Melissa was temporarily staying, to bring her daughter home. While she was at the Huckshorn residence, three of the same men who had stopped by her house that morning showed up at the Huckshorn house and escorted the two women home. Melissa rode behind one of the bushwhackers.

However, the guerrillas accompanied her and her daughter against her will. When the group reached the Fox home, she told them she was going to move away if she could not get rid of them.

Jim Jackson sent word to her that he wanted to have a dance at her house. She sent word back that she could not host such a dance.

In addition to the two shirts Melissa made for Holtzclaw's men, Isabella admitted that her daughter America had helped another woman make two shirts and two pairs of pants for some bushwhackers.

Isabella's husband was killed the previous June by some of Truman's men. He was "enrolled loyal." She herself had been loyal since she "got the light" about a year ago. Although she had once been a Southern sympathizer, she said, she now wished to see the South put down and the authority of the US government restored.[15]

Melissa Fox's January 28 testimony differed but little from her January 23 statement. She now recalled the first time Holtzclaw's men came to her mother's house was in August 1864 rather than September. She made the shirts for Holtzclaw's men because they told her, if she did so willingly, they would pay her—but if they had to force her, they would not pay one cent. This was the only time she had ever helped bushwhackers.

The three visits by Holtzclaw and the single visit by Jackson were the only times guerrillas had ever been at her mother's house. "I never associated or kept company with any person known by me to be a guerrilla," Melissa declared. Perhaps reminded by her examiner of the time she rode through Keytesville behind Samuel Coppidge, she explained that she did so because she feared he would "insult" her if she refused. She had never seen Coppidge prior to that day. She was with him for about two hours on that one occasion.

"I am not a Southern sympathizer, and I sincerely desire the Southern people put down in this war." In fact, she was engaged to William Coleman, a Union private in Company B of the Ninth Missouri State Militia Cavalry. She expected to be married as soon as she could get to Macon City (presumably where Coleman was then stationed).

She did not wish to be sent south, she wanted to take the oath to the Union, and she was willing to give bond if required.[16]

America and Josephine Huckshorn were released unconditionally on February 3 after the evidence in their cases showed they were of "undoubted loyalty." Isabella and Melissa were released on February 8 upon taking oaths of allegiance. America Huckshorn and her daughter were even provided with transportation home, but if Isabella and Melissa Fox were extended a similar courtesy, there is no record of the fact.[17]

A rogue Federal scout had killed Isabella's husband. Her Union neighbors had turned against her and besmirched her and her daughters' reputations. It is remarkable that she even wanted to return to Chariton County. But that's what she did.

And spent the rest of her life there.

Ties to home were incredibly strong for many of the bushwhacker belles.

The Rest of the Story

Melissa Fox's plan to marry William Coleman evidently fell through. She instead wed George Conrad in Chariton County in 1868. In 1870 the couple had a four-year-old boy named George and two one-year-old children in the household. (The older child was perhaps a son that either Melissa or her husband had prior to their marriage.)

Isabella Fox was living next door to George and Melissa in 1870, and America and three of her siblings were living with Isabella.

Ten years later, George and Melissa Conrad still lived in Chariton County, as did Isabella Fox, but Melissa's sister America disappeared by 1880.

In a tragic ending, Isabella and her daughter Melissa died of pneumonia in December 1887, within nine days of each other. Both are buried in Varner Cemetery about three miles east of Keytesville.[18]

Chapter 24
Convicted by Her Own Admission

The large majority of women taken into custody for helping Missouri bushwhackers during the Civil War were arrested at least partly on the testimony of their neighbors, of other civilian witnesses, or of Federal soldiers. Not so in the case of twenty-nine-year-old Montgomery County resident Mary E. Bowles. She was arrested in late December of 1864 and banished solely on the basis of what she told Union officials when she was called as a witness in another person's case.

In late fall 1864, Mary's father, David Bowles, under suspicion for his outspoken Southern sympathies, left home to escape Union persecution. Because of the alleged disloyalty of David and his wife, Julia, Federal authorities confiscated much of their property. The sixty-year-old Bowles also faced an unlikely charge of bushwhacking.[1]

On December 28, Union detective Timothy Cummins served Mary Bowles with a summons to testify in her father's case at the headquarters of the Fourth Sub-District of North Missouri in Troy in neighboring Lincoln County. The next day, Cummins, who also served as a justice of the peace, took a sworn statement from Mary before escorting her to Troy, fifty-five miles northwest of St. Louis.

Mary told Cummins that her father left home the previous fall and rendezvoused with some Southern men under the leadership of Colonel Caleb Dorsey in the Cap Au Gris neighborhood of eastern Lincoln County. He did so only for protection. He came back home twice. He stayed six days the first time and two days the second time. He left for good about the end of October. Mary carried victuals to her father while he was with Dorsey, who was recruiting for the Confederate Army. She also took food to her brothers, the first time about two years ago, when they were camped near their home as Southern partisans. Southern soldiers stayed at the Bowles residence on several occasions since the war erupted.[2]

On December 31, Cummins delivered Miss Bowles to Troy, where assistant provost marshal A. C. Marsh promptly conducted his own interview with the witness. Here is what Mary said.

She lived in the Middletown vicinity of Montgomery County and was twenty-seven years old. (She was at least twenty-nine.) She had three brothers who were or had been in the Confederate Army. She had often fed her brothers, her father, and their friends when they were camped in her neighborhood. Indeed, she had fed Southern men several times since October 1. She considered her brothers, their comrades, and all the other men she fed to be Confederate soldiers, not bushwhackers—a distinction more important to Mary than to her Union accusers.[3]

Based on her own admissions, Mary was charged with giving aid and comfort to bushwhackers. On January 2, 1865, she was sent under guard from Troy to the District of North Missouri headquarters at Macon. On January 4, she had to travel yet again—this time to St. Louis, where she was committed to Gratiot Street Female Prison for "safe keeping." A little over a month later, the provost marshal's office issued an order to parole Miss Bowles upon her oath and send her out of the department. She was released on February 8 and sent to Illinois, the usual place of exile for the Missouri belles who were not shipped south.[4]

About the time Mary was banished from Missouri, her parents' property was put up for public auction because of their alleged disloyalty. Then in late April 1865, David Bowles was captured in Miller County, south of the Missouri River, in company with a squad of guerrillas. He was taken at first to Jefferson City, where he gave a statement on May 5th, and then on to St. Louis, where he was again interviewed on May 11th.

He had gone to Dorsey's camp for protection from some Union home guards, or local militia, who had threatened his life. He went south to Arkansas with Dorsey only to try to coax his sons out of the Confederate Army. (This statement conflicts with other evidence, which suggests that at least one or two of Bowles's sons were also with Dorsey. However, it's possible Bowles had more than two sons in the service at this time, because he had several grown sons.)

Bowles had previously been a Southern sympathizer, but he

now wanted to get his sons discharged because he had become "convinced of the rottenness of the Southern Confederacy." It was too late. Sadly, Bowles learned one of his sons had been wounded and later died. He was unable to get his other son released from the army. Returning to Missouri, he fell in with a band of partisans. They advised him to travel with them for protection. In Miller County, the guerrillas were attacked. Bowles, who did not try to escape, was taken prisoner.[5]

About the time David Bowles was brought to St. Louis, his daughter's case was close to a final resolution, thanks in part to a sympathetic Union officer. Sometime in early May, Thomas Thomas, captain of a Federal militia company, wrote an undated letter to Colonel James H. Baker, provost marshal general of the department. The war had ended a month earlier. Thomas wanted the order banishing Mary Bowles modified to allow her to reside in St. Louis County. About May 21, Baker revoked the order sending Miss Bowles beyond the Department of the Missouri and allowed her to return to St. Louis County. Shortly afterwards, she was presumably released from all obligations of her parole. Although no record of an order to that effect appears to survive, Mary returned home soon after the war.

Mary's father, David Bowles, was released on oath from Gratiot Street Prison on June 7, 1865, and joined her in Montgomery County.[6]

It had been a difficult time for Mary and her father. One of Mary's brothers died serving the Confederacy. David failed in his attempt to get another son out of the service. Mary was arrested, thrown in prison, and banished from Missouri solely on statements she gave in her father's case. Then, to top things off, David was also arrested and jailed as a Rebel sympathizer—even though his loyalties had turned against the South.

The Rest of the Story

During the years immediately after the war, David Bowles filed several successful lawsuits that enabled him to retrieve some of the animals and other property that had been taken from him during the war. His wife, Julia, died shortly after the war. He remarried a widow named Ann Giles.

By 1870, the blended family was living in Jefferson County, but Mary was absent from the household and her whereabouts is unknown.

The following year, however, she was married in Montgomery County to Joshua T. Parrish. Parrish died in 1910 in Lincoln County, seemingly having lived his whole life in Missouri.

What happened to Mary after the wedding has not been ascertained.[7]

CHAPTER 25
The Ordeal of Tabitha Rider

When Tabitha Winkler, barely fifteen, wed twenty-four-year-old Jim Rider on October 2, 1860, she probably never dreamed that her wedding would one day land her in a Union jail, but that's what happened. A little over four years after their wedding, Tabitha was arrested merely for being Jim Rider's wife. "Rider," as she called him, was a murderer, robber, and bushwhacker who shotgunned her stepfather.[1]

The young girl and her new husband, nine years her senior, wed in Livingston County, Missouri. Immediately after their marriage, the newlyweds went to live with Tabitha's aunt Margaret Snead about nine or ten miles south of Chillicothe. They remained there only two or three weeks before going to neighboring Caldwell County to live. The nomadic couple moved at least two more times before the spring of 1861.

When the Civil War erupted. Tabitha's husband "went off and left (her)," as she later testified. He signed up with the Missouri State Guard to fight for the Southern cause. Tabitha went back to stay with her aunt Margaret.[2]

Jim Rider quickly became notorious. After a brief stint with the regular army, he returned to his old haunts in north central Missouri and took to the brush. His mission? Recruit for the Missouri State Guard (and later the Confederacy). Like most Missouri guerrilla leaders, he bore some official authority for such a mission. Also like most partisan leaders in Missouri, he used the recruiting assignment as an opportunity to take up bushwhacking.[3]

There is some truth to the argument that the Missouri partisans were forced to resort to plunder in order to sustain themselves in enemy territory, but it can hardly be denied that many of the recruiting officers enjoyed bushwhacking more than recruiting. Certainly, that seems to be true in Jim Rider's case.

One of Rider's more notorious acts was the murder of his wife's stepfather, forty-seven-year-old Michael West. It happened in the rear lot of a Breckenridge store on the morning of July 9, 1861. Several witnesses testified they heard one or two shotgun blasts. They looked up to see Rider standing over West, holding a double-barrel shotgun in one hand and firing a revolver at the fallen man with the other hand. Tabitha's father was dead. Her mother, Millie (Farnel) Winkler, had married West in December 1859. Bad blood must have existed between Rider and West, because it's unlikely a chance encounter on the street would have escalated to deadly violence. It's hard to tell if Tabitha's relationship with her stepfather and/or her husband was in any way related to the feud.[4]

Sometime in the spring of 1864, Tabitha received a letter from Lucinda Rider, a relative, asking her to come to Saline County. According to Tabitha, Lucinda was Jim Rider's cousin and Lucinda's father, George Rider, was Jim's uncle. But considerable evidence suggests instead that George was Jim's father and Lucinda his sister. Tabitha's depiction of their kinship was likely a mere ruse concocted by Jim Rider to deflect Union suspicion away from his family. Regardless, Tabitha answered Lucinda's summons and reunited with her husband in Saline County. Tabitha later said it had been two years since she had seen "Rider," but she also implied that it was the first time she had seen him since the outset of the war. So, the couple's separation might have been longer than two years.[5]

Tabitha lingered awhile in Saline County with the George Rider family. She started back to Livingston County in the summer of 1864. After crossing the Missouri River, she stopped on a Sunday in Chariton County at the home of a longtime acquaintance named Robert Shannon. Tabitha meant to rest at Shannon's home for a day or two and then ask him to escort her the rest of the way to her mother's home near Chillicothe. On Tuesday, however, her husband showed up and told Tabitha "it would not do" for her to go home. Rider sent her to stay with George Cobb, about ten miles away. Meanwhile, Shannon reported Tabitha Rider's visit to his house to Colonel William Moberly, commanding the local Enrolled Missouri Militia unit at Brunswick.[6]

Tabitha stayed with Cobb about a week. Rider visited her twice.

She returned to Saline County to help George Rider's wife, Evaline, with some sewing.

After a few days, she was shuffled off to a Beatty family. She found her husband there. She remained with the Beattys only a few days before Mrs. Beatty "got afraid to have (her) stay," because she was the wife of the infamous Jim Rider. Mrs. Beatty took her back to Chariton County and left her at Brunswick. Tabitha made her way once again to George Cobb's house five or six miles from town. Rider met her at Cobb's that day. He took her to John Craig's house about nine miles away.[7]

Tabitha remained at the Craig home about a month, and her husband dropped in to see her six or eight times during her stay. One day Rider came and whisked her away to the home of Samuel Elliott a mile and a half distant. Her husband visited her often at the Elliott place, and her stay there stretched to two months, no doubt taking on a sense of permanence to the much-traveled Tabitha. Then Rider showed up and ferried her back across the river to stay with his uncle (or father) in Saline County. After only a week at the George Rider place, she moved once again, this time to the home of a Mrs. Mullins about four miles away. After another week, two of Rider's men came and took Tabitha to the nearby home of a widow lady named Garrett. Mrs. Garrett kept Tabitha about a week before she, like Mrs. Beatty, grew afraid to let the bushwhacker's wife stay any longer. Rider moved her to the house of another woman named Hays, who kept her three or four weeks. Next, Tabitha went back to the home of Mrs. Mullins, who boarded the young woman another week.[8]

Tabitha tired of being shuffled back and forth among Southern-sympathizing residents. She wanted to go home.

She spent one night at the home of John Rider (Lucinda's older brother) and one night at the home of a Mr. Irwin. Her husband came and told her it still wouldn't do for her to go home. Instead, he took her to a widow named Hall, with whom she stayed about a month. While there, Tabitha continued to ask her husband to let her go home, but he refused.[9]

Showing up at the Hall residence one night, Rider took his wife under cover of darkness back across the river to Chariton County and left her at the Samuel Hibler place.

There, Tabitha went by the name "Mrs. James," presumably at Rider's suggestion. She probably adopted the same or a similar alias at other times during the summer and fall of 1864 as her husband shuffled her from one hiding place to another. Tabitha wearied of the life of a fugitive. While at the Hibler home, according to her own later story, she decided to leave and divorce Rider "because he was a bushwhacker." She continually expressed a desire to go home. Mrs. Hibler, no doubt following Rider's directive, wouldn't let her go. Rider himself showed up once or twice to reinforce the decree.

Around the first part of January 1865, Tabitha moved to Sam Hibler's mother's house. She stayed there only part of one night before Rider came with his guerrilla band and finally told his wife she could go home.[10]

Prior to letting her go, though, Rider, with his men, took her back across the river into Saline County and deposited her at the home of a man named George (probably James J. George). Rider left and showed back up the next night. Tabitha, exasperated, told her husband "to go off and let (her) alone."

He left. The next day Tabitha started home. She arrived soon afterwards at her mother's house about six miles from Chillicothe.[11]

After a few days at her mother's home, Tabitha came into Chillicothe on or about January 26, 1865. She would finally file for a divorce. Before she could complete the paperwork, she was arrested by detective Robert Harrison.

He took her to Lieutenant Colonel J. H. Shanklin, commanding the sub-district of Chillicothe. Tabitha admitted she had been with Jim Rider off and on for about six to eight months during the previous summer and fall. She gave the names and residences of many residents who had harbored her and her husband. She also gave the names of some of the men in Rider's band of guerrillas. When she first left home in the late spring of 1864 to meet Rider, she did not believe he was guilty of all the outrages that had been charged against him. But now she was convinced that he was "a regular bushwhacker and robber."[12]

Tabitha was anxious that she might be banished to the South. She "did not wish to go there," as she "had not a friend or acquaintance there." Harrison assured her that, if she fully cooperated with Union

General Clinton B. Fisk, who recommended Tabitha Rider's banishment from Missouri. Clinton B. Fisk, #12357, in the collection of Wilson's Creek National Battlefield. (Courtesy of the National Park Service.)

Tabitha had $120 in greenbacks, a gold watch, a gold locket, and a breast pin at her mother's home. All of this was booty Rider had taken during one of his raids. He gave it to her the previous fall. Rider had originally told her that a doctor or a preacher had given the money and items to him. Harrison and another man escorted Tabitha back to her mother's house, where she gave the loot to Harrison, who said he would turn it over to Captain H. J. Herrick, the local assistant provost marshal.[13]

Tabitha cooperated fully. Despite this, she was banished.

On January 28, Colonel Shanklin reported Tabitha's capture to Brigadier General Clinton B. Fisk, commanding the District of North Missouri. Fisk recommended that she be sent out of the state. "The presence of such," he declared, "only induces the stay of devils like Rider."[14]

The order of banishment was issued shortly afterwards. The news reached Chillicothe. On February 8, Howard S. Harbaugh, editor of the *Chillicothe Constitution*, wrote to General Fisk protesting the order. He pointed out that Tabitha Rider had given valuable information about the guerrillas and had also identified several residents who claimed to be Union men but who were really Rebels. Tabitha had cooperated because Harrison and the jailer, a man named Reed, had told her that she had a choice of either doing so or being sent south. If she informed on her friends, she would be shown clemency, they implied. If Tabitha were banished, it would "forever preclude using her for a useful purpose, but if detained, much good might be accomplished and the woman possibly reclaimed to loyalty herself." Tabitha could make the government quite a bit of money. One of the men she had identified as a Southern sympathizer was worth at least $20,000—money bound to be confiscated.[15]

The banishment order was suspended on February 20. Shortly afterwards it was reinstated with instructions that Tabitha be sent to St. Louis to be shipped out of Missouri.

Tabitha gave a brief statement in Chillicothe on March 2 admitting that she had been with Jim Rider during the previous summer, fall, and early winter. The affidavit was added to her file as evidence against her. The next day, Tabitha was sent to St. Louis, and she was jailed on March 4 at the Gratiot Street Female Prison. She spent the next two months being shuffled back and forth between the prison and the provost marshal's office, where she gave several more statements.[16]

Tabitha gave her most extensive statement on March 9, when she chronicled all of her movements during the time she spent with her bushwhacker husband the previous year. "I never gave Rider or any of his gang any information. I am a loyal woman and opposed to bushwhacking. Have always talked against it."[17]

In mid-March a question arose concerning the money and items Tabitha said she had given to Detective Harrison. Apparently Harrison never turned over the loot to Captain Herrick. The investigation focused initially on the question of whether Tabitha had

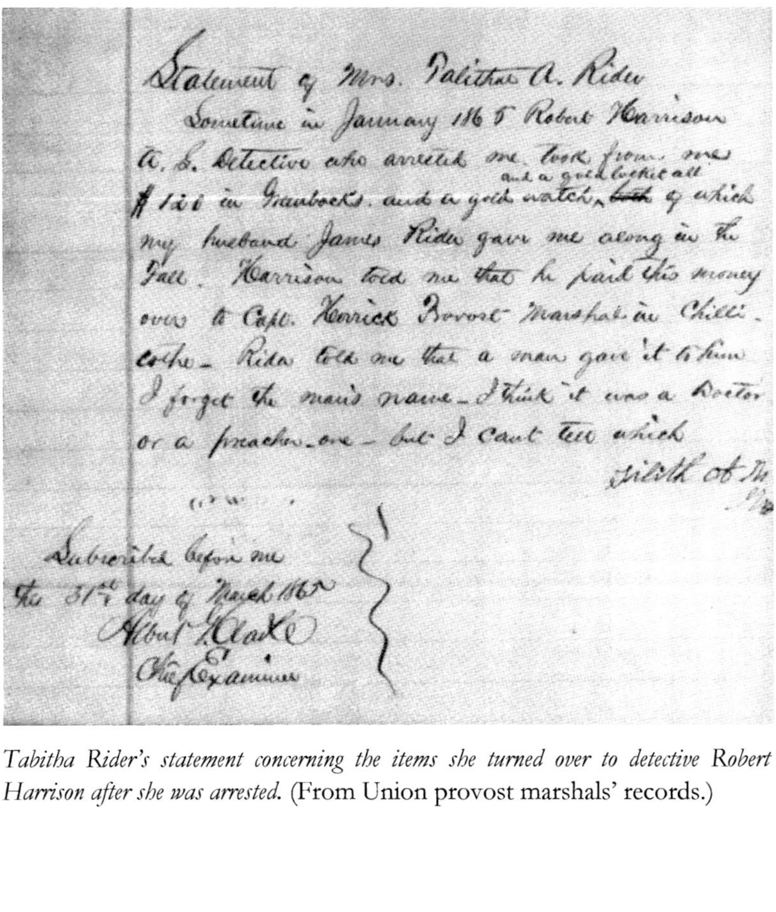

Statement of Mrs. Tabitha A. Rider

Sometime in January 1865 Robert Harrison U. S. Detective who arrested me took from me $120 in Greenbacks. and a gold watch, and a gold locket all of which my husband James Rider gave me along in the Fall. Harrison told me that he paid this money over to Capt. Herrick Provost Marshal in Chillicothe - Rider told me that a man gave it to him I forget the man's name - I think it was a Doctor or a preacher - one - but I can't tell which

Tabitha A. Rider

Subscribed before me the 31st day of March 1865
Albert Clarke
Chief Examiner

Tabitha Rider's statement concerning the items she turned over to detective Robert Harrison after she was arrested. (From Union provost marshals' records.)

tried to bribe Harrison. Both Tabitha and Harrison were summoned to the provost marshal's office on the 16th. Tabitha emphasized that she handed the money and jewelry over to Harrison freely and never offered him a bribe of any kind. Harrison mentioned the booty only in passing, saying that Tabitha had told him Rider gave her $120 in greenbacks and some jewelry after one of his raids.[18]

By the end of the month, the focus of the investigation shifted to Harrison. On March 31, Tabitha was called back to the provost marshal's office to give another statement about the greenbacks and jewelry. She made no mention of the possibility of a bribe. She merely reiterated the fact that she had given the valuables to Harrison. She added that he had told her he would hand the items over to Herrick and later assured her that he had done so.

Whether Harrison faced disciplinary action pertaining to the whereabouts of Tabitha's money and jewelry is not known.[19]

What is known for sure is that, despite having cooperated fully with Union authorities, Tabitha Rider was shipped south on April 30.

During the past year, Tabitha had been moved from one Confederate sympathizer to another—at least nineteen times. After her arrest, Union authorities shipped her to St. Louis and put her in prison. There she was shuffled back and forth to the provost marshal's office—and finally exiled from Missouri.

She only ever wanted to be home.

Tabitha wasn't a bushwhacker belle in that she supported guerrillas. She was just caught up by the tide of their movements and shifted around the state. She must have been exhausted.

The Rest of the Story

After the war, Tabitha came back to Missouri. She remarried in 1868 in Livingston County to Sebron Sneed and started a new family. In 1880, she and Sneed lived in neighboring Daviess County and had seven kids, three of whom were Tabitha's biological children.

What happened to the desperado Jim Rider is unclear. He might have been killed near the end of the war, since there is no post-war record of him and no record that Tabitha ever obtained the divorce she wanted.[20]

Chapter 26
Who Were These Women?

Who were the bushwhacker belles?

Were their actions generally coerced or purposeful? This remains a subject of some debate. And if their actions were not coerced, what motivated them? The answer to the latter question is even less settled than the answer to the former. In an effort to shed light on these issues, let us first examine what else we know about the women who helped Missouri guerrillas.

They had Southern ties.

A cursory study of census records reveals that most of the young men who became Missouri guerrillas were either born in the upper tier of Southern states, such as Kentucky, Tennessee, and Virginia, or else they were born in Missouri to parents who had migrated from the upper South.

The same can be said about most of the women who aided the Missouri guerrillas during the Civil War, as the stories chronicled in the previous chapters show. Even some of the women profiled here who were exceptions to the general rule still had ties to the South. Lurena McCoy was born in Ohio, but her father was born in Virginia. She lived in Virginia herself a few years before coming to Missouri when she was seven years old. Born in New York and reared in Canada, Imogene Jordan Brumfield was one of the few clear-cut exceptions to the rule, but she fell in love with and married a bushwhacker.

So, it is safe to say that most of the guerrillas and their female supporters had historic family ties to the South and identified with Southern culture.

They had relatives fighting for the South.

Their ties to the South were not just historic but also immediate.

Nearly all of them had brothers, husbands, or other family members in the Confederate Army or in the brush. Most had more than one relative fighting for the South. Exceptions were rare.

They were young.

The majority of the bushwhacker belles were young, most in their late teens or early twenties. Occasionally an older woman was arrested, but this usually happened only when the woman had one or more daughters who were arrested at the same time, as in the case of fifty-six-year-old Eliza Spencer. Occasionally a woman in her late twenties or early thirties was arrested, as in the case of Fannie Houx. Sometimes a girl only fourteen or fifteen years old was arrested, but this rarely happened unless a mother or older sister was arrested at the same time, as in the case of Nancy Longacre and her fourteen-year-old daughter, Martha.

In short, most of the females arrested for helping guerrillas were at that stage of life when young people often assert their independence and relish adventure. And fall in love.[1]

They were well connected.

Like the Missouri guerillas themselves, the women who aided them tended to come from stable and well-established families, if not well-to-do families. Some came from families who were politically prominent, at least at the county level. Fannie's Houx's brother was the sheriff of Lafayette County. Sue Bryant's father was the prosecuting attorney of Saline County. Others came from families that, although less prominent, had lived in Missouri for many years prior to the Civil War and were well known in their communities. Nancy Longacre's husband, Benjamin, who died before the war, was the first postmaster of Bluff Springs (forerunner to Kingsville).

Not only did many of the female associates of the guerrillas come from families that had been in Missouri for many years, the majority returned to or stayed in the state after the war. These were women who, for the most part, had strong and enduring ties to their families and communities.

They were ladies.

Union citizens and soldiers often spoke in very derogatory terms of the women who helped guerrillas, sometimes dismissing them as poor, unschooled savages. One observer described them as "ignorant and entirely uneducated" and "entirely controlled by passion." The truth is that many, if not most, of the bushwhacker belles were well educated for their time. Letters they wrote reflected intelligence and emotion. Most considered themselves ladies, and some even prided themselves on their learning. Recall Julia Martin's postscript at the end of her quite literate letter to her friend Sena Bell that she feared it had been poorly written.[2]

They lived in nontraditional households.

The large majority of the women arrested for helping bushwhackers did not have a male head of household at home at the time of their arrest. So, in a literal sense, the women did come from "disorderly" households, as scholars Bynum and Beilein, mentioned in this book's preface, have called them. The families did not conform to the normal order. The corollary, that women with husbands or fathers at home were rarely arrested for disloyal activities, raises an interesting question. Did the women from disordered households, unmoored from social and family restraint, suddenly start engaging in activities—aiding bushwhackers—that they previously would have taken no part in? Or is it more likely they only became targets of Union scrutiny in the absence of a male head of household?

The answer is fairly obvious. Men were seen as the representatives of their households in public dealings, and it was up to the men to control their women. If a man's wife or daughter was suspected of feeding bushwhackers, the man was assumed to have authorized the activity. He was the one who paid the consequences. So, the primary reason that very few women from orderly households were arrested for disloyal activity was not necessarily because they didn't engage in such activity. More likely, it was because their husbands or fathers were there to shield them and to be arrested in their stead, if need be.

It is important to note that a huge number of Southern-sympathizing men in Missouri were away from home fighting for the Rebel cause during the Civil War. In fact, the war so disrupted family life that there were almost certainly more homes where the father or husband was absent than where he was present, at least among

Southern sympathizers. Yet prison rolls show that at least as many male civilians as female civilians were sent to St. Louis prisons for disloyal activity during the war. Missouri's guerrillas were sustained not just by women from disorderly households but also by men and their female family members from orderly households.[3]

They were called prostitutes.

Beilein, in particular, has sought to show that many, maybe most, of the women who were arrested for aiding bushwhackers in Missouri came from households that were not only "disorderly" in a literal sense but also in the sexual sense that the term was often used during the nineteenth century, when a "disorderly house" implied a house of ill fame or prostitution. The theory is that the bushwhackers were sustained primarily by these houses of ill repute and were drawn to them precisely because of the women's loose morality.

Indeed, Union authorities sometimes accused the bushwhacker belles of being prostitutes or maintaining houses of ill repute. Notably the Little sisters, the Spencer sisters, and most of other women arrested with them were accused of being base prostitutes. The Bond sisters were considered "loose characters" and "very bad women." Isabella Fox was thought to keep a house of ill fame, and her daughter Melissa was called a "very lewd woman." However, such accusations were not as widespread as one might suspect from reading the post-war proclamations of authors like the 1891 correspondent to the St. Louis newspaper who asserted that many of the guerrilla women were ready to toss their honor into the scale and do the "deed of shame" merely to gain a bit of information from the enemy. During the war, Union observers routinely characterized the women who helped guerrillas as "bitter rebels," but they did not usually assail their morality.

Even when Union officials accused the bushwhacker belles of being prostitutes, they sometimes did so on mere hearsay. Certainly it's possible Martha Watson from this book's introduction might have been a prostitute. She might have also given her young daughters over to prostitution, as Major Thacher said in early September of 1863. A more likely explanation was that Union soldiers or citizens became exasperated by the females' support of bushwhackers and the rumor that Mrs. Watson's son had been with Quantrill. They may have impugned the women's morality as a way of lashing out at them.

And even when evidence of a woman's alleged prostitution other than mere rumor was offered, the evidence was often flimsy. One of the primary proofs offered by witnesses to sustain their allegations against Isabella Fox of running a house of ill fame was that she had let the guerrillas have a dance at her home. The character of Isabella's daughter was attacked mainly because she had been seen riding on horseback behind a guerrilla. During the Victorian Age, such "unladylike" behavior could get a woman labeled a prostitute. The simple fact of men calling at a home where no male head of household was present was cause for suspicion.

Mary Cull was one of the few female abettors of the Missouri guerrillas, perhaps the only one, who definitely engaged in sexual intercourse outside marriage. However, even she was likely not promiscuous. She became pregnant by Frank Parker while the couple was engaged in 1862, but when she was interviewed two years later, she said she would not marry him now. He had ruined her and had become a "bad man." Although Mary's statement—like those of all the other women who were deposed after their arrests—should be taken with a bit of skepticism, it suggests she did not take premarital sex lightly.

Certainly women did operate as prostitutes in Missouri during the Civil War. But most of them were concentrated in towns like St. Louis and Kansas City, where large bodies of Union troops were stationed. Perhaps a few camp followers trailed Price's army during his 1864 invasion of Missouri or hung out at Springfield when Southern forces occupied that town early in the war. That said, few women, if any, whom we would consider prostitutes today operated in the backwoods of Missouri, providing sexual favors to bushwhackers—or plying Federals with sex to gain information, for that matter. Southern women gave food and shelter to the guerrillas. Bushwhackers sometimes gave them gifts such as jewelry that they had taken during their robberies.

However, it is a leap to conclude that the gifts were in exchange for sex.

In rare instances, this might have been the case, but most of the women who helped the guerrillas would have engaged in premarital sex, like Mary Cull, only with the expectation of marriage, if they would have done so at all. As I've suggested already, most of the young women who helped the guerrillas considered themselves ladies and usually tried to behave as such, despite the great social upheaval of the Civil War. In this regard, they were little different from other young women of the time.

Their fates hinged on factors beyond guilt or innocence.

Beauty, social standing, and charm could help bushwhacker belles facing Union charges. Physical attractiveness could influence not only their treatment when first arrested but also the ultimate disposition of their cases. As we saw in Mollie Goggin's case, she was treated with solicitous attention by almost every Federal officer she encountered, and she eventually had her sentence commuted at the request of officials from her prison.

Also, women from influential families tended to fare better than those from less prominent households. Fannie Houx, convicted on fairly serious charges and sentenced to long imprisonment, spent very little time in confinement, mainly because of the political influence of her brothers. The Little sisters were released upon taking oaths while the women arrested with them were banished from the state, partly because the Littles had the benefit of attorneys and other prominent citizens lobbying on their behalf.

A third extraneous factor that could affect the outcome of the women's cases was how congenial and charming they were in their relations with Federal soldiers. Those who behaved in the "ladylike" manner expected of women sometimes won enough sympathy among their captors to get their sentences mitigated. It was not just Mollie Goggin's beauty that got her released but also her congeniality.

Presumably Mollie Goggin was far from the only young woman arrested for helping Missouri guerrillas who knew how to beguile men, but not all were as ready as Mollie to favor Federal soldiers with their charms. Many were defiant when first taken into custody and brazenly admitted their offenses to the arresting officer. As a *Carthage Weekly Banner* correspondent observed after the war, Southern women of Missouri were more outspoken than men in their dealings with Union soldiers. They felt freer to speak their minds; they knew their sacrosanct status as women would protect them. It usually did.

However, by the time they got to district headquarters or to St. Louis, most retreated into submissive womanhood to lessen the judgment against them. In other words, even those who were not ladylike and congenial at first often became so once they realized their dire circumstances. Recall that Sallie Mayfield's speech, when she first arrived at Leavenworth, was "strongly tinctured with disloyalty," but by the time she reached St. Louis, she displayed a complaisance that belies her post-war image as a defiant Rebel. She claimed she did not even sympathize with the South.

Their punishments varied.

Certainly Union authorities recognized that some of the women were guiltier than others, as the final disposition of their cases clearly shows. Some, like America Huckshorn and her daughter, were released unconditionally after their loyalty was established. Others, whose loyalty remained in doubt, were released to go home upon taking an oath of allegiance. Still others had to give bond in addition to taking an oath. A few, like Nancy Longacre, were found not guilty after their cases came to trial.

For women deemed guilty by Union authorities of aiding bushwhackers—but whose cases stopped short of trial—the most common punishment was banishment from the state. During the middle part of the war, exile to the South for such offenders was fairly common. Many Confederate-sympathizing Missouri women were also sent south at their own request during this time. By mid-1864, the northern states east of the Mississippi River, particularly Illinois, had become a more likely banishment destination for women whom the commanding general judged guilty of aiding guerrillas.

Those tried and found guilty by military commission were usually confined to St. Louis area military prisons for the duration of the war. In only a few extreme instances, when charges beyond simply feeding or harboring guerrillas were involved, did the women receive even harsher punishments. The sentence of ten years in prison Annie Fickle received and the death sentence pronounced on Sarah

Jane Smith both come to mind.[4]

They argued for survival.

When bushwhacker belles were arrested, many adopted more "ladylike" charms to survive. To mitigate the charges against them and lessen their ultimate punishment, they also employed a number of what Fellman has called "survival lies." The stories they told might be more accurately described as *survival arguments*, because the statements were not always lies.

Survival argument: They didn't do it.

Some denied the charges against them from the very beginning. They said there must have been some mistake or claimed they were arrested because a neighbor accused them out of spite. Recall that the Bond sisters, who said they had always been Union sympathizers, blamed their arrest on a personal grudge that Hannah Jenkins held.

It's very likely that some of the women who denied their involvement in aiding bushwhackers were indeed innocent of the charges. It is also true that some of the accusers against them were dubious witnesses whose testimony was at least partly an effort to deflect suspicion away from themselves. Such was the case of Lydia Taylor swearing against the Vaughns. Even Union officials knew women were sometimes arrested on "base rumor and vague suspicions," as judge advocate Major Lucien Eaton observed in the case of the Kincheloe sisters.

Survival argument: They defined bushwhacking differently.

One of the main reasons many of the women arrested for supporting bushwhackers denied the charges against them was that they claimed the men they helped were not bushwhackers but rather regular Confederate soldiers. Southern-sympathizers in Missouri had a different understanding of the concept of "regular Confederate soldier" than did Union authorities. Most of the guerrilla leaders in the state held commissions from the Confederate Army as recruiting officers. This was true of Joe Hart, the guerrilla leader whom Lou McCoy helped. Missouri's partisan leaders did not usually wear Southern uniforms, because to do so behind Union lines would have been suicidal, and their bands of men had usually not been sworn into regular Confederate service. However, most of the leaders did hold some authority from the Confederate Army. Thus, Sue Bryant said, after her arrest, that she knew only one or two guerrillas and had never helped them but that she had helped and would continue to help Confederate soldiers.

The distinction was lost on Union authorities during the war. They considered anyone not part of an organized army and not wearing a uniform a guerrilla.

The distinction between partisan leaders who held Confederate authority and those without such authority has also not generally been recognized or given enough weight in scholarly discussion. Fellman's *Inside War*, for instance, offers many penetrating insights into the psychology of the guerrilla conflict in Missouri, but a few of the author's observations are flawed by his incorrect conclusion that the guerrilla leaders did not hold Confederate commissions—and were proud of their outlaw or near-outlaw status.

To the contrary, most of the guerrilla leaders were not outlaws—at least not in their own eyes. And not in the eyes of their civilian supporters. Not all of the bushwhacker belles would have gone as far as Lizzie DeWitt when she said she did not consider Quantrill's men guerrillas. Almost all, though, had a looser definition of "regular Confederate soldier" than Union authorities.

So, when they denied helping bushwhackers, even when Union officials knew the charges to be true, the women were not necessarily lying but might simply have been having a battle over semantics with their interrogators.

Survival argument: They were mistreated.

Some of the women who were defiant at the time of their arrest justified such behavior by saying they had merely responded to unwarranted insults from Federal soldiers. Jane Ward, when asked about a particular instance when she had become insolent toward Union soldiers, said she did so only because they were cursing her younger brother. She rationalized her cheekiness by explaining, "The Federal soldiers abuse me and, of course, I abuse them." Mary Spencer boldly told Union soldiers that she fed bushwhackers, but she claimed she only said so as an angry response to the accusing soldiers' nastiness.

It is not unlikely that, in some instances, the female abettors of the guerrillas did become sassy toward Federal soldiers mainly in response to gruff treatment. But it is virtually certain that Federal soldiers in Missouri endured more verbal abuse from women than they directed toward women. The soldiers may have resented having to deal with less-than-ladylike women and may even have harbored homicidal or other violent fantasies toward them. However, they rarely acted on their fantasies. Usually they did not even give vent to their anger in the presence of the women.[5]

Survival argument: They lied about their age.

One of the few "survival lies" told by the women arrested for aiding bushwhackers that can readily be proved as a lie was understating their age. When the women were deposed, they were routinely asked how old they were. Comparing their responses to other documents, like census records, shows that many of them intentionally understated their age to gain sympathy from their interrogators. Lizzie DeWitt said she was seventeen when she was twenty-one. Mary Kincheloe gave her age as nineteen when she was more likely twenty-one or twenty-two. Acting like a big sister trying to protect her younger sibling, Mary Cull reported her sister Emily's age at seventeen when Emily was, in fact, about twenty-one.

Union authorities did not want to be perceived as making war on women, much less on mere girls. The bushwhacker belles well knew this.

Survival argument: They helped Union and Confederate men equally.

Another disingenuous strategy the Missouri women sometimes employed was to claim that, while they fed and helped Southern fighters, they also aided Federal soldiers. Thus, when Mary Cull was interrogated, she mentioned a particular time in 1862 that she had given information to Union troops concerning the whereabouts of bushwhackers, and she claimed she always gave such information when it was requested. Fannie Houx tried to have a similar statement entered into the record at her trial by military commission.

Unraveling the bushwhacker belles' testimonies suggests they probably did, on occasion, also help Federal soldiers. But it is almost certain that such aid was not tendered as often or as freely as the assistance they gave to their Southern friends.

Survival argument: Their womanhood made them ignorant and innocent.

Most of the women arrested for supporting bushwhackers did not, like Sallie Mayfield, go so far as to say they favored the Union over the South. But as part of their retreat into helpless womanhood, many readily reclaimed their apolitical standing. Recall that Betty Jackson said that, as a lady, she was not accustomed to being held accountable for anything she might say and did not know what was loyal and what was disloyal. Elizabeth Stone, when asked whether she felt the South was justified in the rebellion, said she didn't know because she knew nothing about politics. Her sister, Mary Kincheloe, expressed a similar sentiment, claiming she didn't care which side won the war.

It would be a mistake to dismiss out of hand such claims of neutrality, because, as I will discuss shortly, most of the women who helped guerrillas were, in fact, not motivated primarily by politics. But it is also safe to say that most of them harbored stronger opinions than those expressed by the Kincheloe sisters.

Survival argument: They were coerced.

Perhaps the most common survival lie told by the women arrested for helping guerrillas was that they were coerced. Isabella Fox said she fed Holtzclaw's bushwhackers because she feared they would steal her horses if she didn't. A number of other women said they fed guerrillas only under the threat of having their homes burned. Portraying themselves as victims was not only one of the most common strategies used by the Missouri belles to mitigate their punishment, but it was also one of the most effective.

Throughout most of the war many Union officials believed the women to be reluctant players in the partisan warfare. To believe otherwise would have been to recognize that the guerrilla conflict in Missouri was a general resistance to the Federal occupation of the state. It was more convenient to believe instead that the guerrilla war was an aberrant and disgusting campaign waged by a fringe element of outlaws.

Thus, General Ewing, in issuing his Order No. 10, cautioned his subordinate officers to discriminate as much as possible between citizens who aided guerrillas because of disloyal motives and those who were compelled to do so by threats. Indeed, Ewing defended his infamous Orders No. 10 and No. 11 for the rest of his life on the grounds that the women displaced by the orders were primarily victims whom he had acted to protect from ruthless guerrillas.

Some of the women portrayed in the previous chapters do fit such a stereotype. It is hard to see Tabitha Rider, for instance, as anything other than a victim of the circumstances in which she found herself. Even some of the other women, like Isabella Fox, might have helped bushwhackers on occasion partly out of fear. In the late summer and the fall of 1864, when Mrs. Fox fed Holtzclaw's men, the Chariton County countryside was swarming with bushwhackers, and it might very well have been risky, as she claimed, to have refused to feed them.

However, contrary to General Ewing's belief, the guerrilla war in Missouri was, by and large, a broad uprising. Later in the war, Union commanders usually recognized the "pretty strong sympathy" for "the bushwhacking fraternity," as General Clinton B. Fisk phrased it, that existed among much of Missouri's civilian population. So, most of the women's claims that they aided the partisans only because they were coerced were no doubt convenient excuses.[6]

Conclusions: So who were they?

If the female abettors of the Missouri guerrillas were not, as a general rule, coerced, what was their primary motivation? To counter the idea that the women who were arrested for disloyal activity in Missouri during the Civil War were victims, a few authors have argued that they acted with power and purpose to aid the overall Southern war effort.

This was certainly true of some of them, particularly those apprehended in and around St. Louis for smuggling mail into area military prisons or otherwise carrying information to the enemy. No doubt it was partially true of some of the women accused of spying for guerrillas, such as Julia Martin.

A simple thirst for adventure might have been a motivating factor as well for Julia Martin and some of the other bushwhacker belles.

However, the large majority of those accused merely of feeding and harboring guerrillas—which was by far the most common charge on which rural Missouri women were arrested—were primarily motivated by ties of kinship. Most of these women had brothers, husbands, sons, or other male relatives among the guerrillas. At the very least, they had neighbors and friends, young men they had known for years, who were guerrillas.

The arrest of Missouri women for feeding and harboring guerrillas was an aggressive Union attempt to brand women's traditional family labor as inherently political. But viewing the women's domestic activity as a focused effort to affect the outcome of the war was mistaken. Just as mistaken as the belief held by General Ewing and other Union officials early in the war that the women were primarily victims. It reinforced the Union's facile notion that the guerrilla warfare in Missouri was not a widespread, household rebellion but instead a barbaric campaign perpetrated by outlaws and their uncivil cohorts. It is true that most of the female supporters of the Missouri guerrillas probably shared their male loved ones' political opinions. But many of the guerrillas themselves were not motivated primarily by political principle, as we discussed earlier in the book.

By and large, the Missouri women fed and sheltered the guerrillas because they loved them, not because they necessarily wanted to aid the overall war effort.[7]

In summary, perhaps the most important conclusion we can draw about the female abettors of the Missouri guerrillas is that it's difficult to make sweeping generalizations about them. They cannot readily be categorized or stereotyped. Each one was an individual. Each was different. They were even less homogenous than the guerrillas themselves. While most were young, their ages varied. Some were defiant, while others were cooperative. Some told bald lies, while others mostly told the truth. Some were obviously guilty of the charges against them, while others should not have been arrested to begin with.

Although few generalizations apply to all the women, we can

safely say this of the female supporters of the guerrillas:

—They were not as noble and longsuffering as their male defenders considered them.

—They were not as daring and adventuresome as post-war scribes sometimes portrayed them.

—They were not as dissolute and coarse as Union observers often depicted them. On this point, it is important to consider that, in general, the women whose stories are chronicled in this book represent only those whom the Union considered the most flagrant violators. Even some of them were not as blameworthy as their accusers made them out to be.

One of the most certain and most important conclusions we can draw about the bushwhacker belles is that they, like the guerrillas themselves, had Southern roots. Only a very few, like Imogene Brumfield, were exceptions to this generalization.

Almost as certainly and even more importantly, the women who helped the Missouri guerrillas, including Mrs. Brumfield, had ties of family and/or close friendship to the men they aided. It follows that most of the women who supported bushwhackers did so because they wanted to help their friends and their relatives, not because they were coerced. It also follows that most of them did not act for political reasons to influence the outcome of the war. For most of them, the war was more personal than that. A number of the women, such as the Mayfields and the Spencers, even lost loved ones. It is little wonder they resented Federals and wanted to help the guerrillas.

This traditional understanding of their motivation for helping the guerrillas—family ties—is not to suggest that the women were not active agents of the warfare and that the Civil War did not empower and liberate them, at least temporarily. To act on behalf of the war effort, regardless of the reason, was an expression of power and freedom. To be arrested, interrogated, and sometimes tried in a military court was certainly to be taken seriously.

For most of the women who aided Missouri guerrillas, however, theirs was a power and freedom they had not sought and did not want. To the contrary, they generally accepted the traditional female role as homemaker and the male role as guardian of the family.

The myth of the guerrilla warrior protecting innocent and helpless woman from brutal invaders had a powerful appeal. Most of the women who had actively aided the bushwhackers were happy to retreat into apolitical womanhood once the Civil War was over and to perpetuate the legend in the way they remembered the conflict years later. Lou Gentry, embracing her victimhood and her role as keeper of the hearth, recalled in 1912 that her arrest had been a cruel injustice inflicted on her by the Federals, and she remembered her first husband, Moses McCoy, as a "true defender of home" who "restored his wife to her children and fireside and then went back to his post in Shelby's command to fight for his country."[8]

Real empowerment for women would have to wait.

Notes

Introduction

1. Union Provost Marshals' File of Papers Relating to Individual Citizens, National Archives Publication M-345, online at www.fold3.com, _____ Watson, Image #292266734, accessed April 27, 2015 (hereafter cited as Individual Citizens, followed by the person's name and the image number); United States Census, 1860, FamilySearch, online at https://familysearch.org/search/collection/1473181 (hereafter cited as US Census, 1860).
2. *St. Paul Daily Globe*, January 4, 1892, quoting the *St. Louis Globe Democrat.*
3. Union Provost Marshals' Papers, Two or More Civilians: 1861-1867, Missouri State Archives, Jefferson City, www.sos.mo.gov/archives/provost/provost.pdf.asp, F1627, #13681, accessed April 25, 2015 (hereafter cited as Two or More, plus the roll number, file number, and accession date if the roll is previously not cited).
4. *Carthage Weekly Banner*, May 6, 1869.
5. Mathew H. Ritchey House, National Register of Historic Places Inventory—Nomination Form, United States Department of the Interior, National Park Service, http://www.dnr.mo.gov/shpo/nps-nr/78003399.pdf, accessed September 7, 2014; Paul R. Petersen, *Quantrill of Missouri: The Making of a Guerrilla Warrior* (Nashville: Cumberland House, 2003), 162.

Chapter 1 The Political Climate in Missouri

1. 1860 Missouri Census Table, online at Civil War on the Western Border, http://www.civilwaronthewesternborder.org/content/1860-missouri-census-table, accessed September 21, 2014.
2. Franc Wilkie, *Missouri in 1861: The Civil War Letters of Franc B. Wilkie, Newspaper Correspondent*, ed. Michael E. Banasik (Iowa City: Press of the Camp Pope Bookshop, 2001), 72. See the July 21, 1853 *Glasgow Weekly Times*, quoting the *Boonville Observer*, for an example of how the supposed propensity of black men to rape white women was used to justify violence against blacks in antebellum Missouri.
3. Michael Fellman, *Inside War: The Guerrilla Conflict in Missouri During the*

American Civil War (New York: Oxford University Press, 1989), 207-208.
4. Jackson's speech is cited in Eugene Morrow Violette, *A History of Missouri* (Boston: D. C. Heath and Co., 1918), 327. The feminization of states and countries, of course, has a long tradition and was not exclusive to Missouri at the time of the Civil War. See, for example, Stephanie McCurry, *Confederate Reckoning: Power and Politics in the Civil War South* (Cambridge: Harvard University Press, 2010) for an excellent discussion of how Georgia and other states of the South conceptualized the homeland as female and how the separate roles of men and women were strictly defined during the Civil War.
5. McCurry, 24; Fellman, 193.
6. See McCurry, page 92, for a discussion of women's close association with flags and other patriotic symbols.
7. Larry Wood, *Other Noted Guerrillas of the Civil War in Missouri* (Joplin, Mo.: Hickory Press, 2007), 11-13.
8. Fellman, 206.
9. McCurry 98; Fellman 195.
10. *St. Joseph Morning Herald*, May 16, 1863.
11. *Ibid.*
12. *War of the Rebellion: A Compilation of Official Records of the Union and Confederate Armies*, Washington, DC: Government Printing Office (1880-1902), 22:2, 460-461. Hereafter cited as *OR*.
13. *Ibid.*, 473.
14. Thomas Curran, "Confederate Women and Military Justice in the St. Louis Area" (Missouri State Archives—Presentation Video Transcripts, 2010), 3-7.
15. Lowry, ix; McCurry, 114-115.

Chapter 2 She Adder and Rebel Damsel

1. Lou Gentry, "About the Fight at Richfield," *Confederate Veteran* 20 (September 1912): 426.
2. *Ibid.*
3. Individual Citizens, Mrs. Moses McCoy, #287556500-287556502. Accessed April 27, 2015. At the time of the Civil War, Richfield and two other small communities had recently consolidated to form Missouri City, but Richfield retained its separate identity during the war, at least in the minds of many residents, and the place was still often called by that name.
4. Lou Gentry, "Experience of a Missouri Woman," *Confederate Veteran* 20 (May 1912), 211, and "About the Fight at Richfield" (September 1912) 426; Individual Citizens, Lurena McCoy #287556490, accessed April 27, 2015; *History of Clay and Platte Counties, Missouri* (St. Louis: National Historical

Company, 1885), 235.

5. Individual Citizens, Mrs. Moses McCoy, #287556500-287556503; Gentry, "About the Fight at Richfield," 426.

6. Individual Citizens, Mrs. Moses McCoy, #287556503-287556504; Gentry, "Experience of a Missouri Woman," 211.

7. *St. Joseph Morning Herald*, May 20, 1863; Gentry, "Experience of a Missouri Woman, 211, and "About the Fight at Richfield, 426; *War of the Rebellion: A Compilation of Official Records of the Union and Confederate Armies*, Washington, DC: Government Printing Office (1880-1902), *OR*, 22:1, 335-336.

8. *OR*, 22:1, 335-336. In Lou's version of this incident, Fletch Taylor tried to shoot Rapp at the hotel, but the landlady deflected the barrel of the pistol so that the shot missed Rapp.

9. Gentry, "About the Fight at Richfield," 427; *OR*, 22:1, 336.

10. *St. Joseph Morning Herald*, May 20, 1863; Gentry, "Experience of a Missouri Woman," 211.

11. *Ibid.*

12. Individual Citizens, Lurena McCoy, #287556486-287556487.

13. Gentry, "About the Fight at Richfield," 427.

14. Gentry, "Experience of a Missouri Woman," 211.

15. Two or More, F1627, #13681.

16. Individual Citizens, Lurena McCoy, #287556484; Gentry, "Experience of a Missouri Woman," 212.

17. "Lurena 'Lou' Alder Gentry," Find a Grave Memorial #96523663, created by Russ Norris, www.findagrave.com, accessed September 13, 2014.

Chapter 3 More in Common than a Name

1. Transcript of Mary, Betty, and Sue Jackson Trial by Military Commission, Records of the Judge Advocate General's Office, Record Group 153, LL 12229, National Archives, Washington, DC. Trial transcripts hereafter cited as RG 153, followed by the file number; US Census, 1860. Lowry describes this case in *Confederate Heroines*, but the author mistakenly identifies Mary Jackson as Bill Jackson's wife. While Bill Jackson might have been related to the Mary Jackson family, any such kinship was apparently not close. Sixty-year-old Mary was definitely not the wife of Bill Jackson, who at the time of the 1860 census was twenty-six and unmarried, and she was just as surely not his mother.

2. RG 153, LL 12229.

3. *Ibid.*

4. *Ibid.*

5. *Ibid.*

6. Two or More, F1601, #6037, accessed April 25, 2015; Individual Citizens, Mary Jackson, #287397272, accessed October 6, 2014; Individual Citizens, Bettie Jackson, #287396407, accessed October 8, 2014; Individual Citizens, Sue Jackson, #287397547, accessed October 6, 2014; RG 153, LL 12229.
7. RG 153, LL 12229.
8. *Ibid.*
9. *Ibid.*
10. *Ibid.* The written statements submitted by Mary and her daughters were either transcribed by an officer of the court, or else the women spoke of themselves in the third person.
11. RG 153, LL 12229.
12. *Ibid.*
13. *Ibid.*
14. "Polly Jackson," Find a Grave Memorial #81971363, accessed April 27, 2015.

Chapter 4 The Heart and Soul of Bushwhacking

1. *History of Vernon County, Missouri* (St. Louis: Brown & Co., 1887) 338-341; *St. Paul Daily Globe*, January 4, 1892; Patrick Brophy, "Lady Bushwhackers Played Active Parts, *Bushwhacker Weekly Magazine*, December 5, 1984.
2. Family Group Sheet for John Mayfield/Ella Justine Burrus, http://www.mcatee.biz/genealogy/familygroup.php?familyID=F3226&tree=MyFamily20 05; United States Census, 1850, FamilySearch, https://familysearch.org/search/collection/14016381850 (hereafter cited as US Census, 1850);
3. US Census, 1860; *History of Vernon County*, 335.
4. *History of Vernon County*, 335.
5. *History of Vernon County*, 335-336; Soldiers' Records: War of 1812-World War I, Missouri State Archives, Jefferson City, online at http://www.sos.mo.gov/archives/soldiers, Hiram
Mayfield. Hereafter cited as Soldiers' Records, followed by the soldier's name.
6. *History of Vernon County*, 336.
7. *Ibid.*
8. *Ibid.*, 338.
9. *History of Vernon County, 338;* Ledger Transcription List—Women and Children Prisoners," transcription of National Archives Microfilm Publication M598, Roll 72, www.civilwarstlouis.com/articles/gratiot/listwomen.aspx, accessed July 26, 2014 (hereafter cited as Ledger Transcription List). The county history gives Sallie Mayfield's age at the time of her husband's death as 23, but since she was seven in the summer of

1850 and seventeen in the summer of 1860, she could not have been more than nineteen in early 1862.
10. *History of Vernon County,* 338.
11. *Ibid.*, 337.
12. *History of Vernon County*, 338; US Census, 1850; US Census, 1860.
13. *History of Vernon County*, 338.
14. *Ibid.*, 313-318.
15. *Ibid.*, 339.
16. *Ibid.*
17. *Ibid.*
18. *Ibid.*
19. *Ibid*, 339-340.
20. *Pittsburgh (Penn.) Dispatch*, September 16, 1891; *St. Paul Daily Globe*, January 4, 1892.
21. Two or More, F1621, #11654, accessed April 25, 2015.
22. *Ibid.* Sallie was called both "Mrs. Gibney" and "Mrs. Waitman" in Union records, but it is clear that "Mrs. Waitman" is the name she was going by at the time of her clash with Union authorities.
23. *History of Vernon County*, 341; Two or More, F1621, #11654.
24. Two or More, F1621, #11654; Bruce Nichols, *Guerrilla Warfare in Civil War Missouri, vol. 3, January-August 1864*, 203.
25. Two or More, F1621, #11654.
26. Two or More, F1621, #11654; US Census, 1860; "William McWaters," http://en.wikipedia.org/wiki/William_McWaters; Ledger Transcription List. Although Jennie Mayfield gave her age as sixteen in the late summer of 1864, both the 1850 and the 1860 censuses suggest that she had to have been at least seventeen at the time.
27. Two or More, F1621, #11654; *History of Vernon County*, 341.
28. Two or More, F1621, #11654.
29. Two or More, F1621, #11654; Griffin Frost, *Camp and Prison Journal* (1867; reprint, Iowa City: Camp Pope Bookshop, 1994), 173.
30. Two or More, F1621, #11654.
31. *Ibid.*
32. *Ibid.*
33. Two or More, F1625, #12766, accessed April 25, 2015; *History of Vernon County*, 341-342.
34. *History of Vernon County*, 342.
35. Two or More, F1625, #12766.
36. Two or More, F1626, #13209, accessed April 25, 2015.
37. *History of Vernon County*, 340; United States Census, 1870, FamilySearch,

https://familysearch.org/search/collection/1438024 (hereafter cited as US Census, 1870); United States Census, 1880, FamilySearch, https://familysearch.org/search/collection/1417683 (hereafter cited as US Census, 1880); "Keys to My Heart: Genealogy of the Sherfick and Wade Families," http://www.mcatee.biz/genealogy/.

Chapter 5 Mary Vaughn and Her Relations in the Brush

1. Two or More Civilians, F1632, #14921, accessed April 25, 2015; "Trouble for the Vaughn's (sic) in Jackson County, Missouri during the Civil War," http://www.doug.vaughn/org/trouble/trouble-main.html.
2. Josiah Vaughn ancestry, http://homepages.rootsweb.ancestry.com/~fuqua/ Main%20Database/mdb1353.htm; "Trouble for the Vaughn's"; Two or More, F1632, #14921.
3. US Census, 1860; Soldiers Records, Dan Vaughn; Two or More, F1632, #14921.
4. "Trouble for the Vaughn's"; US Census, 1860.
5. *New York Times*, March 30, 1863; Individual Citizens, Margaret Clifton, #281795274, #281795278, accessed April 27, 2015; Individual Citizens, Martha Lindsey, #287476038, accessed April 27, 2015; *Kansas City Daily Journal of Commerce*, May 27, 1863; William E. Connelley, *The Life of Preston B. Plumb* (Chicago: Browne and Howell Company, 1913), 145.
6. Individual Citizens, Margaret Clifton, #281795287.
7. *Kansas City Daily Journal of Commerce*, May 27, 1863; *Kansas City Star*, November 28, 1897.
8. *Kansas City Daily Journal of Commerce*, May 27, 1863.
9. *Ibid.*, May 29, 1863.
10. Connelley, *Life of Preston B. Plumb*, 145-147.
11. Two or More, F1625, #12789.
12. *Ibid.*
13. *Ibid.*
14. Two or More, F1656, #20972, accessed April 25, 2015; *Leavenworth Daily Times*, November 12, 1864, citing the *Kansas City Journal*.
15. Unfiled Papers and Slips Belonging in Confederate Compiled Service Records, National Archives Microfilm Publication M347, Roll 335, www.Fold3.com, accessed May 26, 2014, Dan Vaughn, Image #258831956 (hereafter cited as Unfiled Papers, plus the person's name and the image number); Individual Citizens, Daniel Vaughn, #292229193, accessed April 27, 2015; Two or More, F1656, #20972.
16. Individual Citizens, Daniel Vaughn, #292229194.
17. Two or More, F1632, #14921; "Trouble for the Vaughn's."

18. Two or More, F1623, #12344, accessed April 25, 2015.
19. Unfiled Papers, Dan Vaughn, #259931056.
20. Individual Citizens, Daniel Vaughn, #292229192; Two or More, F1623, #12344.
21. "Trouble for the Vaughn's."
22. Two or More, F1630, #14370, accessed April 25, 2015.
23. *Ibid.*, #14544.
24. "Trouble for the Vaughn's."
25. *Oskaloosa (Kans.) Independent*, February 18, 1865; William G. Cutler, ed, *History of the State of Kansas* (Chicago: A.T. Andreas, 1883), 645.
26. Two or More, F1632, #15055; "Trouble for the Vaughn's."
27. Two or More, F1632, #15055.
28. *Ibid.*, F1632, #14921. Lydia Taylor was mistaken in identifying Mary Vaughn as a widow. Mary, in fact, died before Josiah Vaughn, but they had apparently been living apart long enough to cause Mary's neighbor to think she was a widow.
29. Two or More, F1632, #14921.
30. *Ibid.*
31. "Trouble for the Vaughn's."
32. *Ibid.*
33. *Ibid.*
34. *Ibid.*
35. *Ibid.*
36. *Ibid.*
37. *Ibid.*; Joanne Chiles Eakin, *The Little Gods: Union Provost Marshals in Missouri, 1861-1865* (Independence, Mo., np, 1996), 34.
38. Two or More, F1638, #16837, accessed April 25, 2015.
39. Unfiled Papers, Daniels Vaughn, #258831947, accessed May 26, 2014.
40. "Trouble for the Vaughn's"; US Census, 1870.
41. "Trouble for the Vaughn's."

Chapter 6 Anna Fickle: Bribery and Murder

1. *OR*, 41:2, 76; J.W. Buel, *The Border Outlaws* (Cincinnati: Forshee & McMakin, 1882), 35-43; Ledger Transcription List.
2. US Census, 1850; US Census, 1860; John N. Edwards, *Noted Guerrillas of the Warfare of the Border* (St. Louis: Bryan, Brand & Company, 1877), 76; Buel, 35-43.
3. Two or More, F1605, #7320, #7333, accessed April 25, 2015; Individual Citizens, Helvy Fickel, #286431387.
4. *St. Louis Daily Missouri Republican*, March 1, 1864, quoting the *Lexington*

Union; Bruce Nichols, *Guerilla Warfare in Civil War Missouri, Volume 3, January-August 1864*, 49, 126; Soldiers' Records, William M. Sabins; Margaret Mendenhall, trans., *Missouri Ordeal 1862-1864: The Diaries of William Hall Mendenhall* (Newhall, CA: Carl Boyer III, 1985) 180-181; Transcript of Ann Fickle Trial by Military Commission, RG 153, #NN2143. Edwards says in *Noted Guerrillas* that Hinton had already been convicted and sentenced to death at the time Blunt tried to free him, but there appears to be no record of this in Union documents. Also, some reports suggest that Annie was romantically involved with the imprisoned bushwhacker instead of Blunt, but the available evidence seems to favor Blunt as her beau.

5. Two or More, F1659, #21953, accessed April 25, 2015; Mendenhall diaries, 181; *History of Lafayette County, Mo.* (St. Louis: Missouri Historical Company, 1881), 289.

6. Two or More, F1659, 21953; Unfiled Papers, Anna Fickle, #251335566, accessed May 26, 2014.

7. RG 153, NN2143.

8. *Ibid.*

9. Individual Citizens, Anna Fickle, #286431448, accessed May 26, 2014.

10. RG 153, NN2143; Unfiled Papers, Anna Fickle, #251335566, #251335599; Two or More, F1617, #10559, accessed April 25, 2015.

11. *OR*, 41:2, 76-77.

12. Unfiled Papers, Anna Fickle, #251335562-251335563. The *Columbia Missouri Statesman* reported in mid-July of 1864 that Miss Fickle was sentenced to three years at Alton Military Prison, but there appears to be no record of such an action in Union documents.

13. Absalom Grimes, *Absalom Grimes: Confederate Mail Runner*, M. M. Quaife, ed. (New Haven, CT: Yale University Press, 1926), 197-198; Two or More, F1100, Morning Report of Gratiot Street Military Prison, September 7, 1864, accessed April 25, 2015.

14. RG 153, NN2143; Two or More, F1629, #14010, accessed April 25, 2015; Unfiled Papers, Anna Fickle, #251335561; *History of Lafayette County*, 292; Grimes, 196.

15. Annie Fickel Parker death certificate, Missouri Death Certificates, 1910-1963, Missouri State Archives, Jefferson City, online at http://www.sos.mo.gov/archives/resources/deathcertificates/#searchdeat, accessed July 29, 2014; Soldiers' Records, George W. Parker, accessed July 29, 2014; US Census, 1870; US Census, 1880; US Census, 1910, FamilySearch, https://familysearch.org/search/collection/1727033 (hereafter cited as US Census, 1910); Missouri Marriage Records, 1805-2002, www.Ancestry.com, accessed July 29, 2014 (hereafter cited as Missouri Marriage Records).

Chapter 7 Mary Ann Harlow: Bloody Bill Anderson Informant

1. Unfiled Papers, M.D. Erwin, #251305824, accessed July 31, 2014; Individual Citizens, Mrs. Harlow, #286689045, accessed July 10, 2014; Ledger Transcription List.
2. Individual Citizens, M.D. Erwin, #28626922, accessed July 31, 2014; Individual Citizens, Mrs. Harlow, #286689038; OR, 34:4, 564.
3. *OR*, 41:2, 77.
4. Individual Citizens, Mrs. Harlow, #286689042-286689046.
5. Individual Citizens, Mary Ann Harlow, #286689077-286689078, accessed July 10, 2014; Individual Citizens, Mrs. Harlow, #86689036, #86689038, #86689040, #86689048, #86689050.
6. Individual Citizens, Mary Ann Harlow, #286689073; Unfiled Papers, M. A. Harlow, #251767442, accessed July 30, 2014.
7. Unfiled Papers, Mary Harlow, #251767595, #251767601, accessed June 25, 2014.
8. Individual Citizens, Mary Ann Harlow, #286689071, #286689075; Unfiled Papers, Mary Harlow, #251767537, #251767548, #251767587; Two or More, F1625, #12720. Some of the Harlows and Whitsetts were related by marriage; so it's quite plausible that Isaac Whitsett and his wife fled Missouri because their snitching on Mary Ann had caused bad blood in the family or perhaps they feared retaliation by bushwhackers.
9. Bruce Nichols, "North Missouri Event," Missouri in the Civil War Message Board, http://history-sites.com/cgi-bin/bbs62x/mocwmb/webbbs_config.pl?md=read;id=18708; US Census, 1870; US Census, 1880; US Census, 1900, FamilySearch, https://familysearch.org/search/collection/1325221 (hereafter cited as US Census, 1900).

Chapter 8 Bill Anderson Supporter or Bill Anderson Victim?

1. US Census, 1850; US Census, 1860; "Benjamin Isham Longacre," Find a Grave Memorial #42340597, www.findagrave.com, accessed August 2, 2014; Ledger Transcription List.
2. Unfiled Papers, William A. Longacre, #254796116-254796117, #254796122, accessed July 21, 2014.
3. *OR*, 34:1, 1001-1002; Individual Citizens, Nancy Longacre, #287484682-287484683, accessed July 21, 2014.
4. Individual Citizens, Nancy Longacre, #287484682-287484683.
5. *Ibid.*, #287484677-287484678, #287484681.
6. *Ibid.*, #287484676.
7. *Ibid.*, #287484678, 287484680.

8. Individual Citizens, Martha Longacre, #287484672, accessed July 21, 2014; Nancy Longacre, #287484675; Elizabeth Stone, #292110429, #292110432, accessed July 10, 2014. Nancy's son, Thomas, was apparently not sent to St. Louis.
9. Individual Citizens, Nancy Longacre, #287484674-287484675.
10. Individual Citizens, Martha Longacre, #287484671-287484672.
11. Two or More, F1100, Morning Report of Gratiot Street Military Prison, September 7, 1864.
12. Individual Citizens, Nancy Longacre, #287484668-287484669.
13. *Ibid.*, #287484666.
14. Individual Citizens, Nancy Longacre, #287484660, #287484664, #287484684; Unfiled Papers, Nancy Longacre, #254796092; Unfiled Papers, Martha Longacre, #254796037, accessed July 21, 2014.
15. US Census, 1870; US Census, 1880; "Nancy Malory Longacre," Find A Grave Memorial #42239720, www.findagrave.com; Martha Jane "Mattie" Longacre Baker, Find A Grave Memorial #42342503, www.findagrave.com, accessed April 27, 2015.

Chapter 9 Bitter Rebels but Fine-Looking Girls

1. *St. Louis Daily Missouri Democrat*, December 12, 1864.
2. *Emporia News*, July 7, 1860; *Cottonwood Falls Kansas Press*, July 2, 1860; William E. Connelley Papers, Collection 16, Box 13, Kansas State Historical Society, Topeka, Kansas.
3. *Emporia News*, May 17, 1862; Connelley Papers.
4. *Emporia News* July 12, 1862; Connelley Papers.
5. *Ibid.*
6. US Census, 1850; William E. Connelley, *Life of Preston B. Plumb*, 145-146; Fred Barton, "Bill Anderson and Not Charlie Quantrell Was Driving Force Behind Lawrence Raid," undated newspaper clipping, Denver Public Library, Western History Department, William Connelly Collection; Larry Wood, *The Civil War Story of Bloody Bill Anderson* (Fort Worth: Eakin Press, 2003), 26-28.
7. Individual Citizens, Mollie Grandstaff, #287502048-287502049, accessed September 26, 2014; Edward Thomas Fay, "How the Anderson Girls Were Captured," Connelley Papers; Barton, "Bill Anderson and Not Charlie Quantrell."
8. Wood, 31-35.
9. Two or More, F1604, #7173, accessed April 25, 2015; Individual Citizens, Mollie Grandstaff, #287502045-287502047.
10. Individual Citizens, Mollie Anderson, #280145270, #280145283,

accessed May 26, 2014.

11. Individual Citizens, Jane Anderson, #280142557, accessed June 9, 2014.

12. Paul Peterson, *Quantrill in Texas: The Forgotten Campaign* (Nashville: Cumberland House, 2007), 197.

13. Two or More, F1630, #14319. Bush Smith, whom Bill Anderson had married in Sherman, Texas, the previous winter, had remained there when the guerrillas returned to Missouri in the spring of 1864.

14. Two or More, F1658, #21449, accessed April 25, 2015.

15. *Ibid.* Mrs. Bass recalled that the three young women came to her house in mid-November, but it must have been closer to the beginning of the month, if they stayed three weeks or more, as she said, because the Anderson girls were arrested in late November.

16. *Ibid.*

17. *St. Louis Daily Missouri Republican*, December 13, 1864; *St. Louis Daily Missouri Democrat*, December 12, 1864.

18. *St. Louis Daily Missouri Democrat*, January 20, 1865; Connelley Papers.

19. Texas Marriage Records, https://familysearch.org, accessed August 8, 2014; US Census, 1870; US Census, 1880; US Census, 1900; James R. Baker, Jr., *Missouri Partisans*, v. 1. The Author, 2013. Some sources say Jim married Bill's widow, Bush Smith, whose original name was also Mary Erwin, but the evidence suggests that these were two different women. Data from the 1870 census shows that the Mary Erwin who married Jim Anderson would have been only twelve years old in 1864, when Bill Anderson married Bush Smith. A claim made by ex-guerrilla George Shepherd and popularized by J. W. Buel in his 1881 book *Border Bandits* that Shepherd killed Jim Anderson in Sherman, Texas, in 1867 is obviously not true, since records clearly show that Anderson married after that date and was still living in 1870. Unfortunately, the Shepherd yarn is one this author unwittingly continued in an article for the *Missouri Historical Review* in 2003.

Chapter 10 Wife of a Bill Anderson Guerrilla

1. Unfiled Papers, Imogene Broomfield, #248833055, #248833227, accessed August 25, 2014.

2. Unfiled Papers, Imogene Brumfield, #248832900, #248833025, #248833055, #248833227; Two or More, F1630, #14319.

3. Unfiled Papers, Imogene Brumfield, #248832900, #248832925, #248833025. Benjamin Brumfield was killed in mid-November of 1864 by soldiers of the Ninth Missouri State Militia who happened upon his guerrilla band three miles west of Rocheport on the New Franklin Road just after the bushwhackers had killed five Union citizens in retaliation for

the killing of partisan leader Bill Stewart by a Union citizen.
4. *Ibid.*, #248832997, #248833025, #248833156.
5. *Ibid.*, #248833010.
6. Unfiled Papers, Imogene Brumfield, #248833156; *St. Louis Daily Missouri Democrat*, December 12, 1864.
7. Unfiled Papers, Imogene Brumfield, #248832974, #248832997.
8. *Ibid.*, #248832900, #248832925.
9. *Ibid.*, #248832791-248832805.
10. *Ibid.*, #248832821, #248832829.
11. *Ibid.*, #248833055, #248833081.
12. *Ibid.*, #248832772.
13. *Ibid.*, #248833227, #248833233.
14. *Ibid.*, #248832772, 248832960.
15. Individual Citizens, Imogene Brumfield, #286744280, accessed August 25, 2014. The *St. Louis Daily Missouri Democrat* erroneously reported that Mrs. Keeton gave the furs as a gift to one of the Anderson girls as a token of the friendship she and Miss Anderson had established during their mutual incarceration but that regulations "would not permit them to be carried to Dixie." Reason suggests and Union provost marshals' records show that the furs were never intended to be carried to Dixie but rather to Canada, and Martha Keeton was apparently not motivated so much by charity as the newspaper supposed.
16. Unfiled Papers, Imogene Brumfield, #248833270.
17. Individual Citizens, Imogene Brumfield, #286744282.
18. *Ibid.*, #286744284.
19. *Ibid.*, #286744274-286744275.
20. US Census, 1870.

Chapter 11 Confederate Mail Handlers

1. Transcript of Eliza Haynie trial by military commission, RG 153, LL2592.
2. *Ibid.*
3. *Ibid.*
4. *Ibid.*; Individual Citizens, Rachel Haynie, #286864841, accessed April 27, 2015; Individual Citizens, Eliza Jane Haynie, #286864806, accessed April 27, 2015; Unfiled Papers, Rachel Haynie, #251932295, accessed October 15, 2014.
5. RG 153, LL2592.
6. *Ibid.*
7. *Ibid.*
8. *Ibid.*

9. *Ibid.*; Two or More, F1100, Daily Morning Report of Gratiot Street Military Prison, September 7, 1864.
10. Unfiled Papers, Eliza Haynie, #251932076, #251932080.
11. *Ibid.*; Unfiled Papers, Rachel Haynie, #251932293-251932295.
12. Two or More, F1628, #13760, accessed April 26, 2015, and F1630, #14390.
13. US Census, 1870; US Census, 1880.

Chapter 12 Fannie Houx and the Excitement Surrounding Her Case

1. Individual Citizens, Fannie Houx, #287023455, #287023484, accessed July 23, 2014; *Lexington News*, September 19, 2012; US Census, 1860.
2. Individual Citizens, Fannie Houx, #287023445.
3. Transcript of Fannie Houx trial by military commission, RG 153, #NN2733.
4. *Ibid.*
5. *Ibid.*
6. *Ibid.*
7. *Ibid.*
8. *Ibid.*
9. *Ibid.*; Individual Citizens, Fannie Houx, #287023470-287023471, #287023486.
10. Individual Citizens, Fannie Houx, #287023456, #287023476.
11. *Ibid.*, #287023457.
12. RG 153, #NN2733; Individual Citizens, Fannie Houx, #287023456.
13. Individual Citizens, Fannie Houx, #287023451-287023452.
14. *Ibid.*, #287023452-287023453.
15. *Ibid.*, #287023453.
16. *Ibid.*, #287023466; Individual Citizens, Fannie Houk, 287023106, accessed July 22, 2014.
17. Unfiled Papers, Fannie Houx, #254893521, #254893523, #254893525, #254893532, accessed July 22, 2014.
18. Individual Citizens, Fannie Houx, #287023463, #287023497; Individual Citizens, Fannie Houp, #287023122, accessed August 15, 2014.
19. Individual Citizens, Fannie Houx, #287023493.
20. *Ibid.*, #287023463-287023464, #287023489.
21. *Ibid.*, #287023491.
22. *Ibid.*, #287023495.
23. *Ibid.*, #287023462, #287023478, #287023480.
24. US Census, 1870; US Census, 1880; "Frances Pearl 'Fannie' Price Houx," Find A Grave Memorial #68824105, www.findagrave.com, accessed April

27, 2015.

Chapter 13 Susanna Justice: Guerrilla Spy

1. Unfiled Papers, Susan Justice, #252357173, #252357179, accessed August 25, 2014.
2. US Census, 1860; Unfiled Papers, Susan Justice, #252357184-252357185.
3. Unfiled Papers, Susan Justice, #252357177, #252357185-252357186.
4. *Ibid.*, #252357172, #252357176-252357178, #252357189.
5. Two or More, #1100, Morning Report of Gratiot Street Military Prison, Sept. 7, 1864; Unfiled Papers, Susan Justice, #252357182-252187.
6. Unfiled Papers, Susan Justice, #252357175.
7. Individual Citizens, Luzan Justice, #287222388, accessed August 25, 2014; Two or More, #1100, Morning Report of Gratiot Street Prison, Sept. 7, 1864.
8. Individual Citizens, Luzan Justice, #287222387.
9. Unfiled Papers, Susan Justice, #252357180.
10. Unfiled Papers, Susan Justice, #252357179; Larry Wood, "Harry Truman: Federal Bushwhacker" (*Missouri Historical Review* 98:3, April 2004), 201-222.
11. Unfiled Papers, Susan Justice, #252357179; Individual Citizens, Susan Justice, #287222390, accessed April 27, 2015.
12. US Census, 1870.

Chapter 14 Professors of the Christian Religion

1. US Census, 1860; Individual Citizens, Elizabeth Stone, #292110436, accessed July 10, 2014; Individual Citizens, Old Man Kinchloe, #290364355-290364356, accessed July 10, 2014.
2. Individual Citizens, Elizabeth Stone, #292110426; Two or More, F1100, Morning Report of Gratiot Street Military Prison, Sept. 7, 1864.
3. Individual Citizens, Elizabeth Stone, #292110414; Individual Citizens, Mary Kinchelow, #290364408, accessed July 11, 2014.
4. Individual Citizens, Elizabeth Stone, #292110417.
5. *Ibid.*, #292110432, #292110429. Nancy Longacre and her daughter were sent to St. Louis under the same order by which Lizzie Stone and Mary Kincheloe were transported.
6. Two or More, F1100, Morning Report of Gratiot Military Prison, Sept. 7, 1864; Ledger Transcription List; US Census, 1850.
7. Individual citizens, Elizabeth Stone, #292110429-292110430.
8. *Ibid.*, #292110425-292110428.
9. Individual Citizens, Mary Kinchelow, #290364371-290364372.

10. Individual Citizens, Elizabeth Stone, #292110418; Individual Citizens, Mary Kincheloe, #290364365-290364366, accessed July 10, 2014.
11. Individual Citizens, Elizabeth Stone, #292110438.
12. Two or More, F1621, #11554.
13. Individual Citizens, Mary Kinchelow, #290364370; Two or More, F1625, #12784.
14. Individual Citizens, Mary Kinchelow, #290364368-290364369. The brother Ferguson mentioned was no doubt a reference to twenty-year-old James T. Kincheloe. He, in fact, had been a member of Colonel Benjamin Elliott's Confederate regiment since August of 1862 but reportedly rode briefly with Quantrill prior to his enlistment. See Soldier's Records, J. T. Kincheloe, and Michael Banasik, ed. *Cavaliers of the Bush: Quantrill and His Men*. Iowa City: Press of the Camp Pope Bookshop, 2003.
15. Individual Citizens, Lizzie Stone, #292110421-292110422, accessed July 23, 2014.
16. *Ibid.*, #292110420.
17. Individual Citizens, Mary Kincheloe #290364366, #290364373; Individual Citizens, Elizabeth Stone, #292110434.
18. Individual Citizens, Elizabeth Stone, #292110439-292110441.
19. *Ibid.*, #292110439-292110441; Individual Citizens, Mary Kincheloe, #290364376, #290364378.
20. Individual Citizens, Mary Kincheloe, #290364377; Unfiled Papers, Elizabeth Stone, #257429634, accessed August 9, 2014.
21. Individual Citizens, Elizabeth Stone, #292110424, #292110438.
22. US Census, 1870; Find A Grave, http://www.findagrave.com/cgi-bin/fg.cgi?page=gsr&GSfn=&GSmn=&GSln=kincheloe&GSbyre=all&GSdy=&GScntry=4&GSst=26&GScnty=1450&GSgrid=&df=all&GSob=n1&GScnty=1450&.

Chapter 15 The Handsome and Fascinating Mollie Goggin

1. Individual Citizens, Mollie Goggin #286615775, accessed June 9, 2014; Individual Citizens, James Murry #290850397, accessed July 16, 2014.
2. Individual Citizens, Mollie Goggin, #286615722, #286615775; Thomas P. Lowry, *Confederate Heroines* (Baton Rouge: Louisiana State University Press, 2006), 31-32.
3. Individual Citizens, Mollie Goggin, #286615711, #286615815.
4. *Ibid.*, #286615722, #286615789.
5 *Ibid.*, #286615718.
6. *Ibid.*
7. *Ibid.*, #286615718, #286615739, #286615742.

8. *Ibid.*, #286615785, #286615789.
9. *Ibid.*, #286615792.
10. *Ibid.*, #286615715, #286615736.
11. *Ibid.*, #286615700, #286615757.
12. Individual Citizens, Mary Pitman, #291266433-291266434, accessed July 16, 2014; LeAnne Blanton and Lauren M. Cook, *They Fought Like Demons: Women Soldiers in the American Civil War* (Baton Rouge: Louisiana State University Press, 2002), 68-71, 87-90.
13. *Ibid.*, #291266434-291266435.
14. *Ibid.*, #291266435.
15. Griffin Frost, *Camp and Prison Journal* (1867; reprint, Iowa City: Camp Pope Bookshop, 1994) 187, 200, 207, 209-210.
16. Individual Citizens, Mollie Goggin, #286615700.
17. *Ibid.*, #286615704.
18. Individual Citizens, Mollie Goggin, #286615704.
19. *Ibid.*, #286615809; Frost, 218; US Census, 1860.

Chapter 16 The Very Bad Bond Women

1. Two or More, F1611, #8987, accessed April 26, 2015.
2. Two or More, F1611, #8987; Individual Citizens, Harrison Jenkins, #287175344, accessed July 3, 2014.
3. Two or More, F1611, #8987; "Jenkins Family," http://archiver.rootsweb.ancestry.com/th/read/momiller/2000-06/0961842004.
4. Two or More, F1611, #8987.
5. *Ibid.*
6. *Ibid.*
7. *Ibid.*
8. *Ibid.*
9. *Ibid.* US Census, 1860; US Census, 1870; Missouri Marriage Records.
10. *Ibid.*
11. *Ibid.*
12. *Ibid.*
13. *Ibid.*
14. US Census, 1870; US Census, 1880; Missouri Marriage Records.

Chapter 17 The Post Oak "Prostitutes"

1. Two or More, F1622, #11938, accessed April 26, 2015.
2. *Ibid.*; US Census, 1860.
3. US Census, 1850; US Census, 1860; Ewing Cockrell, *History of Johnson*

County, Missouri, v. 2 (Topeka: Historical Publishing Co., 1918), 746; Individual Citizens, Eliza Spencer, #292063503, accessed June 16, 2014. Mary and Emily Cull were both listed as eighteen in the 1860 census, but they were not twins, because Mary had been listed as nine and Emily as seven in the previous census.

4. Two or More, F1622 #11938.

5. *OR*, 34:1, 1057-1058.

6. Individual Citizens, Emily Cull, #280342573, accessed June 16, 2014.

7. *Ibid.*, #280342571.

8. Individual Citizens, Mary Cull, #280342588, accessed June 16, 2014.

9. Individual Citizens, Eliza Spencer, #292063503, #292063505.

10. Unfiled Papers, Jane Ward, #258893606, accessed June 16, 2014.

11. *Ibid.*, #258893628.

12. Individual Citizens, Wealthy Robertson, #291845562, accessed June 18, 2014.

13. *Ibid.*, #291845568.

14. Individual Citizens, Mary Spencer, #292063686, accessed June 16, 2014; Individual Citizens, Hattie Spencer, #292063543, accessed June 15, 2014; Individual Citizens, Jane Spencer, #292063629, accessed June 16, 2014; Two or More, F1622, #11938; US Census, 1860.

15. Two or More, F1622, #11938.

16. Individual Citizens, Mary Spencer, #292063684; Individual Citizens, Hattie Spencer, #292063546; Individual Citizens, Jane Spencer, #292063624; Individual Citizens, Margaret Oliphant, #291020107, accessed June 16, 2014; "Descendants of Duncan Oliphant," http://hershfamily.net/images/Family_Tree_Maker14.pdf.

17. Individual Citizens, Missouri Cull, #280342599, accessed June 16, 2014; Individual Citizens, Mary Cull, #280342586.

18. Two or More, F1622, #11938.

19. Individual Citizens, Mary Cull, #280342581; Individual Citizens, Hattie Spencer, #292063544; Two or More, F1622, #11938; Unfiled Papers, M.A. Harlow, #251767463.

20. Individual Citizens, Hattie Spencer, #292063532-292063533; *St. Louis Daily Missouri Republican*, August 27, 1864 and September 9, 1864; Unfiled Papers, Hattie Spencer, #257426392, accessed June 15, 2014.

21. Individual Citizens, Clara Fannie Little, #287477324, accessed May 26, 2014.

22. Two or More F1622, #11938.

23. *Ibid.*

24. Individual Citizens, Mary Spencer, #292063681-292063682,

#292063687-292063688.
25. Individual Citizens, Hattie Spencer, #292063538-292063541.
26. Individual Citizens, Eliza Spencer, #292063498-292063501.
27. Individual Citizens, Mary Cull, #280342590-280342596.
28. Unfiled Papers, Jane Ward, #298893659, #298893666, #298893675, #298893682.
29. Individual Citizens, Wealthy Robertson, #291845549, #291845552.
30. Frost, 170-171.
31. Individual Citizens, Hattie Spencer, #292063532-292063533; *St. Louis Daily Missouri Republican*, September 6, 1864.
32. Two or More, F1621, #11558.
33. *Ibid.*, F1622, #11938.
34. *Ibid.*, *St. Louis Daily Missouri Republican*, September 28, 1864.
35. Individual Citizens, Eliza Spencer, #292063493, #292063497; Individual Citizens, Hattie Spencer, #292063536; *St. Louis Daily Missouri Republican*, October 19, 1864; Two or More, F1625, #12720.
36. Unfiled Papers, Jane Ward, #258893568, #258893636; *St. Louis Daily Missouri Democrat*, January 20, 1865.
37. Individual Citizens, Wealthy Robertson, #291845547, #291845572.
38. Individual Citizens, Jane Spencer, #292063599-292063600.
39. US Census, 1860; US Census, 1880; Missouri Marriage Records.

Chapter 18 Notorious and Active Rebels

1. Two or More, F1621, #11548; Individual Citizens, Dortha Durrett, #283819551, accessed June 24, 2014.
2. Two or More, F1621, #11548; US Census, 1860.
3. Two or More, F1621, #11548; Ledger Transcription List.
4. Two or More, F1621, #11548.
5. *Ibid.*
6. *Ibid.*
7. *Ibid.*
8. *Ibid.*
9. *Ibid.*
10. Individual Citizens, Dortha Durrett, #283819554, #283819556.
11. Two or More, F1100, Morning Report of Gratiot Street Military Prison, September 16, 1864, accessed April 26, 2015; Ledger Transcription List.
12. Individual Citizens, Julia Martin, #287514030, accessed May 26, 2014.
13. Individual Citizens, Sarah Durrett, #283819530, #293819533, accessed June 24, 2014.
14. Individual Citizens, Dortha Durrett, #283819544, #283819547.

15. Two or More, F1100, Morning Report of Gratiot Street Prison, September 16, 1864, and F1621, #11548.
16. Individual Citizens, Dortha Durrett, #283819549-283819551.
17. Individual Citizens, Sarah Durrett, #283819525-283819528.
18. Two or More, F1621, #11548.
19. Individual Citizens, Sarah Durrett, #283819517; Individual Citizens, Dortha Durrett, #283819521; Two or More, F1621, #11548 and F1625, #12720.
20. Two or More, F1640, #17269, accessed April 26, 2015.
21. Missouri Marriage Records; US Census, 1880; "Benjamin L. Durrett," http://familytreemaker.genealogy.com/users/l/e/a/Chad-Dickeson-Leabo/website-0001/UHP-1046.html.
22. US Census, 1870; US Census, 1880; Soldiers Database, George W. Glasgow; "Abner Martin, Son of Benjamin," http://www.genealogy.com/forum/regional/states/topics/ia/23781/ .

Chapter 19 Four-Time Jailbird "Lizzie" DeWitt

1. Individual Citizens, Elizabeth DeWitt, #283153285, #283153295-283153300 accessed July 10, 2014; US Census, 1850; US Census, 1860; Ledger Transcription List.
2. Individual Citizens, Elizabeth DeWitt, #283153297.
3. *Ibid.*
4. *Ibid.*, #283153285, #283153302; Two or More, F1101, Morning Report of Gratiot Street Military Prison, Sept. 16, 1864.
5. Individual Citizens, Elizabeth DeWitt, #283153295-283153296.
6. *Ibid.*, #283153299-283153300. Lieutenant Couch and two other members of the First MSM Cavalry were killed on April 28, 1864, in Johnson County, reportedly by Quantrill's gang, which had just returned to Missouri after wintering in Texas.
7. *Ibid.*, #283153296.
8. *Ibid.*, #283153296.
9. *Ibid.*, #283153288, #283153302-283153303.
10. Ledger Transcription List; Individual Citizens, Elizabeth DeWitt, #283153285-283153286.
11. Individual Citizens, Elizabeth DeWitt, #283153286-283153287; Two or More, F1625, #12720 and F1640, #17269.
12. US Census, 1870; OR, 41:3, 144.

Chapter 20 Dancing with a Rebel Flag

1. Unfiled Papers, Sue Bryant, #248872322, accessed July 15, 2014.
2. US Census, 1860; Unfiled Papers, Sue Bryant, #24887233.
3. Unfiled Papers, Sue Bryant, #24887233, #248872248; US Census, 1860.
4. Unfiled Papers, Sue Bryant, #248872268; *OR*, 41:1, 219-220; Mrs. John R. Cason, "Missouri Girl's Prison Experiences," *Confederate Veteran*, 13:10 (November 1905), 506-507.
5. Unfiled Papers, Sue Bryant, #248872322 #248872233, #248895094; *OR*, 41:1, 219-220; Cason, "Missouri Girl's Prison Experiences," 507.
6. Two or More, F1625, #12784.
7. Unfiled Papers, Sue M. Brown, #248895290, #248895308, accessed July 18, 2014.
8. Unfiled Papers, Sue Bryant, #248895243, #248895262; US Census, 1860.
9. Unfiled Papers, Sue Bryant, #248895157, #248895171.
10. Unfiled Papers, Sue Bryant, #248895193, #248895211; US Census, 1860.
11. Unfiled Papers, Sue M. Brown, #248895382.
12. Unfiled Papers, George Bryan, #248865724, accessed July 18, 2014; Individual Citizens, Sue Bryant, #280143377, #280143383, accessed July 15, 2014.
13. Unfiled Papers, Sue Bryant, #248865792, #248865817, #248865832.
14. Cason, 507.
15. Unfiled Papers, Sue Bryant, #248872233, #248872248, #248872268, #248872289, #248872416; *Past and Present of Saline County, Missouri*. William Barclay Napton (Indianapolis: B.F. Bowen & Co., 1910), 182. Dick Durrett was probably related to the Durrett sisters of Johnson County, but he was not their brother.
16. Unfiled Papers, Sue Bryant, #248895039, #248895131.
17. *Ibid.*, #248895072, #248895094.
18. *Ibid.*, #248872397.
19. Unfiled Papers, Sue Bryant, #248872397; Individual Citizens, Sue Bryant, #280143377; Cason, 508.
20. Individual Citizens, Sue Bryant, #280143377, #280143383.
21. Cason, 507-508; US Census, 1870; *History of Saline County, Missouri* (St. Louis: Missouri Historical Company, 1881), 763; *Scranton (PA) Republican*, November 15, 1904.

Chapter 21 To Be Hung by the Neck Until Dead

1. Proceedings of a Military Commission, Proceedings of Trial of Sarah Jane Smith, 1864, MC 736, Special Collections, University of Arkansas Libraries, Fayetteville, online at Community and Conflict, www.ozarkscivilwar.org,

accessed September 2, 2014.
2. *Ibid.*
3. *Ibid.*
4. *Ibid.*
5. *Ibid.*; Two or More, F1101, #12749; Individual Citizens, Sarah Jane Smith, #292052056, accessed August 25, 2014.
6. Individual Citizens, Sarah Jane Smith, #292051957.
7. *Ibid.*, #292051940.
8. *Ibid.*, #292051935.
9. Individual Citizens, Jane Smith, #292046405-292046406, accessed August 25, 2014.
10. Individual Citizens, Sarah Jane Smith, #292051946; Two or More, F1890, Roll of Sentenced Prisoners Transferred from St. Louis, Mo. to the Military Prison at Alton, Ill. for execution of sentence, Nov. 25, 1864, accessed April 26, 2015.
11. Individual Citizens, Sarah Jane Smith, #292051971.
12. *Ibid,* #292051962, #292051964, #292051975, #292052010.

Chapter 22 Rebel Arms Supplier

1. Trial Transcript of Nancy Kemp, RG 153, #OO227; Individual Citizens, Nancy Kemp, #287244878-287244879, accessed October 9, 2014.
2. Individual Citizens, Nancy Kemp, #287244886-2872448870; US Census, 1860.
3. Individual Citizens, Nancy Kemp, #287244878-287244879.
4. *Ibid.*, #287244871, #287244881.
5. *Ibid.*, #287244734, #287244873.
6. *Ibid.*, #287244883.
7. *Ibid.*, #287244863, #287244889; RG 153, #OO227.
8. RG 153, #OO227.
9. *Ibid.*
10. *Ibid.*
11. *Ibid.*
12. *Ibid.*
13. *Ibid.*
14. *Ibid.*; Two or More, F1635, #15751, accessed April 26, 2015; Missouri Marriage Records.

Chapter 23 The Rebel Vixens of Chariton County

1. Individual Citizens, Isabella Fox, #286560238, #286560241, accessed July 5, 2014.

2. US Census, 1860; Transcript of J.W. Terman trial by military commission, RG 153, #NN3087; Soldiers Database, Giles Rice.
3. Larry Wood, "Harry Truman: Federal Bushwhacker," *Missouri Historical Review* (98:3, April 2004), 210-213; RG 153, #NN3087.
4. RG 153, #NN3087.
5. *Ibid.*; Wood, "Harry Truman…," 219-220.
6. Individual Citizens, Isabella Fox, #286560238, #286560247; Two or More, 1632, #14928.
7. Individual Citizens, Isabella Fox, #286560237, 286560240; Missouri Marriage Records.
8. Individual Citizens, Isabella Fox, #286560234.
9. *Ibid.*, #286560235.
10. Individual Citizens, Melissa Fox, #286560223; accessed July 5, 2014Isabella Fox, #286560243.
11. Individual Citizens, Melissa Fox, #286560231, Isabella Fox, #286560249.
12. Individual Citizens, Isabella Fox, #286560238.
13. Individual Citizens, Melissa Fox, #286560229.
14. Individual Citizens, Melissa Fox, #286560225; Isabella Fox, #286560245.
15. Individual Citizens, Isabella Fox, #286560240-286560241.
16. Individual Citizens, Melissa Fox, #286560220-286560221.
17. Individual Citizens, Isabella Fox, #286560233; America Huckshorn, #287054656, #287054660, accessed July 12, 2014; Two or More F1632, #14928. Some Union records mention Josephine Huckshorn in conjunction with her mother, America, while others mention her in conjunction with her younger sister Amelia, but America and Amelia are not mentioned together. So, it's unclear whether all three women were arrested or the names America and Amelia were simply confused.
18. US Census, 1870; US Census, 1880; email correspondence with Ann Christian, July 12, 2014.

Chapter 24 Convicted by Her Own Admission

1. Unfiled Papers, David Bowles, #248528138, accessed August 19, 2014; Individual Citizens, Julia Bowles, #280191900, accessed August 19, 20014.
2. Individual Citizens, Mary E. Bowles, #280191917-280191918, accessed August 19, 2014; Unfiled Papers, David Bowles, #248528130.
3. Individual Citizens, Mary E. Bowles, #280191928; Unfiled Papers, David Bowles, #248528131-248528132; *History of St. Charles, Montgomery and Warren Counties, Missouri* (St. Louis: National Historical Company, 1885), 681; Soldiers' Records, John B. Bowles.
4. Individual Citizens, Mary E. Bowles, #280191915, #280191925,

#280191928, #280191930, #280191939; Unfiled Papers, Mollie E. Bowles, #248528389, accessed August 19, 2014; *St. Louis Daily Missouri Democrat*, February 9, 1865.

5. Individual Citizens, David Bowles, #280191848-280191850, accessed August 19, 2014; Unfiled Papers, David Bowles, #248528100-248528102, #248528104-248528105. The property of Southern sympathizers was often confiscated by Federal authorities in Missouri during the Civil War, supposedly as a way of compensating the Union and loyal citizens for property losses inflicted by bushwhackers, whom such Southern sympathizers helped sustain, but also as a way of punishing the offending Rebel sympathizers.

6. Individual Citizens, Mary E. Bowles, #280191915-280191916; Individual Citizens, David Bowles, #280191857.

7. *History of St. Charles, Montgomery…*, 856; US Census, 1870; Missouri Marriage Records.

Chapter 25 The Ordeal of Tabitha Rider

1. Missouri Marriage Records; Individual Citizens, Talitha Alice Rider, #291601895, accessed October 13, 2014.

2. Individual Citizens, Talitha Alice Rider, #291601893.

3. *Ibid.*; Unfiled Papers, James W. Rider, #256635103, #256635200, #256635207, #256635218, #256635239, accessed October 13, 2014.

4. Unfiled Papers, James W. Rider, #256635200, #256635260 #256635272; Missouri Marriage Records.

5. Individual Citizens, Talitha Alice Rider, #291601893.

6. *Ibid.;* Individual Citizens, Robert Shannon, #292008268, #292008270, accessed October 13, 2014.

7. Individual Citizens, Talitha Alice Rider, #291601893.

8. *Ibid*, #291601893-291601894.

9. *Ibid.*, #291601894.

10. *Ibid.*

11. *Ibid.*, #291601890, #291601894.

12. *Ibid.*, #291601894, #291601901.

13. *Ibid.*, #291601890-291601891.

14. Two or More, F1629, #14018.

15. Individual Citizens, James Rider, #291601786-291601787, accessed October 13, 2014.

16. Individual Citizens, _____ Riders, #291601785, accessed October 13, 2014; Talitha Alice Rider, #291601889-291601890, #291601893, #291601895-291601896.

17. Individual Citizens, Talitha Alice Rider, #291601894.
18. *Ibid.*, #291601890-291601891, #291601901.
19. *Ibid*, #291601889.
20. Two or More, F1633, #15158; Missouri Marriage Records.

Chapter 26 Who Were These Women?

1. US Census Records, 1860.
2. Frank Moore, ed. *Rebellion Record: A Diary of American Events, 1864*, vol. 9 (New York: D. Van Nostrand, 1866), 7.
3. I arrived at the estimate of the approximately equal number of male and female civilian prisoners by examining Myrtle Street and Gratiot Street Prison rolls (M598 roll 72 and M416 rolls 89-93).
4. See Two or More, F1654, #26385, for an example of women requesting to go south.
5. See Fellman, 199-201, for a discussion of the restraint normally shown by Federal troops toward the Missouri women.
6. LeeAnn Whites, "Forty Shirts and a Wagonload of Wheat: Women, the Domestic Supply Line, and the Civil War on the Western Border" *The Journal of the Civil War Era* 1, no. 1 (March 2011), 61-62; *OR*, 48:1, 1223.
7. LeeAnn Whites, in "Corresponding with the Enemy: Mobilizing the Relational Field of Battle in St. Louis," in *Occupied Women: Gender, Military Occupation and the American Civil War*, ed. LeeAnn Whites and Alecia P. Long (Baton Rouge: Louisiana State University, 2009), 109, characterizes the Union's requirement that women visiting prisons in the St. Louis area be required to take a loyalty oath as an attempt to label women's domestic labor as inherently political, but the same can said about the arrest of women for feeding and sheltering guerrillas.
8. Gentry, "About the Fight at Richfield," 427.

Bibliography

Books

Baker, James R., Jr. *Missouri Partisans*, v. 1. The Author, 2013.

Banasik, Michael, ed. *Cavaliers of the Bush: Quantrill and His Men*. Iowa City: Press of the Camp Pope Bookshop, 2003.

——, ed. *Missouri in 1861: The Civil War Letters of Franc B. Wilkie, Newspaper Correspondent.* Iowa City: Press of the Camp Pope Bookshop, 2001.

Blanton, DeAnne and Lauren M. Cook. *They Fought Like Demons: Women Soldiers in the American Civil War.* Baton Rouge: Louisiana State University Press, 2002.

Buel, J.W. *The Border Outlaws.* Cincinnati: Forshee & McMakin, 1882.

Cockrell, Ewing. *History of Johnson County, Missouri, v. 2.* Topeka: Historical Publishing Co., 1918.

Connelley, William E. *The Life of Preston B. Plumb.* Chicago: Browne and Howell Company, 1913.

Cutler, William G., ed. *History of the State of Kansas.* Chicago: A.T. Andreas, 1883.

Eakin, Joanne Chiles. *The Little Gods: Union Provost Marshals in Missouri, 1861-1865.* Independence, Mo.: np, 1996.

Edwards, John N. *Noted Guerrillas of the Warfare of the Border.* St. Louis: Bryan, Brand & Company, 1877.

Edwards, Laura F. *Scarlett Doesn't Live Here Anymore: Southern Women in the Civil War Era.* Urbana: University of Illinois Press, 2000.

Fellman, Michael. *Inside War: The Guerrilla Conflict in Missouri During the American Civil War.* New York: Oxford University Press, 1989.

Frost, Griffin. *Camp and Prison Journal.* 1867. Reprint, Iowa City: Camp Pope Bookshop, 1994.

Grimes, Absalom. *Absalom Grimes: Confederate Mail Runner.* M.M. Quaife, ed. New Haven, CT: Yale University Press, 1926.

History of Clay and Platte Counties, Missouri. St. Louis: National Historical Company, 1885.

History of Lafayette County, Mo. St. Louis: Missouri Historical Company, 1881.

History of St. Charles, Montgomery and Warren Counties, Missouri. St. Louis: National Historical Company, 1885.

History of Saline County, Missouri. St. Louis: Missouri Historical Company, 1881.

History of Vernon County, Missouri. St. Louis: Brown & Co., 1887.

Lowry, Thomas P. *Confederate Heroines.* Baton Rouge: Louisiana State University Press, 2006.

McCurry, Stephanie. *Confederate Reckoning: Power and Politics in the Civil War South.* Cambridge: Harvard University Press, 2010.

Mendenhall, Margaret, trans. *Missouri Ordeal 1862-1864: The Diaries of William Hall Mendenhall.* Newhall, CA: Carl Boyer III, 1985.

Moore, Frank, ed. *Rebellion Record: A Diary of American Events, 1864, vol. 9.* New York: D. Van Nostrand, 1866.

Nichols, Bruce. *Guerrilla Warfare in Civil War Missouri, Volume 3, January-August 1864.* Jefferson, NC: McFarland & Co., 2014.

Past and Present of Saline County, Missouri. William Barclay Napton. Indianapolis: B.F. Bowen & Co., 1910.

Peterson, Paul. *Quantrill in Texas: The Forgotten Campaign.* Nashville: Cumberland House, 2007.

—— *Quantrill of Missouri: The Making of a Guerrilla Warrior.* Nashville: Cumberland House, 2003.

Violette, Eugene Morrow. *A History of Missouri.* Boston: D. C. Heath and Co., 1918.

War of the Rebellion: A Compilation of Official Records of the Union and Confederate Armies. Washington, DC: Government Printing Office, 1880-1902.

Whites, LeeAnn and Alecia P. Long, eds. *Occupied Women: Gender, Military Occupation and the American Civil War.* Baton Rouge: Louisiana State University Press, 2009.

Wood, Larry. *The Civil War Story of Bloody Bill Anderson.* Fort Worth: Eakin Press, 2003.

——. *Other Noted Guerrillas of the Civil War in Missouri.* Joplin, Mo.: Hickory Press, 2007.

Print and Online Articles

"Abner Martin, Son of Benjamin." http://genforum.genealogy.com/cgi-in/pageload.cgi?Perry,County::oh::37781.html.

Barton, Fred. "Bill Anderson and Not Charlie Quantrell Was Driving Force Behind Lawrence Raid." Undated newspaper clipping, Denver Public Library, Western History Department, William Connelly Collection.

"Benjamin Isham Longacre." Find a Grave Memorial #42340597. www.

findagrave.com.

"Benjamin L. Durrett." http://familytreemaker.genealogy.com/users/l/e/a/Chad-Dickeson-Leabo/WEBSITE-0001/UHP-1046.html.

Brophy, Patrick. "Lady Bushwhackers Played Active Parts." *Bushwhacker Weekly Magazine* (December 5, 1984). 1.

Cason, Mrs. John R. "Missouri Girl's Prison Experiences." *Confederate Veteran* 13, no. 10 (November 1905), 506-507.

"Descendants of Duncan Oliphant." http://hershfamily.net/images/Family_Tree_Maker14.pdf.

"Frances Pearl 'Fannie' Price Houx." Find A Grave Memorial #68824105, www.findagrave.com.

Gentry, Lou. "About the Fight at Richfield." *Confederate Veteran* 20 (September 1912): 426-427.

——. "Experience of a Missouri Woman." *Confederate Veteran* 20 (May 1912): 211-212.

"Jenkins Family." http://archiver.rootsweb.ancestry.com/th/read/MOMILLER/2000-06/0961842004.

"John Mayfield/Ella Justine Burrus." Family Group Sheet. http://www.mcatee.biz/genealogy/familygroup.php?familyID=F3226&tree=MyFamily2005.

"Josiah Vaughn Ancestry." http://homepages.rootsweb.ancestry.com/~fuqua/ Main%20Database/mdb1353.htm.

"Keys to My Heart: Genealogy of the Sherfick and Wade Families." http://www.mcatee.biz/genealogy/.

"'Kincheloe' Grave Search Results." http://www.findagrave.com/cgi-bin/fg.cgi?page=gsr&GSln=Kincheloe&GSiman=1&GScnty=1450&.

"Ledger Transcription List—Women and Children Prisoners." Transcription of National Archives Microfilm Publication M598, Roll 72, www.civilwarstlouis.com/articles/gratiot/listwomen.aspx.

"Lurena 'Lou' Alder Gentry." Find a Grave Memorial #96523663, www.findagrave.com.

"Martha Jane 'Mattie' Longacre Baker." Find A Grave Memorial #42342503, www.findagrave.com.

Missouri in the Civil War Message Board. History-sites.com/mb/cw/mocwmb/.

"Mo. Census Table, 1860." Civil War on the Western Border, http://www.civilwaronthewesternborder.org/content/1860-missouri-census-table.

"Nancy Malory Longacre." Find A Grave Memorial #42239720, www.findagrave.com.

"Polly Jackson." Find a Grave Memorial #81971363, www.findagrave.com.

"Trouble for the Vaughn's in Jackson County, Missouri during the Civil War." http://www.doug.vaughn/org/trouble/trouble-main.html.

Whites, LeeAnn. "Forty Shirts and a Wagonload of Wheat: Women, the Domestic Supply Line, and the Civil War on the Western Border." *The Journal of the Civil War Era* 1, no. 1 (March 2011), 56-78.

"William McWaters." http://en.wikipedia.org/wiki/William_McWaters.

Wood, Larry. "Harry Truman: Federal Bushwhacker." *Missouri Historical Review* 98, no. 3 (April 2004), 201-222.

Government Documents and Unpublished Sources

Christian, Ann. Email correspondence, July 12, 2014.

Connelley, William E. Papers. Collection 16, Box 13. Kansas State Historical Society, Topeka, Kansas.

Curran, Thomas. "Confederate Women and Military Justice in the St. Louis Area." Missouri State Archives—Presentation Video Transcripts, 2010.

Mathew H. Ritchey House, National Register of Historic Places Inventory--Nomination Form, United States Department of the Interior, National Park Service, http://www.dnr.mo.gov/shpo/nps-nr/78003399.pdf.

Missouri Death Certificates, 1910-1963, Missouri State Archives, Jefferson City, http://www.sos.mo.gov/archives/resources/deathcertificates/#searchdeat.

Missouri Marriage Records, 1805-2002, www.Ancestry.com.

Proceedings of a Military Commission, Proceedings of Trial of Sarah Jane Smith, 1864. MC 736, Special Collections, University of Arkansas Libraries, Fayetteville, online at Community and Conflict, www.ozarkscivilwar.org.

Soldiers' Records: War of 1812-World War I. Missouri State Archives, Jefferson City, online at http://www.sos.mo.gov/archives/soldiers.

Texas Marriage Records. https://familysearch.org.

Transcripts of Trials by Military Commission. Records of the Judge Advocate General's Office, Record Group 153, National Archives, Washington, DC.

Unfiled Papers and Slips Belonging in Confederate Compiled Service Records. National Archives Microfilm Publication M347, Roll 335, www.Fold3.com.

Union Provost Marshals' File of Papers Relating to Individual Citizens. National Archives Publication M-345, www.Fold3.com.

Union Provost Marshals' Papers, Two or More Civilians: 1861-1867. Missouri State Archives, Jefferson City, www.sos.mo.gov/archives/

provost/provostPDF.asp.
United States Census Records. Online at www.familysearch.org.

Newspapers

Carthage (Mo.) Weekly Banner.
Columbia Missouri Statesman.
Cottonwood Falls Kansas Press.
Emporia (Kans.) News.
Glasgow (Mo.) Weekly Times.
Kansas City Daily Journal of Commerce.
Lexington (Mo.) News.
Oskaloosa (Kans.) Independent.
Pittsburgh Dispatch.
Saint Joseph Morning Herald.
Saint Louis Daily Missouri Democrat.
Saint Louis Daily Missouri Republican.
Saint Paul Daily Globe.
Scranton (Penn.) Republican.

Index

Agnes City, Kansas, 95-96
Alder, Lydia, 26-27
Alton, Illinois, 118-119, 153, 155, 212
Alton Military Prison, 118, 126, 152, 155, 212
Anderson, Ellis, 95
Anderson, Jim, 95-96, 102, 105
Anderson, Josephine, 95
Anderson, Martha, 95
Anderson, Martha Jane, 95, 97, 101-105, 107-108, 110
Anderson, Mary, 95, 100-102, 104-105, 107-108, 110
Anderson, William C., 95-96
Anderson, William T. "Bloody Bill," 22, 60, 71, 75, 79-81, 87, 95-96, 102, 107
Aubry, Kansas, 64
Aullville, Missouri, 131
Austin, William, 167

Bailey, James, 36
Baker, A. I., 95-96
Baker, James H., 112-113, 128-130, 178
Balltown, Missouri, 50
Bass, Susan M., 102-104
Bates County, Missouri, 22, 83
Battle of Lexington (Mo.), 221
Bay, John, 61
Belch, Ed, 117-118
Bellamy, Missouri, 47, 49
Bell, J. Warren, 92, 136, 143-145
Bell, Sena, 181-182, 243
Bennett, Simon, 180
Blair, Charles W., 50-51
Blair, William D., 33-34, 36, 38
Blunt, Andy, 72-73
Blunt, James G., 21-22, 59
Bond, John, 160-161
Bond, Ruth, 157, 160-162
Bond, Sarah, 157, 160-162
Boonville Female Seminary, 197, 200
Boonville, Missouri, 197, 200-201, 204
Bowles, David, 229-232
Bowles, Julia, 229
Bowles, Mary, 229-232
Boyce, U. L., 143
Boyd, Leon, 14
Branch, H. B., 128, 130
Breckenridge, Missouri, 234
Bridgeman, William, 47
Broadhurst, Henry, 134
Brown, Egbert B., 38, 74-75, 79-80, 82, 126-127, 150-151, 158, 164, 168, 203-204
Brownell, Frank E., 134, 136
Brown, John A., 140, 143
Brown, W. L., 118-119

Brumfield, Benjamin, 107-109
Brumfield, Imogene, 107-114, 241, 254
Brunswick, Missouri, 223
Bryant, John W., 197, 205
Bryant, Sue, 197-198, 200-205, 242, 249
Buel, J. W., 72
Burk, Margaret, 167, 176
Burns, John, 73
Burris, Nancy, 50, 52

Caldwell County, Missouri, 233
Callaway County, Missouri, 215, 220
Campbell, Jessie, 12
Cameron, Missouri, 134
Carman, Marilla, 223
Carpenter, Robert, 50-51, 53
Carrendon, Madison, 158
Cason, John R., 205
Cass County, Missouri, 22, 46, 69, 191-193
Cassville, Missouri, 207
Catherwood, E. C., 134
Cecil, A. J., 165-166, 173
Cedar County, Missouri, 47-48, 52
Challis, Louisa, 14
Chapel Hill, Missouri, 58-59
Chariton County, Missouri, 137, 221, 223-224, 227, 234-235, 252
Chiles, George, 166, 174
Chillicothe, Missouri, 233-234, 236, 238
Clark, Ephraim, 222
Clay County, Missouri, 56
Clifton, Margaret, 58-59, 69
Clifton, Samuel, 58, 65, 69
Clinton, Missouri, 182
Cobb, George, 234-235
Cochran, M. B., 213
Coffee, John T., 44
Cohn, Gustavus, 82, 136, 142, 194
Cole County, Missouri, 162
Collins, Elizabeth, 218, 220
Concordia, Missouri, 147
Conklin, A. R., 151
Conrad, George, 227-228
Cooper County, Missouri, 149, 188, 197-198
Cooper, James T., 212-213
Coppidge, Samuel, 225, 227
Cornelia, Missouri, 165
Cornwell, Peacock, 217-218
Couch, James, 192
Council Grove, Kansas, 95
Cox, B. M., 61
Coyle, William H., 100
Cramer, Thomas, 181-183, 187
Crawber, Tom, 124
Cull, Emily, 165, 168, 172-173, 180, 250
Cull, Mary, 164-166, 168, 172-173, 178, 194, 245-246, 250
Cull, Missouri, 164, 168, 172
Cummins, Timothy, 229-230
Curty, David, 161-162
Curty, Mahala Bond, 161-162

Dale, Douglas, 122, 124-125, 127
Danforth, L. W., 153-156
Darr, Joseph, Jr., 32, 62, 92, 136-137, 145, 147, 210-211, 216
Day, William, 165, 166, 171-172
Dean, Crat, 192-193
DeBolt, R. A., 108
Derrick, Dick, 202

Dewey, Catalina, 223
Dewey, John, 223-224
Dewey, W. F., 160-161
DeWitt, Elizabeth, 192
DeWitt, Elizabeth "Lizzie," 191-193, 195, 197
DeWitt, William, 192
Dixon, William, 55
Doak, Alexander V., 105
Dodge, Grenville, 112-113, 129, 213, 220
Dorsey, Caleb, 229, 231
Douglass, E. G., 105
Duck, Davis K., 79, 80-81
Dunnegin's Grove, Missouri, 43
Durrett, Dortha, 181, 183-186, 188-189
Durrett, Sarah, 183-184, 186, 188
Dwight, James F., 150

Eads, James, 87-88
Eaton, Lucien, 77, 83, 136-137, 144-145, 178, 248
Eddy, E. A., 140
Elliott, Samuel, 235
Eno, Frank, 56, 83, 125-126, 136-137, 145
Erwin, Marion D., 79-80, 82
Erwin, Mary Lucy, 105
Eshew, Jonathan, 182
Ewing, Thomas, Jr., 21-22, 98, 252-253

Ferguson, Richard L., 126, 143-144, 151-152, 168, 178, 187, 192-194, 198, 204
Fickle, Anna, 19, 71-79, 247
Fickle, Henry H., 71-72
Fickle, Joseph, 71-73
Fisk, Clinton B., 134, 238, 252
Flannery, Isaac, 64
Flannery, Widow, 63-65
Fort Leavenworth, Kansas, 58-62, 65, 133, 247
Fort Scott, Kansas, 43-44, 46-48, 50-51
Foster, Melville U., 89, 183, 186
Fox, Isabella, 221-228, 244-245, 251-252
Fox, Melissa, 221, 223-228, 244
Fox, Peter, 221-223
Frankfort, Missouri, 118
Freeman, Garrett, 183
Frost, Griffin, 154-156, 176
Fulton, Missouri, 216

Gabbert, Eliza, 42-44
Gabbert, John, 46
Gabbert, William, 47
Garnett, Isaac, 216
Garrett, Thomas, 176-177
Gavin, James M., 80, 82, 121-122, 127, 140, 143, 157-158, 162
George, James J., 236
Giboney, Dave, 42, 44, 46, 50
Giboney, William, 56
Gilham, William, 69
Glasgow, George W., 189
Glasgow, Missouri, 108
Goggin, Frances, 156
Goggin, George, 156
Goggin, Mollie, 149-156, 246
Grafenstein, Louis, 28
Grandstaff, Mollie, 97, 99
Gratiot Street Female Prison, 53-54, 67, 82, 104, 118, 140, 145, 184, 202, 205, 210, 230, 238
Gratiot Street Prison, 68, 77, 86, 90, 112, 128, 137, 176, 193, 202, 217, 225, 231

Gray, Charlie, 58, 67-68
Gray, George, 58
Gray, Lucinda Mundy, 97
Grayson County, Texas, 105
Green, John, 140
Greenlee, Bernard, 182
Gregg, William H., 14
Griffin, Bert, 95-96
Grimes, Absalom, 77-78

Hackler, Crud, 165, 173
Halleck, Henry, 210, 212
Hall, J. C. W., 52-53, 61-62
Hall, Willard P., 200, 202-203
Harbaugh, Howard S., 238
Harding, A. J., 136
Harding, Chester, Jr., 29
Harlow, Creath, 80, 83
Harlow, Mary Ann, 79-83
Harrison, Robert, 236, 238-240
Harrisonville, Missouri, 192, 194
Hart, Joe, 25-29, 248
Hayes, John, 51
Haynie, Eliza, 115-116, 118-119, 125
Haynie, Frederick, 116
Haynie, Rachel, 116, 119-120, 125
Heath, H. H., 61, 62, 136
Henry County, Missouri, 172, 181-182, 189
Herman, Henry, 134, 136-137
Herrick, H. J., 238-240
Hibler, Samuel, 235-236
Hickman Mills, Missouri, 57, 62-65
Higginsville, Missouri, 131
Hills, Charles S., 101
Hinch, George, 56
Hines, Jonas, 80
Hinman, John, 49
Hinton, Otho, 72-74, 79
Holden, Missouri, 86, 88-89, 191-192
Holtzclaw, Clifton, 221, 225-227, 251-252
Houts, William S., 174
Houx, Fannie, 121-131, 215, 218, 242, 246, 250
Houx, Frank L., 131
Houx, George, 131
Howard County, Missouri, 101, 107
Huckshorn, America, 223, 225-227, 247
Huckshorn, Josephine, 223, 227
Hurst, James D., 197, 200, 202, 204
Hurt, Martha, 224
Hyatt, Asa, 180

Independence, Missouri, 90

Jackman, Mary, 102, 107
Jackman, Porter, 102, 108, 110
Jackman, Sidney Drake, 102, 108
Jackson, a slave, 122-125, 127
Jackson, Betty, 33-34, 36, 40, 251
Jackson, Bill, 34, 36, 38, 198, 203
Jackson, Claiborne F., 18-19
Jackson County, Missouri, 22, 57-58, 60-61, 67-69, 85-86
Jackson, Jim, 225-227
Jackson, Mary, 33-34, 36, 40
Jackson, Nannie, 34
Jackson, Sue, 34, 40
Jackson, Thomas, 40
James, Frank, 14, 28
James, Jesse, 14
Jefferson City, Missouri, 34, 74, 76, 78, 117, 119, 121-122, 125-127, 149-153, 157-158, 160, 162, 220, 230

Jenkins, Hannah, 158, 161
Jenkins, Henry, 157-158, 160
Jenkins, Lydia, 160
Jenkins, William, 161
Jennings, America, 222, 228
Jennings, Henry, 221-222
Jennison, Charles "Doc," 18
Johnson, Charles P., 176
Johnson County, Kansas, 64
Johnson County, Missouri, 85-86, 92, 140-141, 163, 167, 169, 172-173, 176-181, 183, 188, 191, 195
Jordan, Clara, 110
Jordan, Ida, 110, 114
Jordan, John B., 107, 112
Justice, A. S., 133, 138
Justice, Susanna, 133-134, 136-137

Kaiserman, Sam, 44, 46, 48
Kansas City, Missouri, 22, 59-62, 64, 68, 96-97, 100, 245
Keeton, Martha, 112
Kellogg, D. B., 223
Kemp, Ammon, 216-218
Kemper, W. B., 14, 31-32
Kemp, George, 217
Kemp, Henry, 215-218, 220
Kemp, Nancy, 215-218, 220
Keytesville, Missouri, 221-225, 227, 228
Kincheloe, Louis, 139, 141
Kincheloe, Mary, 139-140, 142-145, 147, 250-251
Kingsville, Missouri, 86, 88, 93
Knights of the Golden Circle, 186
Kuhn, John H., 213

Lafayette County, Missouri, 17, 58, 107, 127, 129, 131, 139-141, 147, 242
Lane, Jim, 18
Lawrence, Kansas, raid on, 22, 60
Lazear, B. F., 139, 143, 191, 193, 197-198, 203
Lee's Summit, Missouri, 69
Lexington, Missouri, 72-73, 75, 79-80, 87, 101, 107, 110-111, 121, 125-130, 140, 143, 182
Lincoln, Abraham, 75, 77
Lincoln County, Missouri, 229
Lincoln, John, 34, 36
Lindsey, Bernard, 58, 65
Lindsey, Emma, 60
Lindsey, Martha, 58-61, 63, 69
Lindsey, Susan, 60
Lionberger, D. C., 200
Little, Clara, 164, 167-171, 176, 177, 180
Little, Fannie, 164, 167-171, 176-177, 180
Little Santa Fe, Missouri, 57
Livingston County, Missouri, 233-234, 240
Longacre, Benjamin, 85, 242
Longacre, Elbert, 86
Longacre, Martha, 89-90, 92-93, 242
Longacre, Nancy, 85, 87-90, 92, 242, 247
Longacre, William, 86
Lotspeich, Rezin, 184
Lundy, Florence, 153-155

Macon, Missouri, 103, 108
Majors, Dave, 46-48, 56
Marchbanks, William, 47, 50
Marsh, A. C., 230
Marshall, Edwin, 188
Marshall, James, 188
Marshall, Missouri, 34, 191, 197-198, 203

Martin, Julia, 181-184, 187-189, 194, 243, 252-253
Mathes, Mark, 11
Maxwell, Eli, 65
Maxwell, Mary "Polly," 60, 65
Mayfield, Brice, 41-43, 46, 48
Mayfield, Clarinda Jane, 42, 50, 52-53, 56
Mayfield, Ella, 41-44, 46-50, 53, 56
Mayfield, Hiram, 41-42
Mayfield, John, 41-42
Mayfield, John "Crack," 42-43, 46
Mayfield, Justine, 41-42, 48, 56
Mayfield, Lenora, 41-42, 46, 56
Mayfield, Lou, 198, 201-202, 205
Mayfield, Margaret, 42, 48
Mayfield, Sallie, 42, 46, 49-50, 52-54, 56, 247
McConnell, Nannie, 50
McCoy, Lurena, 25, 27-29, 31-32, 241, 248
McCoy, Moses, 27-28, 31, 255
McFerran, James, 87-89
McGowan, Mary, 166-167, 174
McIntire, James, 215-218
McNeil, John, 44
McPherson, E. B., 200
McWaters, William Edward, 52
Meredith, John D., 108
Mexico, Missouri, 52, 216
Miami, Missouri, 115-117, 119
Middletown, Missouri, 230
Miller, Alonzo W., 90, 92
Miller County, Missouri, 157, 160, 162, 231
Missouri City, Missouri, 26, 28-29
Missouri River, 86, 115, 224, 234
Missouri State Guard, 19, 42, 57, 86, 172, 233
Missouri State Penitentiary, 150, 220
Moffett, James, 26-27
Moniteau County, Missouri, 149
Montevallo, Missouri, 42-44, 46-48, 52, 56
Montgomery County, Missouri, 188, 215, 229-230, 232
Morgan County, Missouri, 54
Morton, Anderson, 47
Mount Sterling, Illinois, 188, 194
Mundy, Sue, 97
Murray, George, 183
Murray, James, 149
Myrtle Street Prison, 75, 77, 118, 134, 136, 160, 169, 176

Neill, Henry, 143
Neill, L. A., 140
Neosho, Missouri, 42, 44, 46
Nevada, Missouri, 47, 50
New Market, Missouri, 133
Newton County, Missouri, 41-42, 46, 50
Nexsen, George J. W., 89, 110, 112

Oliphant, Barton, 167, 174
Order No. 10, 22, 252
Order No. 11, 22, 252
Order of American Knights, 186, 208
Owesney, W. A., 141-142, 147

Parker, Benjamin F., 21, 60
Parker, Frank, 173, 245
Parker, Wilson L., 115-118
Parks, Joseph, 201

Parman, Joseph, 86-87, 90
Parrish, Joshua T., 232
Parsons, Mosby, 116
Peak, Joseph A., 163-166, 168
Phillips, John F., 163-164
Phillips, Joseph F., 42, 46
Pickett, James A., 108, 223
Piper, John, 81, 198, 203
Pisgah, Missouri, 149
Pitman, Mary, 153-154
Platte County, Missouri, 133-135
Pleasant Hill, Missouri, 194
Pleasonton, Alfred, 82, 88-89, 125-126, 151-152, 168, 198, 203
Plumb, Preston B., 13
Pope, John, 113
Post Oak, Missouri, 163-164, 178, 180
Price, Celeste, 204
Price, Jacob, 125-127
Price, James A., 128-130
Price, Sterling, 19, 133, 182, 186-187, 207, 215, 221, 224
Price, Thomas L., 203-204
Prostitution, allegations of, 163, 165-166, 168, 180-181, 224, 244-245

Quantrill's guerrillas, 19, 60, 105, 249
Quantrill, William, 27, 29, 57, 60, 71-72, 86, 96, 170, 192, 194, 245

Rader, Reuben, 162
Randolph County, Missouri, 95
Ransom, W. C., 58
Rapp, Benjamin, 28
Ray, Joe, 49
Reid, Ann, 72-74
Rex, George, 212
Rice, Giles, 221-222
Rider, Evaline, 235
Rider, George, 234-235
Rider, Jim, 233-236, 238-240
Rider, John, 235
Rider, Lucinda, 234
Rider, Tabitha, 233-236, 238-240
Robertson, Wealthy, 164, 166-168, 175-176, 178
Rocheport, Missouri, 102, 107
Rolla, Missouri, 208, 210
Rosecrans, William, 56, 75-77, 82, 118-119, 125-126, 129, 137, 145, 150, 162, 164, 177-178, 194, 204-205, 210, 212-213
Ruth, Isaac, 173, 193-194

Sabins, William, 72-74
Saline City, Missouri, 33
Saline County, Missouri, 40, 115, 119, 191, 193, 197, 201, 203, 205, 234-236, 242
Sam Gaty, attack on, 58
Samuels, Zerelda, 14
Sanderson, John P., 53, 61-62, 76-77, 142-143, 145, 147, 158, 160, 162, 169, 176, 198, 200-201
Santa Fe Trail, 95-96
Sappington Grove Cemetery, 40
Sapp, W. M., 115-116, 118
Sayre, H. B., 216
Schmitz, Joseph, 26, 28-29
Schofield, John M., 38, 40
Scott, Ferdinand, 28
Scoville, Amelia, 109, 111, 114
Scoville, Byron, 113-114

Sedalia, Missouri, 116, 118, 167, 170-171
Sessions, Darius, 26, 28-29, 31
Shanklin, J. H., 236, 238
Shannon, Robert, 234
Shaw, George W., 102
Shelby, Joseph, 25
Shepherd, George, 72
Sheridan, John, 197
Shinn, George W., 136
Shirley, Bud, 14
Shirley, Myra Maybelle, 14
Sims, Ella, 51
Smith, John H., 165, 167-168
Smith, Sarah Jane, 207, 210-213, 247
Snead, Margaret, 233
Sneed, Sebron, 240
Spencer, David, 172-173
Spencer, Eliza, 163-166, 168, 172-173, 176, 178, 180, 242
Spencer, Hattie, 163, 167-169, 171-172, 176, 178, 180
Spencer, Jane , 164, 167, 180
Spencer, Mary, 163, 167-168, 170, 178, 249
Springfield, Illinois, 54, 56, 83, 178
Springfield, Missouri, 44, 207-208, 210
St. Charles County, Missouri, 54, 183
St. Charles, Missouri, 54
St. Charles Street Prison, 54, 56, 169, 202
St. Clair County, Missouri, 141
Steger, James H., 87-89, 191-192
Stephens, Daniel, 65-66
Stewart, Bill, 165-166, 173
St. Joseph, Missouri, 28-29, 134, 136-137
St. Louis Daily Missouri Democrat, 104
St. Louis Daily Missouri Republican, 104
St. Louis Globe-Democrat, 41, 49
St. Louis, Missouri, 22, 53-54, 61-62, 67-68, 75, 77, 82, 86, 89-90, 100-101, 104, 107-109, 112-113, 118-119, 125, 127-130, 134, 136, 140-141, 143-145, 150-153, 158, 160, 162, 164, 168-169, 176-180, 184, 188, 193, 198, 200-204, 210-212, 221, 225, 230-231, 238, 244-245, 247, 252
Stone, David, 139, 142
Stone, Elizabeth, 139-145, 147, 251
Stone, Wyatt, 142
Street, Joseph M., 103
Swalen, Elias, 162
Swap, Franklin, 126-127, 149, 151-152
Switzler, T. A., 44, 158, 160, 162

Tallon, Peter, 112, 152
Taylor, Fletch, 28
Taylor, Henry, 43-44, 52
Taylor, Lydia, 63-65, 248
Terman, Jacob W. (alias Harry Truman), 136-137, 221-222
Thacher, L. K., 13, 244
Thomas, Nannie, 194
Thomas, Thomas, 231
Thompson, Gideon, 86
Thornton, John C. Calhoun, 133
Thrailkill, John, 224
Tipton, Missouri, 149
Todd, James, 166-167, 174-175
Troutman, Robert, 81

Troy, Missouri, 229-230
Tull, Henry, 63-64
Tuscumbia, Missouri, 157, 160, 162

Union Mills, Missouri, 133
Vandiver, Louis, 26, 28
Vaughn, Dan, 57-65, 67-69
Vaughn, Jim, 57, 59-60
Vaughn, Josiah, 57, 68-69
Vaughn, Mary, 57-58, 62-69, 221
Vaughn, Nancy, 58, 60-61, 63-68
Vaughn, R. C., 129, 141
Vaughn, Richard, 58, 60, 67
Vaughn, Susan, 60-61, 63, 67-69
Vaughn, Thomas, 57-58, 64
Vernon County, Missouri, 22, 41-44, 47, 50, 52, 56
Vickers, Henry, 56

Wade, Catharine, 14
Waller, James, 72-73
Wallis, Elizabeth, 26
Ward, Jane, 163-164, 166-168, 173-175, 178, 180, 194, 249
Ward, Larson, 174
Ward, Thomas, 174
Warrensburg, Missouri, 74-75, 87-90, 92, 125-126, 128, 140, 143, 149, 152, 158, 162-163, 165, 167, 170, 179, 181, 184, 191, 194
Watson, Ellen, 13
Watson, John, 102-103, 108, 110
Watson, Martha, 13, 244
Watson, Sallie, 13
Weaver, William, 182-183
Welch, Warren, 101
Wellington, Missouri, 79, 81, 83, 140
Wellsville, Missouri, 215-216
Westlake, B. F., 188
West, Michael, 234
Weston, Missouri, 133
Whitsett, Isaac W., 80, 83
Whitsett, Mary Jane, 83
Williams, J.P., 82
Williams, Stephen M., 182
Williams, Thomas, 165-166
Windsor, John, 192-193
Withington, Charles H., 96, 101
Wood, Jobe, 158
Worley, Willis H., 82
Wyandotte, Kansas, 59
Wyckoff, John, 87

Yeager, Dick, 86, 87